EMBRYOS
AND
ANCESTORS

EMBRYOS
AND
ANCESTORS

BY

SIR GAVIN DE BEER, F.R.S.

CORRESPONDANT DE L'INSTITUT DE FRANCE
LATELY DIRECTOR OF THE BRITISH MUSEUM
(NATURAL HISTORY)

THIRD EDITION

OXFORD
AT THE CLARENDON PRESS

Oxford University Press, Amen House, London E.C.4

GLASGOW NEW YORK TORONTO MELBOURNE WELLINGTON
BOMBAY CALCUTTA MADRAS KARACHI LAHORE DACCA
CAPE TOWN SALISBURY NAIROBI IBADAN ACCRA
KUALA LUMPUR HONG KONG

© *Oxford University Press 1958*

FIRST EDITION 1940
SECOND EDITION 1951
THIRD EDITION 1958

REPRINTED LITHOGRAPHICALLY IN GREAT BRITAIN
AT THE UNIVERSITY PRESS, OXFORD.
FROM CORRECTED SHEETS OF THE THIRD EDITION
1962

PREFACE

IN 1930 I published a book under the title *Embryology and Evolution*, in which I made an attempt to show that after rejecting the theory of recapitulation, a much better synthesis could be made of our knowledge of embryonic development and evolutionary descent, opening up new fields for observation and co-ordination of studies in embryology, genetics, and evolution. Ten years later I presented the evidence again in an expanded form under the title *Embryos and Ancestors*, and in 1951 I published a revised edition.

During the intervening years a great deal of new evidence has become available, and these fresh data have fitted into place in my scheme like pieces of a puzzle, for I have seen no reason to alter the plan of my former book in the slightest degree. The present book is my previous one brought up to date and enlarged.

It has been very encouraging to me to note the lively interest in these problems shown in recent years. The first necessity in biology will always be further observation and experiment; but as Professor Woodger points out, progress in thought is necessary as well. Outworn theories are not only dull in themselves, but they are actually harmful in thwarting the framing of new working hypotheses which take account of recent progress made in the various experimental branches of biology. Such an outworn theory I believe Haeckel's theory of recapitulation to be. Similarly, the germ-layer theory has ceased to cover the facts.

The present time when the theory of evolution celebrates its centenary is particularly appropriate for a critical appraisement of the relations between embryology and evolution.

I should like to acknowledge my debt to M. Jean Rostand who translated my previous book into French. Few exercises are as helpful for testing the soundness of one's deductions and conclusions as the expression of them in another language, particularly his.

I wish likewise to record my indebtedness to Sir Julian Huxley, the late Professor W. Garstang, Professor Sir Ronald Fisher, and Professor J. B. S. Haldane for their helpful criticism, and to Mr. R. B. Benson, Dr. M. Burton, Dr. L. R. Cox, Mr. R. Essex, Mr. P. Freeman, Mr. R. Freeman, Dr. I. Gordon, Dr.

J. P. Harding, Dr. A. T. Hopwood, Mr. P. F. Mattingley, Dr.
K. P. Oakley, Dr. W. J. Rees, Mr. N. D. Riley, Dr. Malcolm
Smith, Dr. L. F. Spath, Dr. C. J. Stubblefield, Dr. George
Taylor, Dr. H. Dighton Thomas, Dr. E. Trewavas, Dr. E. I.
White, and Dr. H. Muir Wood for valuable information. My
thanks are likewise due to Miss M. Skramovsky who compiled
the Index.

In order to avoid overloading the text, I have added dates to
the names of authors only in those cases where the multiplicity
of references under their name might lead to confusion.

G. DE B.

CONTENTS

LIST OF ILLUSTRATIONS

I

STAGES OF DEVELOPMENT AND STAGES OF EVOLUTION

EMBRYOS undergo development; ancestors have undergone evolution, but in their day they also were the products of development. Our first task must therefore be to define these two sets of events to which living things are subject. We shall concern ourselves mostly with animals, but what we shall have to say about them is, in general, applicable also to plants.

Stages of development and the scale of beings

The life of an animal may be said to start from the egg which has just been fertilized. The egg is a more or less spherical object and it bears no resemblance to the animal that laid it, or into which it will develop. The processes of development are therefore concerned with the transformation of the egg into that form which we recognize as 'the animal'. The transformation is gradual, and so the shape of the spherical egg is modified little by little into another shape, and this is changed into yet different ones which succeed one another until the definitive or adult shape is reached. During its development, therefore, the animal passes through a series of successive stages, and it is the sequence of these stages which we mean when we speak of the animal's *ontogeny*. Some of the ontogenetic stages are familiar to every one, such, for example, as the caterpillar of the moth or the tadpole of the frog. But, on the whole, the stages of development of animals are more or less unknown to the layman, and he must rely on the embryologist, whose business it is to collect and study these interesting phases of an animal's existence.

Another series of stages can be made out from animals by comparing the full-grown or adult shapes of one kind of animal with those of other kinds, and finding that they can be arranged in an order of increasing or decreasing complexity. Such an order was not unknown to the Greeks, who called it the *scale of beings*. At the top of Aristotle's scale was man, below whom came whales, viviparous quadrupeds (other mammals), oviparous quadrupeds (reptiles and amphibians), and birds, and, below these, a medley of animals which Aristotle regarded as being without blood, and in which we can recognize what we call the invertebrates, consisting of octopuses, lobsters, insects, snails, starfish, and sponges, in descending order. A couple of thousand years later, the scale of beings received complete expression at the hands of Bonnet, who strung out all the animals, plants, and minerals which he knew, on a long ladder, of which they formed the rungs.

It was natural that the thought should arise of comparing the two series which we have now just seen—the sequence of ontogenetic stages and the successive shapes of animals on the scale of beings. This idea seems to have occurred to Harvey, for, when speaking of development, he says: 'Nature, by steps which are the same in the formation of any animal whatsoever, goes through the forms of all animals, as I might say egg, worm, embryo, and gradually acquires perfection with each step.' The same notion is expressed in the following passage of John Hunter: 'If we were capable of following the progress of increase of the number of the parts of the most perfect animal, as they first formed in succession, from the very first to its state of full perfection, we should probably be able to compare it with some one of the incomplete animals themselves, of every order of animals in the Creation, being at no stage different from some of the inferior orders.' So also Serres: 'Man only becomes man after traversing transitional organizatory states which assimilate him first to fish, then to reptiles, then to birds and mammals.' Similar ideas were also expressed by Meckel, and their views were frequently referred to as the 'Meckel–Serres law', which was later amplified by Agassiz into the 'law of parallelism' between systematic classification, embryonic development, and palaeontological succession.

According to these views, therefore, the ontogenetic series and the scale of beings run parallel with one another, and the developmental stages of an animal are held to correspond to the definitive or adult stages of animals lower down on the scale.

The laws of von Baer

While the scale of beings was gradually being amended and expanded as new animals came to the notice of naturalists, the foundations of an accurate descriptive knowledge of the ontogenetic stages through which animals pass in their development were not laid until the work of von Baer (1828). As a result of his extensive researches, von Baer came to a number of conclusions which are expressed in the form of four statements which have come to be known as the 'laws of von Baer'. As they are of the greatest importance from the present point of view, they are here repeated:

1. In development from the egg the general characters appear before the special characters.
2. From the more general characters the less general and finally the special characters are developed.
3. During its development an animal departs more and more from the form of other animals.
4. The young stages in the development of an animal are not like the adult stages of other animals lower down on the scale, but are like the young stages of those animals.

By his 1st and 2nd laws von Baer expressed the fact that in the development of the chick, for instance, there is a stage at which he could recognize it as a vertebrate but could not say what kind of vertebrate it was; and that at a later stage when he could recognize it as a bird it was still impossible to distinguish which kind of bird. Indeed, of a couple of embryos which von Baer had preserved in spirit, he was unable to say whether they were reptiles, birds, or mammals, so similar are the young stages of these animals. The 3rd and 4th laws express von Baer's most important contribution, which is that animals are more similar at early stages of their development from the egg than when they are full-grown, and that this resemblance between early stages becomes progressively diminished as they grow older. Instead, therefore, of passing through the adult stages of other animals during its ontogeny, a developing animal moves away from them, according to von Baer, and the ontogenetic stages do not run parallel to the sequence of forms of the scale of beings.

Stages of development and the succession of ancestors

The introduction of the concept of evolution was obviously destined to make important changes in the consideration of the relations of ontogeny to the scale of beings. For the scale of beings then ceased to be a mere static row of shapes of adult animals, and, instead, became a line of ancestors which by modification in descent have evolved into other (and usually more complex) forms. The modifications undergone by the shape of the adult animals in successive generations during evolution could now be regarded as a series of stages in the history of the race, which series became known as the *phylogeny*. The problem now was to see how ontogeny and phylogeny were related.

As was natural, Darwin relied greatly on the evidence which embryology provided in support of evolution. The subject was included in the section of the *Origin of Species* devoted to 'Mutual affinities of organic beings', where stress was laid on the fact that resemblance between embryos whose adults differ supplies evidence of affinity and receives its natural explanation by the descent of such forms with modification from a common ancestor. This argument is indisputable, and is the logical consequence of von Baer's laws interpreted in the light of evolution. It may be noted that it is no part of the argument that the embryos of the descendants should be equated with the adults of the ancestors, and in his Sketch of 1842 and Essay of 1844, Darwin made no such claim. In the *Origin of Species*, however, Darwin adopted Agassiz's view of the correspondence between fossil 'ancient animals' and 'the embryos of recent animals', a resemblance which Agassiz, a disbeliever in evolution, could never explain, whereas Darwin could by converting the 'ancient animals' into ancestors.

The next step was taken by Fritz Müller. For him, ontogeny could follow one of two methods. During its development from the egg, an animal might either pass through the ontogenetic stages and beyond the final adult stage of the ancestor ('overstepping'), or it might diverge more and more from the ontogenetic stages of the ancestor (progressive deviation). The former mode reflects the theory of parallelism of Harvey and Serres, the latter gives expression to von Baer's theory of the greater resemblance between animals when they are young. It is important to notice that Müller based phylogeny on ontogeny, for it is the changes in ontogeny (i.e. alteration in the processes of development of the descendants as compared with those of the ancestor) which make the adult descendants differ from their ancestors, and so add a new link to the phylogenetic chain.

The theory of recapitulation

This was the state of affairs when Haeckel took up the matter and expressed his views of the relation of ontogeny to phylogeny in the form of his famous theory of *recapitulation* or *biogenetic law*. According to this (1866: II. 300; 1875 B:9), *ontogeny is a short recapitulation of phylogeny*, and *phylogeny is the mechanical cause of ontogeny*. The adult stages of the ancestors are repeated during the development of the descendants, but they are crowded back into earlier stages of ontogeny, therefore making the latter an abbreviated repetition of phylogeny. These repeated or 're-capitulated' ancestral adult stages reflect the history of the race, preserved by heredity, and so Haeckel (1875 A) applied to them the term *palingenetic*. As an example may be mentioned the stage in the unhatched bird and unborn mammal when visceral slits or pouches are present. Haeckel urged that these visceral slits represented gill-slits of the adult stage of the ancestral fish, which in the birds and mammals has been pressed back into early stages of development.

Applying his formula to a wider field, Haeckel (1874) concluded that since nearly all the Metazoa pass through a gastrula stage during their development, therefore the adult ancestor of the Metazoa was a gastrula or 'gastraea', represented today by the coelenterates. This will be discussed in later chapters (pp. 164 and 166).

At the same time, it could not be denied that in some cases, at least, the young stages of a developing animal presented shapes and structures which no adult ancestor could possibly have possessed, such as the birth-membranes of a mammal for instance. In these cases Haeckel concluded that the recapitulation of palingenetic stages was temporarily in abeyance and that a new or *caenogenetic* stage had been intercalated in the ontogeny as an adaptation to environmental conditions which the mode of life of the young animal imposed. The caenogenetic stages, therefore, were unhistoric falsifications and had no ancestral or evolutionary significance.

Haeckel believed that there was a difference in mechanism of production between changes in the adult stage which he regarded as inherited, and changes in the young stages which he regarded as adaptively acquired interpolations in the life-history.

It will be noticed that the biogenetic law abandons von Baer's principle of progressive deviation or rather relegates it to the state of the caenogenetic exceptions, and that it is really a reversion to the theory of parallelism and the 'overstepping' of Müller, to which it adds the idea of causation in that the succession of palingenetic stages in ontogeny is due to these stages having succeeded one another in phylogeny. The biogenetic law makes it necessary to believe that the new variations (by means of which evolution was brought about) occurred at the end of the ontogeny of the ancestor, or in other words, that the evolutionary novelty first appears in the adult. Phylogeny, then, according to Haeckel, is brought about by the successive tacking of new final stages on to the existing adult stages of animals, and the processes of development in ontogeny are 'due' to this progressive accumulation in phylogeny. What 'due' may mean we shall see in the next chapter.

Apparent confirmation of Haeckel's views was provided by the work of Hyatt and Würtenberger on ammonites. These fossil animals had shells which were constantly added to during their life. The above-named authors thought that they could show that the characters which appeared on the older parts of the shell of an ancestral ammonite were to be found on the younger parts of the shell of subsequent and descendant ammonites. At all events, this view commended itself to Weismann (1904), who summed up his opinion as follows: 'The ontogeny arises from the phylogeny by a condensation of its stages', which he also expressed as 'a retraction of the phyletic (phylogenetic) acquisitions of the mature animal deeper and deeper into the germinal history of the species.'

The theory of recapitulation has been provided with an elaborate terminology. 'Tachygenesis' is the speeding-up and compression of ancestral stages in developments, 'lipogenesis' is the omission of certain stages, 'bradygenesis' the lengthening of certain stages.

Until recently the theory of recapitulation still had its ardent supporters. From the embryological point of view MacBride (1914) insisted that 'the larval (i.e. early) phase of development represents a former condition of the adults of the stock to which it belongs'. Further, he affirmed, when comparing the young stage with 'the adult ancestral stage which it represents . . . one receives the impression that one is dealing with a reaction which, constantly repeated through thousands, nay myriads of generations, tends to set in sooner and sooner in the course of development; just as in the life of the individual, the *formation of habit* causes reactions to require for their evocation less and less of the original stimulus'. From another point of view Smith Woodward, speaking as a palaeontologist, says that he is 'convinced that whenever he is able to trace lineages he finds evidence of the recapitulation of ancestral characters in each life-history', and 'he is equally convinced that the phenomena he observes when tracing lineages can only be explained by assuming that acquired characters are inherited'. These two authors thus proposed to relate phylogeny to ontogeny by means of the inheritance of acquired characters. Quite apart from whether we accept or reject the inheritance of acquired characters (and we shall have something to say about this in the next chapter), it must be borne in mind that the relation between ontogeny and phylogeny is to be looked for and found in heredity.

Such is the history of the development of thought which has led to the theory of recapitulation. This had a remarkable sway and was even championed by Bernard Shaw. It was responsible for the statement that 'during its life-history an animal climbs up its family tree'.

The rejection of the theory of recapitulation

Since much of the argument in this book is based on the observations of von Baer, it is all the more regrettable that, as Lovejoy and Oppenheimer have shown, his repudiation of the theory of recapitulation should have led to his rejection of evolution as well. Keibel and Mehnert pointed out that the order in which characters appeared in phylogeny is not always faithfully reproduced in ontogeny. For instance, teeth were evolved before tongues, but in mammals now tongues develop before teeth. In their ontogenetic development in mammals today teeth have obviously been retarded relatively to tongues, and the realization of this fact is of great importance because the argument is still occasionally heard that *because* a structure is formed early in embryonic development, *therefore* it must have appeared early in evolution. As will be seen below, this does not follow at all.

To the alteration and reversal of the sequence of stages the term *heterochrony* is applied, and it creates the suspicion that the alleged retraction of adult characters into younger stages of development (if it really occurs) is not simply due to the piling up of new variations at the end of the life-history, for the successional order of the pile is not necessarily respected. It also suggests that it is not legitimate to speak of a 'stage' being shifted back to a later or on to an earlier period in the life-history. It is not the 'stage' which is shifted *en bloc*, but certain characters which may be peculiar to the stage. It must also be remembered that what an embryologist calls a 'stage' is merely an arbitrarily cut section through the time-axis of the life of an organism. A 'stage' is thus really an abstraction of the four-dimensional space-time phenomenon which a living organism is.

Even before the theory of evolution had been propounded, T. H. Huxley had in 1855 demonstrated the fallacy of Agassiz's 'law of parallelism'. He showed that there is nothing embryonic in the earliest fossils known, such as trilobites, graptolites, or brachiopods, which would justify their comparison with young stages of development in later forms. Nor is the cartilaginous skeleton of selachians to be regarded as nothing but an arrested embryonic structure. Huxley therefore concluded that 'there is no real parallel between the successive forms assumed in the development of the life of the individual at present, and those which have appeared at different epochs in the past'.

Another line of attack on the theory of recapitulation was made possible by the increase in detailed knowledge of young stages of development. Sedgwick (1894) showed that the earlier stages of development of quite closely related animals such as the hen and the duck could be distinguished, and that in the case of *Peripatus* it is the difference between the embryos of two of the species which makes it possible to distinguish between them, the adults being indistinguishable.

Sedgwick (1909: 178) next showed that there is no evidence for the view that evolutionary novelties only appear in the terminal or adult stages of life-histories, as Haeckel's theory of recapitulation requires. 'The evidence seems to show, not that a stage is added on at the end of the life-history, but only that some of the stages in the life-history are modified . . . one would not expect often to find, even if new stages are added in the course of evolution, that they are added at the end of the series when the organism has passed through its reproductive period. . . . Inasmuch as the organism is variable at every stage of its independent existence and is exposed to the action of natural selection there is no reason why it should escape modification at any stage.' The realization of the fact that evolutionary novelties can make their appearance at any stage of the life-history was an important step in the exposure of the inadequacy of Haeckel's theory of recapitulation. Darwin had already stated this quite clearly in the *Origin*: 'in a state of nature natural selection will be enabled to act on and modify organic beings at any age, by the accumulation of variations profitable at that age, and by their inheritance at a corresponding age'.

W. His concluded that even at their early stages, developing animals possess the characters of the class, order, species, and sex to which they belong, as well as individual characteristics. O. Hertwig went on to point out that the very egg itself must have specific characters although they may be invisible, and that the eggs of two different animals are really as distinct from one another as are their adults, the distinctions becoming more and more visible as development proceeds. The egg of the mammal and the unicellular ancestor are not really comparable, and in a remarkably thorough analysis Hertwig revealed this flaw in the logic of Haeckel's argument. In the same vein F. R. Lillie pointed out that not only the final result, but all the stages of ontogeny are modified in evolution.

W. Garstang (1922) elaborated this view very skilfully, and so showed that there has been an evolution along the line of fertilized eggs (or zygotes), in consequence of which animals have modified their ontogenies and so changed the shape of the final stage of development, viz. the adult. But a series of adult forms modified in this way is phylogeny, and so phylogeny is the result of ontogeny instead of being its cause. Garstang thereby arrived at the same point of view as Hurst, who wrote: 'I do deny that the phylogeny can so control the ontogeny as to make the latter a record of the former.' The same opinion has since been expressed by Ekman, Franz, Fuchs, Nauck, Schindewolf, and Shumway. Similarly, Berg allowed that ontogeny anticipates phylogeny.

Among other adverse critics may be mentioned Naef, who by

his 'law of terminal alteration' redirected attention to von Baer's principle of greater resemblance between young stages; Sewertzow, whose principle of 'anaboly' resembles the 'overstepping' of Müller, and whose 'archallaxis' savours of the principle of deviation; and Franz, who proposed four methods ('biometabolic modes') by means of any of which ontogeny may be related to phylogeny.

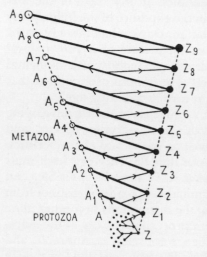

FIG. 1. The relations between ontogeny and phylogeny. $Z-Z_9$, the succession of zygotes; $A-A_9$, the succession of adults (phylogeny); Z_1-A_1, Z_2-A_2, the succession of ontogenies. From W. Garstang, *J. Linn. Soc. Lond. Zool.* **35**, 1922.

In a paper which deserves far more attention than it has received, A. P. Pavlov attacked the theory of recapitulation with firm evidence from the field of palaeontology, which is all the more important because it concerns ammonites, i.e. the same material as that which led Hyatt and Würtenberger to formulate their views. Pavlov showed that far from always recapitulating the adult stage of the *ancestor*, the young stages of the ammonite frequently foreshadow the adult stage of the *descendant*. This is the very reverse of recapitulation and it means that evolutionary novelties of phylogenetic significance may make their first appearance in the *young* and not solely in the adult as Haeckel contended. These ammonites cannot be made to support the theory of recapitulation without reversing the stratigraphical sequence of the beds in which they are found.

Pavlov's observations have been independently confirmed by Spath whose researches led him to precisely similar conclusions: 'It may be necessary to assume an inverted geological order if our views of the biological order of ammonites are to continue to be governed by discredited "laws" of recapitulation' (1924:194); and 'when the horizons of all these stocks are definitely known, it is hoped to get good additional evidence for a final rejection of the views on ammonite development connected with the names of Hyatt and Würtenberger' (1925:268).

That such rejection is imperative follows in no uncertain manner from Spath's demonstrations that Hyatt's series of ammonites, which were supposed to prove the theory of recapitulation, not only involve tampering with the stratigraphic succession, but are based on demonstrable fallacies, assumptions and *non-sequiturs*: 'Hyatt's deduction of his cycle of coiling from the individual development of a single example of *Gyroceratites fecundus* . . . was indeed the masterpiece in overstepping the bounds of reasonable evaluation of ontogenetic evidence' (1936).

In spite of these facts, it is astonishing with what tenacity the theory of recapitulation has been retained by some palaeontologists. As a result of detailed studies on Jurassic ammonites, Brinkmann had been led to the conclusion that the so-called biogenetic law is by no means of universal application. While in some lines ontogeny appears to run parallel with phylogeny, in others this is not the case. Here, 'phylogeny has lost its influence over ontogeny'. Did it ever have any?

Although he did not abandon the theory of recapitulation, J. P. Smith disarmingly confessed that 'in the sense in which the term has been used by most adherents of the theory, it [ontogeny] *never* recapitulates'.

Even George, a defender of the biogenetic law, was forced to admit that 'the application of the law must be tentative rather than final; it is approximate, rather than exact; it suggests and implies rather than fulfils'.

Swinnerton in a careful and critical study recognized that not only ancestral adult but also young characters can be recapitulated, or, as we prefer to say, repeated; and he made clear that the repetition of a character is far from being the reconstitution of an ancestral stage.

With devastating logic W. K. Gregory (1925) said that 'if the biogenetic law were universally valid, it would seem legitimate to infer that the adult common ancestor of man and apes was a peculiar hermaphroditic animal, that it subsisted exclusively upon its mother's milk, and that at an earlier phylogenetic period the adult ancestor was attached to its parent by an umbilical cord.'

Ehrenberg also pointed out that in so-called cases of recapitulation, the young stages of the descendants resemble the young stages of the ancestors more closely than they resemble the adult stages of those ancestors, a conclusion which is in complete agreement with Garstang's results. Similarly Jezhikov recognized that the stages seen in the development of the descendants are not necessarily to be regarded as representative of the adult ancestors, and that the uncritical acceptance of such a view has led to the conclusion that evolutionary novelties only appear in the adult, which he rejects. Lebedkin also concluded that recapitulation is not inevitable.

Kryžanowsky, one of the many recent authors to consider the theory of recapitulation, subjected it to a searching analysis. He knew of 'no single case in which evolutionary modification of ontogeny has taken the form of addition of new terminal phases to the final phases of the old ontogenies'. He objected on logical grounds to a comparison between phylogeny on the one hand, and the final stages of ontogeny on the other. Phylogeny he, like Garstang and Swinnerton, regarded as the succession of *complete* ontogenies, and since *all* evolutionary ontogenetic novelties are repeated in some phase or other of subsequent ontogenies (i.e. have 'phylogenetic' significance), Haeckel's distinction between palingenetic and caenogenetic characters falls to the ground.

More recently Hadži (1944) has attacked Haeckel's biogenetic law in its stronghold of the gastraea theory, for he has produced cogent arguments for the view that the original ancestral Metazoa were not in the least like gastrulae and that the coelenterates are not primitive at all.

It has been claimed by some enthusiasts that phylogenetic processes are repeated in regeneration and asexual reproduction. From what is now known of the extreme diversity of methods by which, and of tissues from which, processes of regeneration are carried out, this argument gives the reverse of support to the theory of recapitulation.

In the plant kingdom the biogenetic law was at first accepted by Strasburger and Goebel; but the first rebellion against the theory of recapitulation was made by Nicoloff who showed that the young stages of plants could not be relied on to give information concerning their ancestry. Guillaumin contended that the biogenetic law could not be of universal application because of the numerous cases where the young leaves of plants are more advanced in their evolution than the older ones. Gaussen and de Ferré have gone further and claim that evolutionary novelties may make their first appearance in the young stages of plants which are prophetic of the conditions in the fully-formed stages of their descendants. Finally, Wardlaw has shown that the size and complexity of a leaf may be determined by nutrition and has warned against applying the theory of recapitulation to plants.

It is obvious, then, that with regard to the relation which may exist between ontogeny and phylogeny, there is a basic divergence of opinion. While some continue to place phylogeny as a cause acting in and behind ontogeny, others prefer to reverse this relation. The matter is important, for it concerns the kernel of biology—development, evolution, and heredity. And, far from the question being one of merely academic interest, it is of the greatest practical importance, for the prestige so long enjoyed by the theory of recapitulation has had a great and, while it lasted, regrettable influence on the progress of embryology. This will be shown in due course. The following pages are therefore devoted to an attempt to synthesize the existing state of knowledge in these three fields and to produce a consistent formula which will co-ordinate them all.

The words which Sedgwick wrote many years ago (1894) are true today: 'If after fifty years of research and close examination of the facts the recapitulation theory is still without satisfactory proof, it seems desirable to take a wider sweep and to inquire whether the facts of embryology cannot be included in a larger category.'

II

ONTOGENY

IN the development of any organism we have to distinguish between the internal factors which are at work inside it and the external factors which constitute its environment. Now the internal factors were present in the fertilized egg, and so they can also be regarded as the transmitted factors, passage of which from parent to offspring constitutes heredity. When, therefore, we ask the question: Do the internal factors which are present in the fertilized egg suffice to account for the normal development of an animal? we are also questioning if heredity is solely responsible for the sequence of processes which constitute ontogeny. And since phylogeny can only be related to ontogeny through heredity, we are testing the validity of Haeckel's statement that phylogeny is the mechanical cause of ontogeny.

Internal and external factors in embryonic development

Fortunately, our knowledge of the processes of development has recently been very greatly increased by the extension of the application of experimental methods to the study of embryology. It may be definitely stated that the internal factors which were inherited from the parents are *not* sufficient to account for the development of an animal. To illustrate this all-important point, we may refer to the fact that ever since the Silurian geological period, roughly 300 million years ago, vertebrate animals had two eyes, as can be proved from a study of the fossils. Since (then as now) there must be internal factors concerned with the production of the two eyes, these have been transmitted to every generation for a very considerable period. But these factors are not self-sufficient, for if a few pinches of a simple salt (magnesium chloride) are added to the water in which a fish (*Fundulus*) is developing, that fish will undergo a modified process of development and have not two eyes, but one, as Stockard showed. Countless similar examples might be given, but this one suffices to show that by themselves the internal and therefore transmitted factors are not able to 'produce' a normal animal.

Numerous experiments have shown that the internal factors

of an animal are possessed equally by the cells in all its parts. So the cells of the head of a worm can by regeneration produce a tail, and the cells of the tail can regenerate a head. But if the cells of the head possess the internal factors which control the production of a tail as well as the internal factors which control the production of a head, how is it that in normal development these cells do produce a head and not a tail? C. M. Child solved this problem by showing experimentally that the first thing which has to be settled in a developing egg is the polarity, i.e. which part of the egg will give rise to the front and which to the hind end of the future animal. As soon as the polarity is established, local diversities arise and result in the qualitative differentiation of the different parts. Now in many cases the determination of this polarity seems to be the result of the action of factors which are *external* to the fertilized egg. In other cases it is possible that the polarity of the egg is derived from that of the oogonium which gave rise to it, but this merely pushes the question of the origin of polarity back in time. However this may be, it is clear that all the way through development the internal factors produce nothing of themselves, but they enable the animal to react in definite ways to the external factors and by this means give rise to structure after structure in the process of development. Heredity does not account for the individual, but merely for the potentialities some of which are realized in the individual. In other words, the internal and transmitted factors are by themselves unable to 'produce' an animal at all.

The 'inheritance' and 'acquisition' of characters

The first rigorous analysis of the relation of internal and external factors in development is due to Lankester, who showed that they can only be regarded as co-operating in the production of all the characters of an organism. The same point of view was developed by E. S. Goodrich (1924), who stressed the distinction which has to be drawn between the process of transmission of the internal factors from parent to offspring, and the process of production in the offspring of characters similar to those which were possessed by the parent. 'An organism is moulded as the result of the interaction between the conditions or stimuli which make up its environment and the factors of inheritance. No single part is completely acquired, or due to inheritance alone. Characters are due to responses, and have to be made anew at every generation.' Similar views were expressed by Conklin (1922).

These conclusions, which are based on definite experimental evidence, have a far-reaching importance. In the first place, they show that the question—Are acquired characters inherited?— has no meaning, for all the characters of an organism are both inherited and acquired; they would not be developed at all unless the organism possessed the requisite internal and inherited factors, and unless the external factors were sufficiently 'normal' to evoke the 'normal' developmental responses. A change in either the internal or the external factors will result in a departure from normal development. What the questioner really mean is—Can an effect originally produced as a response to an environmental stimulus come subsequently to be produced regularly without that stimulus? In other words, can external factors become internal? When, therefore, Hyatt defined an acquired character as 'a modification which makes its appearance in the adult or later stages of development and is obviously dependent for its origin upon other than hereditary causes', he is really describing the effect of an external factor, but that does not justify him in excluding the participation of internal factors in producing that effect.

Furthermore, these conclusions invalidate completely the distinction which Haeckel tried to draw between palingenetic characters which were supposed to be 'inherited' and caenogenetic characters which were supposed to be 'acquired'.

We shall return below to the question whether external factors may become internal, and may go on now to note that the conclusions at which Child and E. S. Goodrich arrived lift a great burden off the problem of heredity. The structure of an animal shows a number of exquisitely delicate adjustments; the splinters inside a bone are situated exactly where they are required to withstand the pressure to which the bone is subjected; the fibres of a tendon lie accurately along the line of strain between a muscle and the bone to which it is attached; centres of nerve-cells in the brain are situated close to the ends of the nerve-fibres from which they habitually receive impulses, and when in phylogeny there is a change in the nerve-fibres from which any given nerve-centre habitually receives its impulses, the nerve-centre is found to be situated near its new source of stimulation. It is this appearance of change in the position of nerve-centres during evolution which Kappers designated under the term neurobiotaxis.

It was a source of much perplexity to the student of heredity to try to understand how the factors controlling the production of such intricate and refined adjustments could be transmitted to the fertilized egg and produce these effects. He need not have worried about the production of the effects, for that lay in the province of the experimental embryologist, and not in his. As it turns out, it is the pressure in the tissues which causes the cells along the lines of stress to produce splinters of bone, and that is why these splinters are in the 'right' place; it is the very pull exerted on the tissues by the muscles which determines the production of a tendon with its fibres orientated along the lines of strain; it is the very ends of the nerve-fibres which have the property of stimulating nerve-cells to divide and so produce a nerve-centre in proximity to them, as Detwiler proved. The nerve-centres arise afresh in each generation, and by arising in a different place under the stimulation of a different set of nerve-fibres, the apparent effect of a migration in phylogeny receives its explanation.

All that is required is the transmission by internal factors of the capacity to react in these ways to new stimuli which evoke one response after another.

It is therefore obvious that ontogeny cannot be regarded simply as an extrapolation into the future of a chain of events which happened in past and previous generations. Each ontogeny is a fresh creation to which the ancestors contribute only the internal factors by the means of heredity. And this historic past is not the phylogenetic line of ancestral adults, but the line of the germ-plasm supplying the fertilized eggs for each and every generation. The action of the internal factors is to ensure that if the external factors are normal and do evoke any response in development and produce an animal at all, that animal will develop along the same lines as its parent. The internal factors are only a partial cause of ontogeny.

The internal factors are therefore also a partial cause of the resemblance found between related animals, and of the fact that in animals, even only distantly related, their young stages are

often found to resemble each other. This is the explanation of
the repetition in the ontogeny of the descendant of developmental stages in the ancestor, i.e. of successions of ontogenies
with no or little change.

The origin of change in ontogeny

We may now turn to the question whether the internal factors
which are operative in ontogeny can in any way be regarded as
the result of the modifications which the ancestors underwent in
evolution resulting in phylogeny; or, in other words, whether
phylogeny is in any way a 'cause' of ontogeny. If these modifications which the ancestors underwent were the result of changes
in the internal factors, then the question can be answered at
once, or rather it does not arise, for in this case the phylogeny
will itself have been the product of the internal factors working
in ontogeny. But if, on the other hand, the modifications which
the ancestors underwent in phylogeny were due to changes in
the external factors, then these external factors could only become the cause of the internal factors which control those same
modifications in subsequent ontogenies in so far as these factors
can be converted from external into internal factors (i.e. in old
terminology, in so far as 'acquired' characters can become
'inherited').

The work of Muller and others has shown that it is possible
to produce mutation, i.e. a permanent change in the internal
genetical factors, as a result of exposing the animal to special
external stimuli such as X-rays, and similar effects are now
known to result from temperature-changes and from treatment
with certain chemical substances. But these external stimuli
do not produce any modification in development at all before
they affect the internal factors. Exposure of flies to X-rays does
not affect the characters of the bodies of these same flies, although
it can 'produce' an internal factor, i.e. evoke a mutation which
will ensure that later ontogenies result in animals modified in a
particular way. These experiments have shown the possibility
of 'direct induction' of a change in the internal factors by
external factors. They have not shown the possibility of 'somatic
induction', i.e. of a change in the internal factors produced by
a corresponding change in the structure of the body, which
latter change was itself produced by external factors. Still less

have they shown that the cause of change in the internal factors, i.e. of mutation, is in any way adaptive.

The severe physical resistance (external factor) to which the muscles of the young blacksmith are exposed results (if his genetic constitution permits) in the development of a large biceps, but it will not cause his son to be born with or to develop a biceps larger than that of any ordinary man unless he, too, takes to wielding the blacksmith's hammer. To put the matter as succinctly as possible, no case has yet been satisfactorily proved in which, as a result of external factors, first the development of an animal has undergone a modification and, at the same time, these external factors have become internal and transmitted so that the same modification has come to be invariably produced in all the subsequent ontogenies of descendant animals without the necessity for the external factors which originally evoked the modification. It has never been shown that a modification evoked during successive ontogenies by the effects of use (or disuse) has become imprinted on the genes so that the modification becomes inborn and arises without the stimulus of use (or disuse) which originally evoked it. Until such a case has been proved, it cannot be believed that the effects of external factors and of use and disuse on body or mind are transmitted or play any part in ontogeny in subsequent generations.

There are some remarkable instances in which structures (such as callosities of the skin) may in some cases be inborn and in others evoked by the effects of use. Duerden has shown that when the young ostrich hatches, it possesses a number of callosities already developed. These callosities are situated on the breast, the pubic region, and on each ankle-joint. Now, the callosities on the breast and pubic region are functional, for the ostrich rests its body on them when it crouches. But the callosities on the ankle-joints are not used, for the legs tilt inwards and so the callosities do not bear on the ground. Instead, the weight of the body 'rests upon an adjacent inner projection of the ankle, and the skin and scales here gradually thicken and form an accessory pad'.

The interest of this case lies in the following facts. All these callosities are 'inherited', i.e. internal factors controlling their formation are transmitted, but whereas in some (the accessory pads) this formation is evoked by external factors (friction and use) after hatching in each generation, in the others (breast, pubic, and ankle-joint callosities) these particular external factors are not required, for the formation takes place before hatching and is inborn. But this is no evidence for the assertion that the internal factors which control the development of the latter type of callosity are the result of the action of the external factors (friction and pressure) on the body of the ancestor. Even if the functional necessity preceded the genetical change, all that we can say is that mutations and recombinations of genes have produced a hereditary change; and since the inborn callosities imitate the evoked callosities formed by friction, Medawar has introduced the useful term *genocopy* to describe such hereditary variations. We can say no more and no less about the origin of genocopies than we can about the cause of any other hereditary variations: they are due to mutations and recombinations of genes, preserved by natural selection.

We can, however, say one thing more about cases like that of the ostrich's callosities. The capacity to form callosities in response to external factors is due to the possession of relevant internal factors or genes. It has been shown by C. H. Waddington that the degree of response to external factors can in some cases be altered by deliberate selection and either increased or decreased. This is an example of the well-known fact that selection and reshuffling of the genes can alter characters under the major control of particular genes. The interest of this for the present case lies in the fact that the capacity to respond to an external stimulus can be increased to the point where the response is made to some intermediate (but inherited) process of development, with the result that the original external factor is no longer required. This is no 'inheritance' of an 'acquired' character, but the production of a genocopy by selection.

Somatic induction, or the transmission of the effects of use and disuse, constitute the kernel of the Lamarckian point of view; and it is curious that while we still lack evidence of this, Lamarck ruled out that of which we have evidence, viz. direct induction, though, in fact, he was correct in rejecting the view that direct induction can produce an adaptive inherited response to the environmental stimulus.

It would be very convenient if it were possible to accept an explanation of the origin of change in internal factors and of their adaptive nature on the lines of Lamarck's hypothesis of the effects of use and disuse, but the evidence is dead against it. Nor can the effects of use or disuse explain the origin of the capacity of organisms to react to use and disuse, as Abercrombie has so aptly remarked. It is necessary to adopt a humbler position and admit that the causes of origin and change in the genetical factors of organisms are unknown. Once they have arisen or changed (mutated), selection plays an all-important part in moulding their effects.

Finally, there is the question of the part played by the external factors which, by exerting selection on each generation of a phylogenetic lineage, have been partly responsible for the descendants having evolved into what they are. Holmes has suggested that the action of these past external factors is also reflected indirectly in the ontogenetic development of the descendants whose survival they have conditioned. But this selective action on the part of the past external and environmental factors can hardly be included under the heading of phylogeny, which may therefore be said to play no part in ontogeny.

III

THE SPEEDS OF THE PROCESSES OF DEVELOPMENT

W^E have seen in the previous chapter that development is brought about by means of the interaction of internal and external factors. Granted that the external factors remain constant and normal, we have now to inquire into the way in which the internal factors produce their effects. These internal factors have recently been subjected to very intense study, but mostly as regards the mechanism of their transmission from parent to offspring. They are mendelian factors or genes, and are regarded as discrete units situated in or on those universal constituents of the nuclei of cells—the chromosomes. A change induced in one of these genes is called a mutation, and the gene is then fixed in this changed condition until it mutates again. It is now accepted that these mutations, and recombinations of genes at the fertilization of eggs by sperms, are responsible for the appearance of novelties in evolution.

The way in which the genes are sorted out and distributed between parent and offspring is well known as a result of Morgan's (1926) continuation of Mendel's work, and forms the subject-matter of the science of genetics. In the process of their transmission the genes are carried in the germ-cells, the egg and the sperm. Germ-cells, like all cells, only arise by the division of pre-existing cells, and the production of ripe germ-cells occupies two cell-generations. It is during these two cell-generations (which culminate in fertilization) that the distribution of genes takes place, and so the geneticist who studies this distribution in hereditary transmission is really following the genes through two cell-generations only. But it takes fifty-six generations of cells to produce a body like that of a man out of a fertilized egg (itself a single cell), and during these fifty-six generations the genes are playing their part in company with the external factors in moulding the animal through the successive stages of ontogeny. We now want to know how this part is played.

This question is only beginning to be asked, and the lines on which it is to be answered were first indicated by Goldschmidt (1927, 1934). In his work on the determination of sex in the gipsy moth he showed that the structure of the adult, according to whether it is male or female, depends on the relative speeds at which two sets of genes produce their effects. These two sets may be referred to as the male-producing and the female-producing genes. In other words, genes as factors do not only have qualitative values; each gene also has a specific quantitative value and reaction-rate. Various races of the gipsy moth have male-producing (and female-producing) genes of different quantitative value. By introducing into an egg containing a weak female-producing gene a sperm containing a strong male-producing gene (as may be done by crossing moths of different races), it is possible to convert would-be females into males more or less completely. The conversion takes place at a certain time in development when the stronger male-producing gene overtakes its rival (the female-producing gene). Up to this point the female-producing gene has been ahead and the animal has been developing along female lines, but from the point of conversion onwards, the male-producing gene is leading and the animal then finishes its development along male lines. The stronger these male-producing genes, the sooner do they overtake their rivals, the earlier the time of conversion from one type of development to the other, and the more complete will be the conversion from female to male. Such animals which have switched over from a period of development in one sex to a period of development in the other are called intersexes, and a series of degrees of intersexuality can be established, from very slight to complete sex-reversal. In this series it can be noticed that the various organs and parts of the body do not all switch over from maleness to femaleness together, but one after another in a definite order, along a scale of increasing intersexuality. An organ which has finished its development before the time of conversion remains wholly female. Since the conversion takes place only after a definite point in time, the organs which are affected in cases of a slight degree of intersexuality should, on the theory, arise late towards the end of ontogeny, while those organs which arose earlier, i.e. before the time of conversion, will not be affected. In order to get at these latter organs and to switch them over from female-ness to maleness, it is necessary to have the overtaking of the female-producing genes by the male-producing genes happening sooner, which will be the case if the latter are very strong. The theory, therefore, rests on the assumption that the various organs develop in a certain definite order in time. Now this assumption can be tested independently of the evidence on which the theory is based (which was the varying degrees of intersexuality), by simply studying the development of the gipsy moth. When this was done, it was found that the order of development of organs is precisely that which the theory demanded. There is therefore a definite experimental basis for the statement that genes can control the structure of the body and can alter that structure by varying the rate at which they work.

An analogous case was investigated by E. B. Ford and J. S. Huxley in the brackish water-shrimp *Gammarus*. Some of these animals have black eyes and some red, and whether they have eyes of one or the other colour is determined by genes. These genes produce their different effects by varying the speed at which they allow the deposition of black colouring matter covering the red, and the time of onset of the processes.

Another example is that of the colour of the caterpillars of the gipsy moth, studied by Goldschmidt. The pattern on the back of the caterpillars in some races becomes obscured by black pigment, and the rapidity of the deposition of this pigment is under the control of genes. Similarly, the time of onset of the deposition of pink pigment on the shell of the snail *Cepaea* is controlled by genes, as Diver has shown. Genes likewise control the rate of formation of the pigment cells in the skin of goldfish, as H. B. Goodrich and I. B. Hansen found.

The difference in size between large and small rabbits is due to different rates of cell division, which rates, as Castle and Gregory have shown, are under the control of genes. Differences of shape are the result of different rates of growth in different directions, and these have been shown in gourds and pepper-corns to be controlled by genes. Details of these and other cases were given by Sinnott and Dunn.

That the general idea is true that the genes produce their different effects by working at definite speeds, can further be shown by raising or lowering the temperature of the environment which accelerates or retards the rate of action. This is why a primrose, which at a temperature of 20° C. has red flowers, will have white flowers if it is grown at 30° C. It also supplies the reason why the fur of the extremities (ears, paws, and the tip of the tail) of Siamese cats is dark, for the temperature at these places is lower than in the body generally.

We therefore reach the conclusion that by acting at different rates, the genes can alter the time at which certain structures appear, viz. in the case described, male structures in would-be female gipsy moths, and black eyes in *Gammarus*. This conclusion is of considerable interest, for it enables us to see how changes and indeed reversals in the order of development of structures can take place. To this phenomenon the term *heterochrony* may be applied. It may be imagined that a character *A* was evolved in phylogeny before a character *B*, but there is no reason why in ontogeny character *B* should not arise before, simultaneously with, or after, character *A*, according to the relative speeds of the genes at work, and the environmental conditions. A character which appeared in a late or adult stage of the ancestor might develop early in the ontogeny of the descendant, and vice versa. The contrast between the evolutionary and the embryological histories of tongues and teeth is a case in point.

Haldane (1932 A) devoted a study to the times in ontogeny at which genes exert their effects, and he showed that a gene may act: (1) on the germ-cells, (2) on the fertilized egg, (3) on the embryo, (4) on the larva, (5) on the developed but immature organism, (6) on the adult, (7) on the maternally-produced structures associated with the next generation (e.g. albumen, shell, placental decidua), (8) on the germ-cells of the next generation, (9) on the fertilized egg of the next generation. Haldane also provided examples of nearly all these possibilities from both the vegetable and animal kingdoms, and he stressed the importance of the effects of heterochrony in changing the stages in ontogeny at which the genes may act.

Supposing that in a smooth-shelled ammonite such as *Liparoceras cheltiense* there appeared a gene of class (4) controlling the formation of ribs on the innermost whorls of the shell, the result would be as in *Androgynoceras sparsicosta*. If heterochrony prolonged the action of the gene into class (5), only the outermost whorls would be smooth as in *Androgynoceras subhybrida.* If the action of the gene were further prolonged into class (6) the entire shell would be ribbed as in *Androgynoceras lataecosta.* These ammonites all exist and form an evolutionary sequence.

Following up this line of thought, it may be asked what the effect would be if a gene of class (9) controlling rapid growth of the young stages of the next generation were to become accelerated so as to exert its effects in the later stages of its own generation. Presumably the result would be a tumour.

In the vertebrates the development of several structures is under the control of chemical substances, the hormones, which are produced in special glands and circulate in the blood. In the frog the thyroid hormone is of great interest, for it is concerned in the development of the limbs, the lungs, and the tongue, i.e. in the production of those structures which will turn the tadpole into the frog and so bring about the change which is called metamorphosis. If extra thyroid hormone is administered to a tadpole, it will metamorphose too soon; if its thyroid gland is removed, it will not metamorphose at all, and the limbs, lungs, and tongue are not developed. The time at which metamorphosis normally occurs varies in different frogs and toads, and J. S. Huxley (1923) has shown that the differences in development of the following animals can be explained on the basis of the different rates at which the thyroid gland develops in each:

Bufo calamita (toad) metamorphoses in early summer.

Rana temporaria (common frog) metamorphoses in midsummer.

Rana clamitans metamorphoses in its second year.

Rana catesbeyana (bull-frog) metamorphoses in its third year. The thyroid gland develops fastest in the first which metamorphoses while it is still of small size, and slowest in the last which reaches a much larger size before it metamorphoses.

There is little doubt that the speed at which the thyroid gland develops is itself under the control of genes, for Riddle, working on the thyroid of pigeons, came to the conclusion that the 'normal mechanism of heredity can operate in the perpetuation of small changes in the endocrine organs'. The differences between the toads and frogs just mentioned can therefore be indirectly referred to the different rates of action of the genes.

In mice, Smith and MacDowell discovered a gene which

controls the formation of the eosinophil cells of the pituitary gland. When these cells are absent, the mice are dwarfs, presumably because the cells produce the growth-promoting substances. These results have been confirmed by de Beer and Grüneberg. At all events, we have here definite evidence of the genetic control of endocrine function.

In the mammals the hormones acquire an increased importance in regulating the speed of development, and deficiency in the thyroid, for instance, is well known to be associated with the under-developed condition known as cretinism. When the balance of the different hormones is upset, the tempo of development may be seriously affected, as in the condition described by Gilford as progeria, in which a man became senile and extremely decrepit by the time he had lived only seventeen years. Compared with other mammals, the speed of development in man is very slow, as can be seen from the table on page 74.

Some animals go on developing throughout their lives, but most cease altering their shape at a certain stage in ontogeny which is called the adult, and which is characterized by the fact that the reproductive organs are then ripe and ready to propagate the race. Now, the time at which the adult stage is reached is also governed by the rate of action of the genes, either directly, as in the gipsy moth, or indirectly by means of hormones, as in the case of the frogs and newts. It is possible, therefore, for there to be a competition between the genes which control any particular character and those which determine the assumption of the adult stage; and unless the former work fast enough and get in in time, the character will not be able to show itself. This is what actually happens in those cases in which an animal becomes sexually mature while still in the young stage, a phenomenon known as *neoteny* or *paedogenesis*. An example of this is furnished by the axolotl, which is really the tadpole stage of a newt (*Siredon*) and possesses gill-slits and external gills. In this state it can become sexually mature, and so some features of its structure, such as the bones of the skull, never become properly developed. Another example is the worm *Polystomum integerrimum*, which is parasitic on the frog, usually in its bladder, where it takes three years to reach maturity. But should it infect an early tadpole stage of the frog, it remains in the gill-chamber and becomes sexually mature in five weeks. The structure of this

neotenous form differs from that of the normal worm in that it
has but one male reproductive gland instead of several, and
other structures such as the intromittent organ, vagina, and
uterus are vestigial or absent. Many animals have become permanently committed to a neotenous state; so the newts *Proteus*,
Necturus, and *Typhlomolge* resemble the axolotl, and *Polystomum
ocellatum* resembles the neotenous form of *Polystomum integerrimum*.
On the other hand, by delaying the time at which the adult
state is normally reached, it is possible to cause structures to
appear which would not ordinarily have done so. So in the case
of the female gipsy moth, Goldschmidt was able to delay the
onset of maturity sufficiently long for the male-producing genes
to overtake the female-producing ones, and so bring about the
formation of male structures in an otherwise normal female. It
will be shown later that something like this has possibly taken
place in the evolution of certain kinds of animals.

The problems raised by the study of the different times in
ontogeny at which the differences develop in the characters that
distinguish different related groups of organisms from one
another are of the greatest interest. A start was made in this
field by Haecker with his studies on 'phenogenetics', and it has
now been developed on a more rigorous basis by Grüneberg and
others who have worked on types of which the genetical differences are accurately known. These studies bridge the gap between embryology and genetics, and when they have been
pursued further they will doubtless be found to provide much
new information on the problems associated with heterochrony.

We may safely conclude that the speeds at which the internal
factors work are of great importance in development, and that
variations in the relative speeds of the various factors may play
an important part in the relations of ontogeny to phylogeny.

IV

PHYLOGENY

PHYLOGENY is the scale of beings rehabilitated as a result of the theory of evolution into a row (or rather a number of rows) of adult forms which are related to one another, not from adult to adult, but from the fertilized egg which gives rise to one adult to the fertilized egg which produces the next. The adult forms in phylogeny are therefore disconnected from one another and incapable of influencing their successors, since this would require that the effects of use and disuse could become converted into internal factors and so affect the ontogeny and production of the adult of the next generation.

Phylogenetic transformations

It was pointed out by Garstang (1922), Swinnerton, and Kryža-nowsky that the restriction of the term phylogeny to the adults of the series is arbitrary, and that phylogeny should be regarded as the succession of complete ontogenies. This is true, and it must be noted that the upholders of the theory of recapitulation had adults in mind when they thought of phylogeny. But the cases in which the ontogenies of the animals in a phylogenetic series are known (ammonites, gastropods) are few. It is, therefore, more convenient to restrict phylogeny provisionally to mean the succession of adults. If all animals had been preserved as fossils, and if all these fossil remains had been discovered, we should be able to trace a continuous series of adult ancestral forms which would represent the phylogeny of the race which we were studying. Unfortunately this is not the case for the fossil record is still imperfect, and we only have a number of more or less isolated forms to indicate the track which phylogeny has taken. Nevertheless, the study of the phylogenies of a number of animals such as the horse, elephant, and camel have yielded very interesting series showing the progressive modifications which these races have undergone during evolution. Now, on comparing the various members of a phylogenetic series, it appears that the differences between the structures of the adults are largely differences of proportion, and of number, of the

parts relatively to one another. D'Arcy Thompson says in this
connexion that 'it is certain that, in particular cases, the evolution of a race has actually involved gradual increase or decrease
in some one or more numerical factors, magnitude itself included—that is to say, increase or decrease in some one or more
of the actual and relative velocities of growth.' In other words,
phylogeny in these cases has been brought about by variations
in the relative rates of action of the genes, which formed the
subject of the last chapter, or by allowing genes of given relative
rates of action to work for longer (or shorter) times.

The comparison of one adult form with another can be made
very instructive by inscribing the shape of one form on a grid-
system of Cartesian co-ordinates. If the skull of *Hyracotherium* (an
early fossil regarded as ancestral to the horse) be inscribed in
this way and the drawing be compared with that of the skull of
the horse, it is found that the points in the horse's skull corresponding to those in that of *Hyracotherium* have been displaced.
By a harmonious transformation of the grid, the skull of *Hyracotherium* can be distorted and made to resemble that of the horse.
But there are intermediate steps in this distortion, and we
actually have fossil horses which fit these intermediate steps perfectly (*Mesohippus* and *Protohippus*. See also p. 59). We may agree
with D'Arcy Thompson when he writes: 'It is the ratio between
the rates of growth in various directions by which we must
account for the external form of all, save certain very minute,
organisms'; and we may conclude further that it is an alteration
in this ratio between the rates of growth which has produced a
phylogeny such as that of the horse. It is not necessary to imply
that evolution has only consisted in quantitative variation of
already existing structures; on the contrary, qualitative variation in the form of structural novelties must also have appeared.
But once the internal factors for these novelties have become
established, they will be subject to quantitative modification
and heterochrony.

Clandestine evolution

It is, perhaps, worth stressing the fact that if a novelty appeared and only affected the young stages of ontogeny in a race,
that race would not show any phylogenetic progression if that
is measured only by adult modification. It is therefore possible

to imagine that a certain amount of 'clandestine' evolution of qualitative novelties may take place in the young stages of development while the adult stages are undergoing little change. Such an evolution of structures in the young is well known, and called caenogenesis, or youthful adaptation. If neoteny then occurs, and the animals become sexually mature in the young condition which caenogenesis has produced, the phylogeny will undergo an unexpectedly abrupt modification and start off in a new direction altogether. Now, the fossil record has been of the greatest value in tracing the phylogenies of horses within the mammals, and of mammals and reptiles in general within the vertebrates; or, to take another group, of ammonites within the molluscs. But no fossils have been found which bridge the gaps between the larger groups (or phyla) of animals; between the vertebrates on the one hand and the starfish on the other, or between either of these and the molluscs or worms. Doubtless there were many forms whose fossil remains have not been found; there must have been still more which were not fossilized because they did not have any hard parts capable of being preserved, and these will include young stages in which caenogenesis has taken place. Therefore it is probable that these gaps, that these discontinuities in the phylogenetic series of adults, may to a certain extent also be due to 'clandestine' evolution in the young stages, followed by neoteny and the sudden revelation of these hidden qualitative novelties. In the following pages an attempt will be made to show that this has occurred in some cases at least.

Evolution in straight lines

Attention may now be paid to those cases of phylogenies in which the modifications of successive adults appear to have taken place in definite directions. A case in point is that of the titanotheres, a group of extinct mammals. The earliest fossil titanotheres had no horns on their heads. Later fossils had horns, and in each of the four races into which the titanotheres seem to have split, these horns became progressively larger and larger, until they reached ridiculous dimensions and were probably responsible for the extinction of the race which then occurred. This incorrigible tendency to produce larger and larger horns, to vary continuously in the same direction, is an example of the phenomenon to which has been given the names of *orthogenesis* or *programme evolution*.

While some authors have attempted to assign orthogenesis to the action of mysterious forces, its explanation in many cases has been furnished by J. S. Huxley (1924, 1932) from a study of the relative sizes of parts of animals at different absolute sizes. In the case of the claws of some crabs, the ratio between the size of the claw and the size of the body increases with increasing body-size, or, in other words, the maximum size which the claw reaches in its development increases relatively faster than the body. Many other instances may be given of the same phenomenon, which is called *allometry* (previously known as *heterogony*). In all these cases the relative growth-rates of the allometric organ (in the case mentioned, the claw) and of the body remain constant during long periods, and may be expressed mathematically. The expression is $y = bx^{\alpha}$, where x is the size of the body, y the size of the allometric organ, b is a constant dependent on the particular case, and α is a constant. When the value of α is greater than 1, we have positive allometry as in the case of the claws just described; when the value of α is less than 1, we have negative allometry which is important in connexion with the reduction of organs; when the value of α is equal to 1, we have isometric growth of organ and body.

The interest of this demonstration from the present point of view is that any increase in the size of the body will necessarily entail an exponential increase in the size of the allometric organ as a correlated variation, brought about by an increase in the rate of action of the factor controlling the formation of the allometric organ. In confirmation of this, H. F. Osborn (1915) showed that it is a fact that the body-size of the titanotheres did increase, and that in those forms in which the horns were small they only appeared in the adult, whereas in the later-evolved forms in which the horns were large they were already present in young stages. Further, it may be concluded that unless the size of the body has reached a certain minimum value, the allometric organ will not show itself at all. So while the early titanotheres were too small to show horns, they transmitted the factors for horn-production to the four races to which they gave rise, in each of which horns appeared independently when the body became large enough.

'Orthogenesis' of a structure in phylogeny may, in some cases, therefore, be regarded as due to the existence of a particular quantitative relation between the rate of action of the factors controlling the production of that structure and the rate of action of the factors controlling the size of the body.

It should be added that except for these cases in which, as shown in this chapter, the appearance of evolution in straight lines is explicable as due to correlation with allometric growth, the idea of orthogenesis is erroneous. As Simpson has shown with a wealth of detail, evolution only goes on in a straight line if natural selection favours it at each stage. There is no evidence for any 'force' tending to direct evolution other than natural selection, and the course which it has set has usually been tortuous in the extreme. The most that can be said for 'orthogenesis' is that if an evolutionary novelty has conferred advantage on the variant which shows it, an accentuation of the same variation may possess even more survival value, but only up to a certain point.

Lastly, it may be noticed that if an animal with an allometric organ were to decrease the size of its body, that organ would become vestigial and would finally disappear. This has actually been proved by Champy in the case of the sword-like extension of the tail of the fish *Xiphophorus*, which becomes progressively reduced as the body decreases in size, in the adults of successive generations bred in captivity. Further consideration of these phenomena will be given in Chapter IX.

V

HETEROCHRONY

WE have seen in previous chapters that the strengths of
the internal factors of development can vary and exert
their effects at different rates, with the result that the
time of appearance of a structure can be altered. To this shifting
along the time-scale the term *heterochrony* is applied. It is thus
possible for two organs to reverse the order of their appearance
in successive ontogenies, and, by varying the rates at which
animals become mature, adult structures can be reduced to a
vestige and discarded, or youthful structures can become adult
and so be introduced into the phylogeny.

A word must be said about the term 'youthful'. From the time
the egg is fertilized until the young animal emerges from the egg-
membranes, i.e. hatches, it is known as an embryo, and this
period is called embryonic. After hatching, and until it has assumed the adult form, the young animal is known as a larva, this
period being called larval, and often characterized by remarkable adaptations to the environmental conditions in which the
larva lives.

While originally the embryonic period was very short, as animals became more complicated in evolution they took longer to
develop, which meant that the time at which the young animal
was hatched and could start fending for itself was delayed. As
an adaptation to this delay a store of food was provided by the
mother for consumption by the embryo in the form of yolk in
the egg, or provision was made for the continuous supply of
nutriment from the mother to the embryo by means of a placenta. By these means the embryonic period was prolonged at
the expense of the larval, and structures which had been larval
in previous ontogenies would (unless they were delayed also)
come to be embryonic. When, therefore, it is desired to speak of
a structure or character which appears in early stages of development, it may be either embryonic or larval. Which it actually is
does not matter for the present purposes, and so, in order to
avoid making a distinction where none is meant, in the following
pages the word 'young' will be used merely to express an early

stage of development, and the structures which appear at that stage will be called 'youthful'.

The distinction between adult and young, i.e. between structures which appear late or early, is drawn principally because it is the structures of the adult which form the phylogenetic series.

There can now be no doubt that evolutionary novelties may have made their first appearance at any stage of the life-history, early or late. It is useful to have terms to designate these possibilities, and *neanic* may be used for characters which first appeared in early stages of ontogeny, and *ephebic* for those which first appeared in the adult. This distinction would not have been admitted by Haeckel, since the theory of recapitulation required that only those characters which appeared in the line of adults had evolutionary significance.

The effects of heterochrony will make it possible for any character, neanic or ephebic, to appear later or earlier, or just at the same corresponding time, when compared with a previous ontogeny. Applying this to youthful and to adult structures, we get six possibilities. A delayed appearance of new structures will mean their reduction to vestiges, unless the time at which the adult stage is reached is also delayed; whence a seventh possibility. Lastly, a distinction must be made between those youthful structures which concern only the young stage and those which persist and also affect the adult. Heterochrony, therefore, provides eight possibilities of variation in the way in which structures may appear in the ontogeny of a descendant as compared with the ontogeny of the ancestor. These eight possibilities may be regarded as morphological modes of evolution.

It is, of course, impossible to measure the relative rates of action of the factors in controlling the development of structures in the ontogenies of all animals, especially those which are extinct and known only by fossil remains. However, there is the method of comparison; for if a structure is found in the adult stage of one animal and in the young stage of another, it is obvious that the structure has developed faster in the latter. If, further, the former animal is for other reasons regarded as a representative of the ancestral type from which the latter animal descended, then it may be concluded that the phylogeny of the latter animal has been brought about by a relative acceleration in ontogeny of the rate of action of the factors controlling the development of the structure in question. All the eight possibilities outlined above may be tested in this way. It is, of course, true that the external factors can also operate in modifying the rates of action of the internal factors, but they will on the whole act more or less equally on all the internal factors, and will not, therefore, be of such importance as the internal factors in producing hetero-chrony. In the following considerations the external factors are regarded as constant during the phylogeny; the possible effects of their variation will be considered later.

Morphological modes of evolution

Characters which are present or make their appearance in the young stage of an ancestral animal (neanic characters) may in the ontogeny of a descendant appear:

A. In the young stage only, producing youthful adaptations or *caenogenesis*, without affecting the phylogenetic adult series.

B. In the young and adult stage, producing a substitution of a new adult condition for the old, resulting in progressive *deviation* in the ontogeny of the descendant from that of the ancestor.

C. In the adult, by a relative retardation of the development of the bodily structures as compared with the reproductive organs, resulting in *paedogenesis* or *neoteny*.

Characters which are present in the young and adult stages of an ancestor may in the ontogeny of a descendant appear:

D. In the young stage only, resulting in the *reduction* of the character to a vestige.

Characters which are present or make their appearance in the adult stage of an ancestor (ephebic characters) may in the onto-geny of a descendant appear:

E. In the adult stage, resulting in those differences which dis-tinguish individuals, varieties, and races: *adult variation*.

F. In the post-adult stage, i.e. too late, resulting in the reduc-tion of the character to a vestige by *retardation*.

G. In the same stage, which is no longer adult, the new adult stage being relatively delayed, resulting in 'overstepping' the previous ontogenies or *hypermorphosis*.

H. In the young stage, producing precocious appearance of the ancestral character and *acceleration*. The accelerated character may or may not persist into the adult stage of the descendant.

Cases B and C, which produce phylogenetic effects by introducing youthful characters into the line of adults, may be combined under the term *paedomorphosis*, first proposed by Garstang (1922: 100). Cases E, G, and H, which produce phylogenetic effects by modifying characters which were already present in the line of adults, may conveniently be included under the term *gerontomorphosis*, first proposed in the 1st edition of this book (1930: 38). Cases G and H will give *recapitulatory* or *palaeogenetic* effects, while cases B and C will lead to results which may be described as *antirecapitulatory* or *neogenetic*.

In the following pages examples will be given of each of the eight possibilities outlined above. Attention may, however, be called here to a point which concerns the manner in which heterochrony may have been brought about. If it be true that a structure is formed at a certain time as a result of a reaction of a certain speed, then if the speed is increased the structure will be formed earlier. But the time of appearance of the structure may be governed not only by the speed but also by the magnitude of the reaction, i.e. by the amount of agent which is reacting, and this may also affect the size of the structure. It appears, therefore, to be necessary to take into consideration differences of capacity as well as differences of intensity in the reactions of the internal factors in producing structures. This is shown by the work of Ford and Huxley, who found that the condition in which the eye of *Gammarus* is pale (i.e. contains relatively little black colouring matter per unit area) can be obtained not only by a decreased rate of deposition of the black pigment (i.e. by decreased intensity) but also by an increase in the area of the eye (i.e. insufficient capacity). Conversely, in cases in which the area of the eye is small (as in dwarfs) a gene of low intensity has sufficient capacity to allow a rich deposit of black colouring matter as was proved by Ford (1928).

The time of appearance of a character will also be dependent on the time of onset of the formative processes, and Ford and Huxley have found genes in *Gammarus* which control this time.

In some cases the time of appearance of a character may be delayed by the action of another factor which acts as a temporary inhibitor. The female-producing genes act as temporary inhibitors to the production of male characters in the gipsy moth

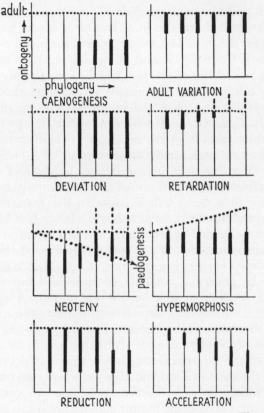

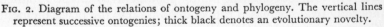

FIG. 2. Diagram of the relations of ontogeny and phylogeny. The vertical lines represent successive ontogenies; thick black denotes an evolutionary novelty.

up to the time at which the male-producing factors win, and the animal is switched over from one sex to the other.

The part which heterochrony, or the 'changing of the gears' of developmental processes, might play in evolution is well shown by Berrill's (1945) studies on the lower chordates. 'If the gearing ratio of the ascidian egg is shifted to that of *Amphioxus*, the segmentation will proceed beyond the 9th cleavage before gastrulation begins, and consequently a blastula similar to that of *Amphioxus* will be formed, and invagination into a large segmentation cavity will occur. . . . If gastrulation were postponed one division later, the blastocoel might survive gastrulation, as it does in echinoderms. Differentiation of chordaplasm and myoplasm would be equally retarded, so that a notochord consisting of the order of 600 cells [as in *Amphioxus*] instead of about 40 [as in ascidians] would result, muscle-tissues being equally affected.'

It may also be noticed that Darwin appealed to the principle of heterochrony to explain the evolutionary problem presented by the fact that parthenogenesis occurs in the mature female of coccid insects, the pupa of *Chironomus* [*Tanytarsus*], and the larva of *Cecidomyia* [*Miastor*]: 'we have only to accelerate parthenogenetic reproduction by gradual steps to an earlier and earlier age, . . . and we can perhaps account for the marvellous case of the *Cecidomyia*.' (*Origin of Species*, World's Classics Edition, p. 506.)

Another aspect of the importance of heterochrony in the evolution of insects may be seen in the progressive retardation or even inhibition of growth of the adult organs in the highest forms, to which Chen has drawn attention. In these the development of the adult organs is delayed until a late stage and then takes place rapidly by means of imaginal discs.

VI

CAENOGENESIS

THERE are a number of cases in which different animals resemble one another when adult, but are markedly unlike one another in the early stages of their development. These are exceptions to the 4th law of von Baer. Some of the characters which these animals show in their early stages could not possibly have been present in the adult stage of any ancestor, and so it is certain that they arose as neanic characters during early stages of development. This fact is important, for it proves that evolutionary novelties can and do appear in early stages of ontogeny. Here belong the cases of embryonic and larval adaptation to which Haeckel (1875 A: 409) applied the term *caenogenetic*, a few of which will now be considered by way of illustration.

Embryonic membranes, structures, and larval forms

No one will deny that the amnion and the allantois (embryonic membranes), which are of such essential importance to the development of every reptile, bird, and mammal, could never have featured in any adult ancestral form, and must have evolved in the early stages of ontogeny. It is also worth noticing that the evolution of the mammals could not have taken place if it had not been for these embryonic novelties.

It is equally certain that the glochidium larva of the freshwater mussel *Unio* which is temporarily parasitic on a fish; that the larval stage of *Haemocera* which is parasitic in a worm while the adult stage is free and resembles normal copepods; that the inflated larva of *Sitaris* which floats on the honey of the bee *Anthophora* which it parasitizes while the adult is a normal cantharis beetle; that all these youthful adaptations were introduced into early stages of ontogeny and reflect no adult characters at all.

Other examples are provided by the embryonic structures which enable the embryos to hatch out of their egg-cases, such as the egg-bursters of insects described by van Emden (1946), the glands on the snout secreting enzymes which dissolve the embryonic membranes found in some fish and amphibia, and the egg-teeth and caruncles of vertebrates described by Hill and de Beer

(1949). In the honey-guides, birds of the genus *Indicator* which, like the cuckoos, lay their eggs in the nests of foster-parents, this adaptation is carried still further and the caruncle is prolonged into a sharp hook which is used to kill the parasite's foster-brethren, as Friedmann has shown. The hooks are then shed.

The nauplius is a larval form commonly found in the Crustacea; the trochosphere is a larval form of frequent occurrence in Annelida and Mollusca. These larval forms as well as many others such as the pilidium, veliger, pluteus, actinotrocha, must be regarded as larval adaptations to dispersal, and not, as recapitulationists contend, as the representatives of ancestral *adult* forms. As Woltereck (1905) convincingly showed, the trochosphere is to be regarded as the representative of the ancestral *larval* form. The trochosphere could not be the form of the adult ancestor of Annelida and Mollusca, nor could the nauplius represent the form of the *adult* ancestor of Crustacea, for that ancestor must have had its body divided into several segments, while the nauplius has only three segments. That so many Annelida and Mollusca do have a trochosphere larva is due to the fact that they have a common ancestor (which in its ontogeny had a trochosphere larva), whatever that ancestor may have been like when adult. The same conclusion applies to the nauplius which is evidence for the affinity between the groups of Crustacea which have it in their life-histories, but is no indication whatever of the structure of the adult Crustacean ancestor. Raw has made it very probable that the protaspis is simply the larva of trilobites, and represents no adult ancestor.

The cotyledons of flowering plants are the first leaf-like structures to appear in the seedlings, and the fact that they are formed early in the ontogeny and are usually simple in structure led to the view that they represented the definitive foliage leaves of the ancestors. This argument has been shown by Guillaumin to be unsound. In the first place he has pointed out that the palaeontological evidence is all against the supposition that the original foliage leaves of ancestral flowering plants were simple in structure. On the contrary, they were complex in the earliest phanerogams of all classes, as may be seen from the following examples: among gymnosperms in the Silurian Cordaites, in Devonian Pteridosperms, in apetalous dicotyledons of the Lower Cretaceous, and among monocotyledons in palms of the Upper

Cretaceous. Simple leaves are probably not primitive but the result of reduction in evolution, and it is absurd to suppose that the cotyledons of living plants represent the complex primitive ancestral foliage leaves.

Even more important is the fact that cotyledons are 'larval' structures, adapted to serve the seedling during the critical period of germination by functioning as organs for storing reserve food-materials (in non-endospermic seeds), or as organs for transmitting stored food-materials to the growing points (in endospermic seeds), and sometimes also as precocious organs for carbon-assimilation. In other words, the cotyledons are caenogenetic structures, comparable with the embryonic membranes in animals, evolved and present only in early stages of the life-history and without any phylogenetic significance whatever.

Developmental processes without relation to evolutionary history

A decisive case is provided by the method of cell-division which the fertilized egg undergoes in the development of certain Platyhelmia (flat-worms), Annelida (true worms), Mollusca, and Nemertina: the method known as 'spiral cleavage'. In all these cases, the new cells are formed by division from the old cells in certain regular positions which follow a definite rule. But this rule cannot conceivably represent any *adult* feature of any ancestor; it is merely a developmental device for splitting up the single fertilized egg-cell into a larger number of smaller cells, and for sorting out the raw materials that will go to form the various regions of the future embryo.

In many cases it is possible to prove that the ontogenetic development of an organ is different from what its evolution must have been. For instance, the mammalian liver develops as a compact mass of cells permeated by bile canaliculi, subsequently penetrated by blood-vessels. But the phylogeny of the vertebrates suggests that the liver was originally probably a simple outpouching of the gut which, in higher forms, became subdivided into a number of branches separated by blood spaces. Ontogeny here does not retrace the steps of phylogeny, but leads straight by the most direct means, as Drooglever Fortuyn showed, to the final result.

Another excellent example, pointed out by E. S. Goodrich (1930), is furnished by the lung. During the whole length of its phylogenetic history, the adult lung must have possessed a thin and highly vascular membrane through which gaseous exchanges took place. But in embryonic development the lung is represented by a mass of dense mesenchyme into which the lung-buds gradually grow, followed by blood-vessels. Thus the respiratory epithelium, which must have existed at the start of the evolution of the lung, is not formed until the end of embryonic development.

Similarly, the metanephric kidney arises in ontogeny from two quite separate series of rudiments: the buds of the ureter, and the mesenchyme out of which the Malpighian corpuscles are differentiated. But in the phylogenetic series of adults these corpuscles must always have been connected with the branches of the ureter, or function would have been impossible.

Thus the embryonic development of the liver, the lung, and the metanephric kidney cannot represent any adult ancestral conditions, and must be regarded as caenogenetic innovations, evolved in early stages of development. The same is true of the mode of development of the pharynx, thyroid, and thymus in man, as Weller has shown.

Other examples of cases in which ontogenetic events are directly opposed to phylogenetic history have been given by Nauck. In the phylogeny of birds the angle between the coracoid and scapula has been reduced and become more or less acute. In the ontogeny of the chick the angle is of 78° at 13 days incubation, rises to 138° at hatching, and drops to 64° in the adult. There is no phylogenetic background for this phenomenon, which is purely caenogenetic. Other instances are provided by the temporary and subsequently reversed embryonic changes in the retroversion of the head of the tibia, or the displacement of the bladder in man.

A particularly instructive example is provided by the shape of the head in mammalian embryos. These have round, bulging foreheads and short jaws, but they rapidly elongate and give rise to the long snout and flat head characteristic of such animals as the rabbit and the wolf. That such an embryonic condition could not possibly represent any ancestral adult condition was decisively shown by W. K. Gregory (1936): 'If the biogenetic law were infallible it would not be necessary to continue palaeontological exploration in quest of successive stages in evolutionary history. If we wished to learn the form of the skull and of the jaws in the remote ancestors of the Canidae, for instance, it would only be necessary to look at the bulging forehead and feeble jaws of the young animals. From such material we could easily infer that the adult ancestral dogs were very unlike the existing jackals, wolves, and police dogs, which hitherto have been regarded generally as relatively primitive in skull form, and we should have to conclude that the Pekingese dog, with its bulging forehead and weak jaws, stands much nearer to the ancestral type.' Which would be absurd. The shape of the head of the embryo and young dog has no phylogenetic significance whatever and is purely caenogenetic. The same argument applies to cats and pigs.

In most chordates the neural tube arises as a groove, the sides of which fold over to form a tube. But in *Petromyzon, Lepidosteus, Lepidosiren*, and Teleostei it arises as a solid rod, in which a canal subsequently hollows out. Clearly, one of these methods must be caenogenetic and the same is true of the methods of formation of the lateral-line canals in Chondrichthyes and Osteichthyes. As Allis has pointed out, in the former the organs and lines sink beneath the epidermis and are subsequently hollowed out, and, in places, exposed to the surface. In the latter, the lines are formed as grooves and, in places, subsequently closed over. One of these methods must be caenogenetic.

The coelomic cavity can arise during development by one or other of two different methods. In some groups it is formed as an outpouching of the gut-cavity, when it is termed an enterocoel, as for example in echinoderms and lower chordates. In other groups it is formed by the hollowing out of a cavity in a solid band of cells, when it is called a schizocoel, as in annelids and molluscs. MacBride (1914) attempted to read a deep phylogenetic significance into the method of origin of the coelom. Assuming the diverticula of the gastro-vascular cavity of adult ctenophores to be comparable to enterocoelic pouches, he concluded that the enterocoelic method of formation of the coelom was primitive and that it was evidence for the evolution of coelomate animals from an adult like a ctenophore. The schizocoelic method, in his view, must be secondary because in his search for the adult ancestral significance of all the features of embryonic development, he could not otherwise answer his question: 'what changes in successive generation of adults can we suppose to be represented by the separation of a gut-cell from its neighbours, and by its proliferation to form a mass of cells which later become hollowed out to form a cavity?'

MacBride's dilemma was unnecessary, for as Goodrich (1930) pointed out, the formation of coelomic sacs does not represent any adult ancestor, and the question whether they arise as enterocoelic pouches or schizocoelic cavities has no significance for the phylogeny of adult ancestors, although it may indicate affinity between those embryos and larvae in which they develop in the same manner.

Hadži (1949, 1953) has cut the ground from under Mac-Bride's argument by showing that 'coelomic' cavities must have been present in Protozoa, and that when the original Metazoa became cellularized, these cavities became surrounded by cells and formed in different ways (see p. 167), which recapitulate no adult ancestor.

It has been pointed out by de Beer (1938, see p. 150) that differences are found in the causal processes and formative stimuli directly concerned in the formation of organs and structures. For instance, in the Tunicata the formation of the neural tube is not dependent on the presence of the notochord; in higher chordates it is dependent. In the frog *Rana esculenta* the formation of the lens is not dependent on the presence of the eye-cup; it is dependent in *Rana fusca*. In each case one of these alternative methods of development must be caenogenetic.

Dissimilar young: similar adults

There are many cases in which the younger stages of development of different animals are dissimilar, while their adults are much more alike. Hurst drew attention to the fact that while the adult forms of the insects *Culex*, *Chironomus*, and *Corethra* do not differ widely, their larval stages show much greater differences from one another. One species of *Culex*, viz. *Culex moucheti*, has a larva which differs widely from that of other Culicines and closely resembles that of the Sabethines, as Hopkins has shown.

Among the saw-flies, *Palaeocimbex quadrimaculata* is a species of great interest, for in three different geographical regions the larvae are markedly different although the adults are indistinguishable. This may be seen from the descriptions of the larval forms in Central Europe and in the Mediterranean region given by Enslin, Sarra, and Bodenheimer. Another good example is provided by the species *Nematus miliaris* and *N. fagi*. Both species appear together in Europe, with adults to all external appearance (including the genitalia) similar, but with very different

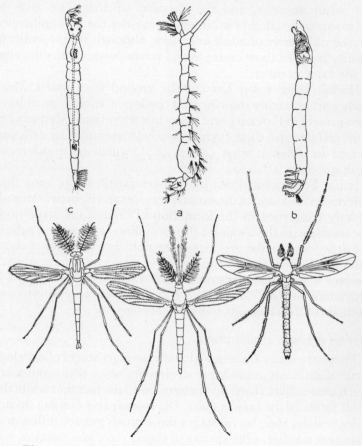

FIG. 3. The young and adult forms of three flies, to show the similarity between the adults and the differences between the young. *a, Culex; b, Chironomus; c, Corethra.* From Miall.

larvae. *N. miliaris* has conspicuous social larvae feeding on willow, whereas *N. fagi* has inconspicuous solitary larvae feeding on beech, as Brischke and Zaddach have shown.

A situation of great interest is provided by the gall-flies, among

which there are numerous examples where the differences that
are known between species relate to the structure of the galls
which they produce on the host-plant. In so far as these galls are
the result of secretions of the insect during egg-laying, they may
be said to reflect adult characters. But their structure is also
determined by the presence within them of a larva and may be
said to reflect differences between the physiological characters
of the larvae. Examples are provided by *Rhodites rosae* and *R.
mayri*: both occur on roses, and the adults are not easily distinguishable; the galls, on the other hand, are very different.

The same phenomenon is exhibited by the flies of the genus
Austrosimulium. According to Mackebras and Mackebras, the
species *tillyardi*, *laticorne*, *multicorne*, and *longicorne* are inseparable
in the adult state and can only be distinguished by the respiratory organs of the pupa.

Topsent observed that in sponges of the genus *Halichondria*,
specific distinctions have to be based on differences exhibited
by the young forms while the fully-grown forms are very similar.
Thus in *H. panicea* the larva is elongated, rounded anteriorly,
pointed posteriorly, covered with cilia of moderate length;
spawning-time: May and June. In *H. bowerbanki* the larva is
ovoid, the cilia at the hinder end are very long, and spawning-
time is August and September. But in the adult sponges the
spicules, structure of the skeleton, size, and shape in the two
species are indistinguishable.

Spath has found the same state of affairs in ammonites, and as
these animals figure very largely on the platform of the recapitulationists, no evidence concerning them can be neglected. Spath
(1926: 137, 139) states that 'as in many other ammonites, whilst
the adult of *Gagaticeras* are remarkably similar, the more plastic
young show great variability'. 'It is clear that a simple application of the biogenetic law to *Gagaticeras* would lead to results as
absurd as in the case of a new-born monkey. To add to our overwhelming detail, while there may be pronounced raricostation
throughout several depressed whorls of young *Gagaticeras* already
at a diameter of a few millimetres, in other immature specimens
there is not only fine and close costation, but the whorls are
round or even compressed at smaller diameters. . . . The larger
whorls are almost indistinguishable. . . . Whilst we should not
hesitate to identify—specifically—all the adults, ontogenetic

peculiarities, such as variations in whorl-shape, might be adduced to justify the assumption of the most diverse phylogenies and skipping of hypothetical stages.'

Similarly (1923: 65): 'if, as seems probable, new characters appear discontinuously or suddenly in the young, i.e., on the inner instead of the outer whorls of an ammonite, thus reversing the supposed regular sequence of stages in the life-cycle, all clues may be lost that might reveal genetic affinity, and we are forced to classify ammonites more and more according to geological occurrence'.

Swinnerton has pointed out that the differences between the various forms of protoconch in ammonites ('asellate', 'latisellate', 'angustisellate') do not appear to affect later ontogeny, and are examples of caenogenesis. He has also shown that the fixation of an organism like *Ostrea* to its substratum must be regarded as a caenogenetic event.

It may be remembered that Sedgwick (1894) was unable to establish any specific difference between *Peripatopsis capensis* and *P. bálfouri* except on the structures of the early stages of development. The larval development of *Polygordius lacteus* and of *P. neapolitanus* is very different, but the adult worms, according to Woltereck (1904), are practically indistinguishable. In the former species, which inhabits the North Sea, the trunk of the future adult develops in a sort of amniotic cavity within the body of the trochosphere larva which in such a case is described as an endolarva. In the latter species, however, the trunk of the future adult develops as an external aboral extension of the trochosphere larva, here known as an exolarva.

In nemertines, Schmidt has described a remarkable case of larval dimorphism in *Lineus gesserensis ruber*. In addition to the normal type of development from large eggs which give rise to inert embryos with small blastopores and thick epidermis, there is another type in which small eggs give rise to mobile embryos with thin epidermis and large blastopores through which they engulf their brother-eggs. The adults are similar except for a difference in colour.

The fly *Chironomus salinarius* has two alternative larval forms, and Buxton has drawn attention to dimorphism of eggs and larvae in several species of *Anopheles*.

Other examples of cases in which the young forms differ more

than the adults are provided by the moths *Acronycta tridens* and
A. psi, the frogs *Rana tigrina* and *R. cancrivora*, the isopods *Chiriodo-tea sibirica* and *C. entomon*, the saw-flies *Lophyrus pini* and *L. similis*.
Examples of dissimilarities between embryos or larvae of

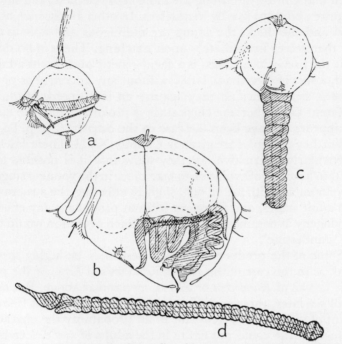

FIG. 4. Larval divergence in *Polygordius*. (*a*) Trochosphere of *P. lacteus* and
neapolitanus. (*b*) Larva of *P. lacteus*. (*c*) Larva of *P. neapolitanus*. (*d*) Young
metamorphosed worm of *P. lacteus* and *P. neapolitanus*. (After R. Woltereck, in
Archiv für Entwicklungsmechanik, **18**, 1904.)

closely related species or of identical species under different environmental conditions, have been given by Giard under the head
of 'poecilogony'. The freshwater variety of *Palaemonetes varians*
develops in a manner very different from the seawater variety.
    Great variation may be found between the products of hatch-
ing among closely related forms. *Penaeus* hatches as a nauplius,
Palaemonetes as a zoea, *Homarus* as a 'mysis-larva' while *Potamo-bius* has suppressed its larval stages and hatches as a miniature
adult; yet all of them are Decapod Crustacea. This case of
marked differences in development attracted the attention of

Darwin. Other examples may be found among the species of *Peripatopsis* where, as S. M. Manton has shown, there are oviparous and viviparous forms with eggs small or large, yolkless or heavily yolked.

In many birds the young are nidicolous, helpless, and slow to acquire ability to live by themselves. In other birds, such as the fowl and the duck, the young are nidifugous and able to fend for themselves immediately upon hatching. There is no doubt that the precocious 'chick' is a caenogenetic and recent adaptation, a sort of terrestrial 'larva' without any ancestral or phylogenetic significance. It may acquire an importance of quite a different kind when the chick stage is prolonged into the adult, as appears to have been the case in the ostrich. (See p. 82.)

Further examples are given in Chapter XVII. These cases are particularly instructive, for they show that it is possible for a certain amount of evolution to take place in the younger stages of development without or only slightly affecting the structure of the adult stages, and therefore without producing any effect in phylogeny as commonly understood. Such evolution would then be 'clandestine'.

Some of the products of caenogenesis may be highly specialized, as in the case of the glochidium larva of *Unio*, or the parasitic larvae of *Haemocera* or *Sitaris*, mentioned above. But as we shall see later, these specialized cases are unimportant from the point of view of phylogeny, for in all probability the characters of such larvae could not figure in the adults of any descendants.

'Ontomutations'

Because the methods of cleavage of the egg and the localization in it of the various organ-forming substances (pp. 136, 163) vary greatly in different groups of animals, Dalcq has concluded that evolution must have involved sudden drastic changes in the organization of the egg which he has called 'ontomutations'. Their results would have been to change the earliest processes of development and to produce structures such as the embryonic membranes of amniote vertebrates (p. 40). Ontomutations would therefore have been caenogenetic changes. Dalcq has concluded further that these changes must have been abrupt and given rise to new groups of organisms *per saltum*. But since the organization of the egg and the localization of organ-forming substances can vary greatly in closely related organisms (pp. 136, 151, 162), and embryonic development can take short cuts (p. 42) without evolutionary significance, it may be questioned whether such differences in the egg originated the evolution of these groups instead of accompanying or following it, and still more whether the clear-cut differences between the eggs of such groups today is evidence for the suddenness of their appearance in evolution.

Conclusion

It is clear, then, that evolutionary novelties do arise in the early stages of development and may restrict their effects to those stages. It is equally clear, as Morgan (1924) pointed out, that the internal factors controlling the production of these novelties can be and are transmitted like any other internal factors, i.e. are genes. We therefore reach the conclusion that these youthful characters are prone to the effects of heterochrony by acceleration or retardation of the rates at which the internal factors act, and might therefore be expected to appear in the adult as well as in the youthful stages. This possibility will be considered in a subsequent chapter.

A word is, perhaps, necessary to justify the retention here of the term 'caenogenetic'. It is meant solely to designate the origin of an evolutionary novelty in early stages of ontogeny. Shorn of the implications which Haeckel attributed to it, it might seem as though the term were better dropped. But the terminology is already complicated and confused, and since the obvious alternative term 'neogenetic' is already used in another sense (see p. 37), it appears to be simplest to retain 'caenogenetic' and restrict its meaning as above.

VII

DEVIATION

IN this chapter we must consider those cases in which the young stages of development of different animals resemble one another more than they resemble the adult stages, and more than the adult stages resemble one another. We shall therefore have to deal with the cases which led von Baer to propose his principle of the greater resemblance between young stages, and Müller to propose the method of progressive deviation. They are the basis of Sedgwick's rejection of the theory of recapitulation and they also form the basis of Naef's law of terminal alteration and Franz's third biometabolic mode. Sewertzow's principles of deviation and of archallaxis are also included here; the latter representing an extreme condition of the former, leading to deviation so precocious that the young of the descendant no longer resembles even the young of the ancestor. Jaekel's principle of metakinesis is similar, and Kleinenberg's 'substitutions' are also examples of deviation. The cases considered here are of great importance because they have been used erroneously to support the biogenetic law and to claim that the young of the descendant is a picture of the adult of the ancestor.

Examples of deviation

One of the most interesting cases is that of the gill-slits, or rather of the visceral pouches, which appear in the embryonic stages of reptiles, birds, and mammals. These structures resemble the visceral pouches which appear in the *embryonic* stages of fish. The visceral pouches of embryo reptiles, birds, and mammals bear·little resemblance to the gill-slits of the adult fish. Any one who can see can convince himself of the truth of this. All that can be said is that the fish preserves its visceral pouches and elaborates them into its gill-slits, while reptiles, birds, and mammals do not preserve them as such, but convert them into other structures such as the Eustachian tube, the tonsils, and the thymus glands. There *is* similarity between the embryos of fish and of reptiles, birds, and mammals, but the later stages of ontogeny have diverged. In the reptiles, birds, and mammals other adult stages

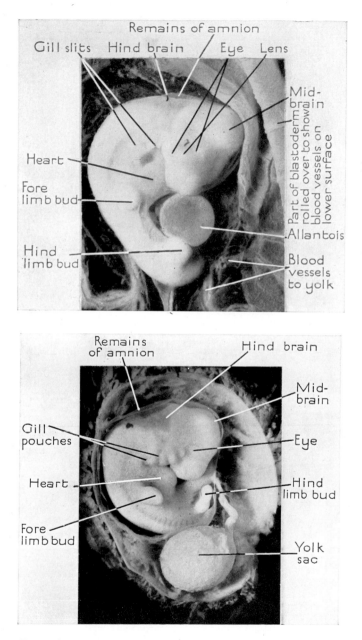

FIG. 5. An embryo of a chick (*A*) compared with that of a human being (*B*) to show the similarity between the young of animals whose adults are markedly different. After Haldane and Huxley, and by permission of Professor A. Thompson, Department of Human Anatomy, Oxford.

Photograph, W. Chesterman and D. A. Kempson

have been substituted for the adult stage of the fish. During the phylogeny of the reptiles, birds, and mammals, therefore, factors have arisen in the ontogenies which control the development from the embryonic stage onwards and which have produced progressive deviation.

Archaeopteryx had a long tail of twenty vertebrae, to sixteen of which corresponded a pair of rectrices feathers. In the adult stage of modern flying birds the tail is very much shortened: the six or seven pairs of rectrices are inserted transversely, and the half-dozen terminal tail-vertebrae are reduced and fused together to form the pygostyle. In the young modern bird, as Steiner found in an embryo of the owl *Syrnium aluco*, the rudiment of the tail is relatively elongated with a row of rectrix-rudiments along each side. This does not mean that the conditions in the embryo bird of today represent those of adult *Archaeopteryx*, but of *Archaeopteryx*'s embryo. What makes this case particularly interesting is the fact that the embryos of the flightless birds or ratites do not show this 'Archaeopteryx-stage'; for it had previously been thought that the ratites were more primitive than other living birds. It is now clear (p. 82) that the ratites are not primitive at all.

The red blood-corpuscles of mammals are nucleated before birth and non-nucleated afterwards. Lower vertebrates have only nucleated corpuscles. This does not mean that the embryonic mammalian corpuscles represent those of adult ancestral vertebrates, but simply that postnatal mammals' blood-corpuscles have lost their nuclei.

The adult stages of hermit-crabs have curved abdomens while those of normal adult crabs are symmetrical. The larval stages of hermit-crabs are symmetrical, but this symmetry represents that of the *larval* stages of normal crabs and not that of the adult stage of Galatheid crabs from which hermit-crabs are regarded as descended.

The endostyle is present in Tunicates and in *Amphioxus* from the late larval stage to the end of adult life. In *Petromyzon*, as W. Müller first showed, it is present only in the ammocoete larva. There is no doubt that the ancestors of *Petromyzon* had an endostyle in the adult, since it is an adaptation to the ciliary method of feeding which the primitive chordates practised. But this does not mean that the ammocoete larva recapitulates the endostyle of the adult ancestor; it repeats the development of the ancestral larval endostyle and it is the adult of *Petromyzon* that has lost it.

We can in another case prove conclusively that a larval form which resembles the *larval* form of another animal which is regarded as ancestral, actually differs from the *adult* form of that ancestral animal. *Portunion* is a crustacean of the order Isopoda, and in its adult stage it is parasitic in crabs. The larval stage of *Portunion* resembles the larva of normal non-parasitic Isopoda, and like the latter, it has seven pairs of limbs on its thorax. But the normal Isopoda when they are adult have eight pairs of limbs on their thorax, and so it is definitely clear that the larva of *Portunion* takes after the larva of normal Isopoda (which are regarded as its ancestors) and not after the adult. 'It is the adult *Portunion* which has lost its legs, not the young *Portunion* which has acquired them from its adult ancestors' (Garstang, 1922).

Entoconcha is a member of the gastropod order of molluscs, and in its adult stage it is parasitic in sea-cucumbers. The larval stage of *Entoconcha* is a veliger similar to that of the larval stages of more normal Gastropoda, and so here again we find that the larval stage is a reflection of the larval stage of the ancestor and of nothing else. That *Entoconcha* and normal Gastropoda should both have veliger larvae proves that *Entoconcha* is a gastropod, just as a parallel line of reasoning proves that *Portunion* is an isopod crustacean.

The sole is a so-called flat-fish because in its adult state it has turned over on its side and lies flat on the sea-bottom. It also undergoes a certain amount of structural modification resulting in the migration of the eye on the underside over to the upper side, and consequent asymmetrical distortion. But the larva of flat-fish is symmetrical and swims upright, and so is the larva of normal fish. The symmetry of the larva of the flat-fish corresponds to that of the larva of normal fish and only indirectly to that of the adult stage of normal fish. It is true that normal fish remain symmetrical, while flat-fish become asymmetrical in the adult condition, and therefore the larva of flat-fish bears a stronger resemblance to the adult of normal fish than it bears to its own adult. But this is because the normal fish has not changed, whereas the flat-fish has, in substituting its type of adult structure for that of its ancestor.

The skull of the sharks is cartilaginous throughout their life; the skull of higher vertebrates (e.g. mammals) is cartilaginous only in the embryonic stage, and the cartilage is replaced by bone in the adult. This cartilaginous skull of the mammalian embryo resembles that of the embryo shark, not that of the adult shark. The essence of this fact was correctly discerned by Reichert over a hundred years ago. In the human embryo the cartilaginous skull is insignificant by comparison with the size of the brain. It is quite obvious that these conditions reflect those of the ancestral embryo and not the ancestral adult, for, as Lewis so very aptly remarked: 'Who would claim that our primitive ancestors had more brain than skull, except perhaps the few who believe in the downfall of man?'

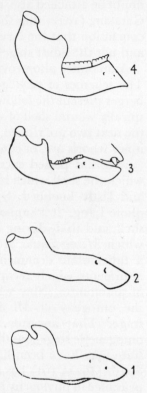

An interesting case is that of the mandible of the elephant, described by Eales. During ontogeny the mandible of the modern elephant elongates until, about the time of birth, it projects some way in front of the foremost tooth. The phylogeny of elephants is fortunately well known, and there is no doubt that the ancestral elephants underwent a similar type of development of the mandible, which, up to this point, the ontogeny of modern elephants repeats. But from this point modern elephants deviate and the mandible shortens, apparently by absorption of the anterior projection and probably by differential growth. There is therefore no evidence that it is the adult ancestral characters which the ontogeny of modern elephants repeats.

FIG. 6. The development of the mandible in *Elephas africanus* showing the reduction of the chin. 1, foetus of mandible—length 2 cm.; 2, foetus of mandible—length 5·6 cm.; 3, newborn; 4, adult. Ratio of magnifications, 30:12:3:1. From N. B. Eales, *Proc. Zool. Soc. Lond.*, 1931.

In the same way, *Antedon*, a crinoid which is free and unattached in its adult stage, passes through a larval stage when it is attached by a stalk. Other crinoids are attached by a stalk in their adult state, and their larvae must without any possible doubt be attached also, although they have not yet been studied. Garstang (1922) thus showed that all the evidence points to the conclusion that the larval stage of *Antedon* represents the larval and not the adult stage of its stalked ancestors.

Ammonites also provide evidence for deviation in ontogeny. The schemes of phylogeny drawn up by Hyatt and Würtenberger present the following situation. *Microceras densinodus* has a spirally wound shell of which the four inner whorls are smooth, the next two are ribbed, and the outer whorls are knobbed. The inner whorls are, of course, the earliest to be formed, and so the animal has passed successively through ontogenetic stages in which the shell which it secreted was first smooth, then ribbed, and lastly knobbed. So, on the theory of recapitulation, to quote Lang, 'it is supposed that the ancestral form had a plain shell, and that, during its evolution, the stock or lineage from which *M. densinodus* arose acquired, first a ribbed, and then a tuberculate ornament'. This example is typical of all the arguments which recapitulationists seek to base on the study of ammonites. Now why should the ribbed-shelled stage in the ontogeny of *M. densinodus* represent an ancestral *adult* stage? That ancestor may have had a ribbed-shelled *early* ontogenetic stage, but there is no evidence at all of what its adult state may have been like. Indeed, in some species of *Psiloceras*, Spath (1924: 191) has shown that the ribs make their first appearance in phylogeny in the inner whorls, i.e. in the early stages of ontogeny. After presenting further evidence of this type Spath (1923: 65) concludes: 'There is no necessity for assumption of a previously existing costate stage in tuberculate ammonites, or of a slender-whorled evolute stage before a stout-whorled involute stage, except to make them fit arbitrary cycles and lineages; for the evidence generally points to some indifferent root, common to the two extremes.' These arbitrary cycles and lineages are based on the theory of recapitulation the truth of which is taken for granted; they do not prove it. In this connexion it may be recalled that these hypothetical lineages may involve a reversal of the geological order, which is of course absurd.

A similar conclusion was arrived at by Franz, who pointed out that the smooth-shelled snail *Paludina neumayri* probably gave rise in the Pliocene period to *Tulotoma*, which has ribs on the outer whorl of its shell. The inner whorls of *Tulotoma*'s shell are smooth, as are the inner whorls of the shell of *Paludina*, but none of the characters of the outer (adult) whorls of the shell of *Paludina* have appeared on the inner whorls of *Tulotoma*'s shell, although they have had all the time since the Pliocene period to do so. These examples therefore present evidence of similarity between young stages and divergence between adults: not of recapitulation.

The evolution of gastropod molluscs

The gastropods are molluscs with twisted bodies, and as their ancestors must have been symmetrical, the chief problem of the evolution of gastropods is the origin of the torsion of the body and shell through 180° which is so characteristic of them. Such a form as the limpet develops into a more or less symmetrical veliger larva which suddenly undergoes a twist through 180°, the process of torsion occupying sometimes as short a time as two or three minutes. Crofts has shown that the mechanical cause of the torsion is the single asymmetrical larval muscle of the head and left side of the foot. Garstang claimed that there is great advantage accruing to the larva from being twisted. Whereas before the torsion it was not able to withdraw its head into the safety of the mantle-chamber, it can do this after the torsion. Torsion may thus be a larval adaptation, and so Garstang (1928 A) made a strong case for the view that gastropods have twisted bodies because twisting appeared as a neanic evolutionary novelty in the *larva* of their ancestor. This twisting would therefore be a caenogenetic character which differs from those which we considered in the last chapter only in that its effects persist into the adult stage instead of only affecting the larval stages of the ontogeny.

The evidence from palaeontology is in favour of this view, and Brookes Knight has shown that in the Lower Cambrian *Helcionella* is untorted, while *Oelandia* is torted. 'Torsion may have first taken place between these two genera in earliest Cambrian or in pre-Cambrian times.'

This theory of the origin of the torsion of gastropods has two advantages. In the first place, it does away with the difficulties which arise in any attempt to explain the origin of torsion on the assumption that it arose gradually during the adult life of some early mollusc. No adaptive significance can be conceived for such an event, whereas, as we have seen, the process may be adaptive if it takes place in the larva. In the second place, Garstang's theory provides an explanation for the total lack of forms showing any intermediate stages in this torsion. Torsion can take place easily in the young larva and twist the body of the animal through 180° at one stroke, but if it took place in the adult, it would have had to take place gradually, providing intermediate stages. That intermediate stages are not *a priori* im-

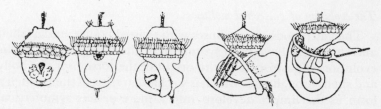

Fig. 7. Stages in the development of the limpet, showing that the animal starts symmetrical, and subsequently undergoes torsion while still young, resulting in the twisted structure which is characteristic of gastropods. After torsion the larva is able to withdraw its head into the protection of the mantle-chamber. (From Garstang.)

possible is proved by the fact that intermediate stages in detorsion in later gastropods are not wanting. There is no danger whatsoever of mistaking these detorting forms for the 'torting' forms for which we search in vain.

The skull of the horse

Another example of an evolutionary novelty occurring early in embryonic life and affecting all later stages is the skull of the horse. It was for a time thought from Robb's researches that in the development of the face of the modern horse, the changes of shape which it undergoes in ontogeny as a result of allometric growth were a repetition of those which the evolutionary series of horses underwent in phylogeny, which would have been an example of recapitulation. Further research, however, by Reeve and Murray has shown that this is not the case. In the modern horse the allometric growth-coefficient of the face relatively to the skull has a value of 1·5 up to a face-length of 10 inches, after which the growth of the face is isometric with that of the skull. In the fossil horses, however, the growth-ratio of the face in early forms with short teeth from *Hyracotherium* through *Mesohippus* to *Merychippus* is about 1·8. In later forms with long teeth, from *Pliohippus* to *Equus* the growth-ratio is about 1·5. This means that with the evolution of long hypsodont teeth, the proportions of the skull were reorganized, and this was brought about not by any increase in the allometric rate of growth of the face, but by an increase in size of the rudiment of the face at a very early stage of development, followed throughout ontogeny by a lower growth-ratio than had been the case in the ancestors. The ontogeny of the horse's face therefore does not repeat, let alone recapitulate, its phylogeny. In the modern horse, the length of the face is not reached by the young passing through the shapes of the skulls of its ancestors, but is the result of exaggerated anticipatory growth in early embryonic life. As such, this is an example of deviation.

Deviation in plants

Examples of deviation are also found among plants. In several flowering plants, adaptation to dry conditions has led to the development of xerophytic characters involving the reduction of leaves and stomata, giving a cactus-like appearance. This has occurred independently in many groups such as the Cactaceae, the Euphorbiaceae, the Asclepiadaceae, and, among conifers, the Pinaceae. In many of these cases, the early-formed foliage leaves are normal, and it is at later stages of development that the xerophytic adaptations appear. These early stages are repeating the corresponding early stages of the ancestral forms, they are not recapitulating the adult stages of the ancestors. This is well shown by the conditions in *Chamaecyparis*, a pine. The young seedling has leaves (pine-needles), whereas the mature form only has scales. The youth-form can be fixed and retained indefinitely by using side-branches as cuttings; it is then known as *Retinispora* under which name it is cultivated. The youth-form never or only very rarely flowers, which shows that it corresponds to the youthful, not the adult stage of the ancestors. It is therefore the adult *Chamaecyparis* which has lost its leaves, not the young *Chamaecyparis* that has acquired them from its adult ancestor.

Another case of deviation at the earliest stages of development is to be found in plants. The monocotyledons must have been descended from poly- or dicotyledonous ancestors, since the condition in which two or more cotyledons are present is more primitive than that in which there is only one. Takhtajan has pointed out that this must have involved the substitution of one cotyledon for two at the very earliest stages of development.

The monocotyledonous organization also involves many other structures which likewise appear at very early stages. These deviations have resulted in the production of a whole sub-class.

Changes in the number and position of structures

Next, we may consider some cases in which animals differ from others in the number of certain parts. *Colossendeis* is a pycnogonid with four thoracic segments and pairs of legs. *Decolopoda* is similar but it has five thoracic segments and pairs of legs. It is difficult to conceive of the extra segment and pair of legs of *Decolopoda* having arisen gradually, for segments are either present or absent. Nor can *Decolopoda* be regarded as the type from which *Colossendeis* arose by gradual loss of a segment, for four seem to be the regular and five the exceptional number of segments in the thorax of pycnogonids. In any case, there is still the difficulty of the change of number. There remains the possibility that the extra segment of *Decolopoda* was formed during the early stages of ontogeny, when the material for the future thorax was divided into five instead of into four. In *Dodecolopoda* it is divided into six. Other instances are given by Hedgpeth.

Similar conclusions can be drawn from other examples. I have myself observed that in the development of the chick it is possible for the number of segments, ribs, and vertebral bodies to be greater by one whole unit on one side of the body as compared with the other which was normal. It was also plain that the discrepancy could not be accounted for by fusion of two segments on the side with the smaller number, nor by secondary splitting on the other side. It must be concluded that the process of segmentation has split up the material of the chick's body into a different number of segments on each side. In Bateson's words, there has been a fresh 'distribution of differentiation' on one side. If both sides had been partitioned as was the side with one segment too many, the animal would have been comparable to *Decolopoda* in this respect, and formed as a result of an embryonic variation. It is possible that the extra gill-slits which are present in *Heptanchus* (7), *Hexanchus* (6), *Chlamydoselache* (6), *Pliotrema* (6), and in *Eurypharynx* (6), over and above the number (5) which is typical in fishes, may be explained in this way as Versluys suggested, but there are difficulties in this case.

E. S. Goodrich (1913) showed that the position of the fins of fish has been transposed up and down the body in phylogeny, but that there is no shifting during ontogeny. The fin arises in a new position from its first appearance in ontogeny, which shows that there has been no recapitulation; instead, progressive deviation has resulted in the substitution of a new position for that of the ancestor. Sewertzow also presented similar evidence, which he used to illustrate his principle of archallaxis.

The same phenomenon has been shown by Butler to occur in the teeth of mammals. Transitions from the pattern of typical molars to that of the teeth in front of or behind them take the same form in related species, but do not always affect the 'same' teeth ('sameness' means identity of numerical position in the jaw). It follows, therefore, that a particular tooth-type can in phylogeny move backwards or forwards in the jaws. But there is no shifting during ontogeny. The teeth arise in their new position from the start of the ontogenetic development of each individual.

Conclusion

It was pointed out by Sedgwick that 'the evidence we have seems to indicate that evolutionary modification has proceeded by *altering* and not by *superseding*: that is to say that each stage in the life-history, as we see it today, has proceeded from a corresponding stage in a former era by the modification of that stage and not by the creation of a new one. . . . The evidence seems to show, not that a stage is added on at the end of the life-history, but only that some of the stages in the life-history are modified.' This view has been substantiated to an ever-increasing extent with the progress of knowledge, and it expresses in succinct form why Haeckel's biogenetic law is rejected. The embryo of the descendant passes through modified stages of the ancestral ontogeny; it does not pass through and beyond the ancestral adult stage.

Kryžanowsky considers *all* modifications of ontogenies in evolution to have taken the form of deviations and substitutions. He distinguishes between 'autogeneous' and 'heterogeneous' substitution. In the former, existing ontogenetic phases are

partially or wholly substituted for other, earlier or later, existing
phases. Here belong the cases which we have included under the
headings of neoteny, retardation, and acceleration. In Kryžanowsky's second category, new phases are partially or wholly
substituted for existing phases at early, middle, or late stages of
ontogeny. This category covers the cases which we include under
caenogenesis, deviation, reduction, hypermorphosis, and adult
variation.

The evidence presented in this chapter proves that von Baer's
principles as expressed in his third and fourth laws have a wide
application. The origin at early ontogenetic stages of variations
which are ontogenetically permanent, i.e. affect the adult as
well as the young, is proved. These variations differ from caenogenetic variations merely in that the latter only concern the early
stages of ontogeny. But this difference amounts to nothing more
than the lengths of time during which the internal factors controlling the variations are acting, as would result from alterations
in the intensity and capacity of the factors.

Nearly all the cases mentioned in this chapter have been
adduced to prove the theory of recapitulation, and it has been
my task to show that they do not prove it. What they do prove is
embryonic similarity and repetition of characters in *corresponding* stages of the ontogenies of ancestor and descendant, which
reveals the affinity between different animals, but supplies no
evidence of what the adult ancestral form was like.

Deviation is a mode of evolution which allows larval characters in the ancestor to influence the adult stage of the descendant.
This is a principle to which Garstang gave the name paedomorphosis. As this is the exact opposite of Haeckel's principle of
recapitulation and is of great importance in phylogeny, it will be
referred to again.

VIII

NEOTENY

OUR object now is to consider those cases in which the adult form of an animal bears features by which it resembles the young form of its ancestors, or to put it the other way, those cases in which the young features of the ancestor have been retained in the adult stage of the descendant. Interpreting these cases in terms of heterochrony, they imply a *relative* retardation in the rate of development of the body (soma) as compared with the reproductive glands (germen), so that in respect of certain characters the body does not undergo as much development in the ontogeny of the descendant as it did in that of the ancestor. This state of affairs may, of course, be brought about in many ways, to which, in the past, different names have been given: 'paedogenesis', von Baer (1866); 'neoteny', Kollmann; 'epistasis', Jaekel; 'progenèse', Giard; 'foetalization', Bolk; 'proterogenesis', Schindewolf. Many examples of these phenomena have been given by Boas.

The term *paedogenesis* was introduced by von Baer in 1866 to cover cases of precocious sexual maturity of the reproductive organs while the organism is still in the condition of a larva or even an embryo, as in *Polystomum* or *Miastor*. The term *neoteny* was introduced by Kollmann in 1883 to cover cases in which animals retain their larval form and habits either temporarily or permanently and become sexually mature in that condition without undergoing the final developmental changes which produce the adult, as in various amphibia. The term *foetalization* was introduced by Bolk in 1926 to cover cases in which characters in the adult descendant remain in the same condition as in the foetus or young of the ancestor, as is seen in man.

In principle, therefore, paedogenesis (and similar terms like progenèse) applies to cases where the larva develops precocious sexual maturity; neoteny (and similar terms like proterogenesis) to cases where the sexually mature animal retains larval characters. In both, characters of the body are retained in a condition of partially arrested development as compared with the ancestor; and such characters are said to have undergone foetalization.

Since there can be no hard and fast distinctions between paedogenesis and neoteny, and paedogenesis is of no significance in progressive evolution, all these cases are included here under the term neoteny. Neoteny is the most important mode by which larval and youthful characters in the ancestor can influence adult characters in the descendant, a principle to which Garstang gave the term *paedomorphosis* in 1922.

Examples of paedogenesis

With the rate of development of the body remaining constant, this effect will be produced if the development of the reproductive system is accelerated. Here belong the well-known cases of paedogenesis, of which the most striking are those of *Polystomum integerrimum*, which has already been mentioned; of the cestode *Archigetes sieboldi*; and of the acanthocephalian *Echinorhynchus clavaeceps*. The same phenomenon can be observed in *Miastor*, one of the flies. Here, the larva or grub produces the next generation without ever developing any further.

The parasitic copepods also show paedogenesis. A normal copepod passes through six nauplius stages and five copepodid stages. *Achtheres ambloblistis*, as described by Wilson, hatches in the first copepodid stage, and after finding a host moults into the adult which corresponds to a third copepodid stage of normal copepods. Here again, therefore, it can be proved that the larva of the descendant represents the *larval* and not the adult stage of the ancestor. *Salmincola salmonea* hatches as a first copepodid, and according to Gurney: 'Development does not proceed any further, the larva attaching itself to the host in this first stage. The adult is therefore a paedogenetic first copepodid.' These cases also provide an example of the phenomenon to which Eimer gave the name of 'genepistasis', meaning that of two related forms one can undergo more development than the other.

Ripe germ-cells have been found in larval stages of ctenophores (*Eucharis*), Scyphozoa (*Tetraplatia*), and actinians. These cases fall, however, under the heading of '*dissogony*', for the organisms will become sexually mature again at the adult stage.

Examples of neoteny

In many cases retardation of the development of the body relatively to that of the reproductive system has taken place, and we get an animal like *Siredon mexicanum* which may become mature when its body is still in its larval stage, known as the axolotl. Such a case is usually called neotenous, and this one is of particular interest. The axolotl retains its external gills and gill-slits, and this is exactly what a number of other newts have done. But whereas the axolotl is only faculta- tively neotenous, since it can undergo metamor- phosis, lose its external gills and gill-slits, and assume the adult charac- ters of *Amblystoma* under either natural or experi- mental conditions, *Typh- lomolge, Necturus, Proteus*, &c., are permanently neotenous. There are other newts in which neoteny does not occur, and it is clear that the neotenous condition of the axolotl is an evolu- tionary novelty resulting from heterochrony. The same conclusion may be applied to the other neo- tenous forms which must

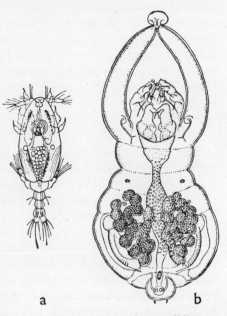

a   b

Fig. 8. *Achtheres percarum. a*, 'copepodid' stage; *b*, adult. After W. T. Calman, *Crustacea*, A. & C. Black, London, 1909.

have been derived from newts which only became mature after metamorphosis. The evolution of the neotenous urodeles, there- fore, has involved the retention of characters (external gills, gill-slits) in the adult stage which belonged to the larval stage of the ancestor.

Another case of neoteny is that discovered by Cousin in the cricket *Gryllus campestris*. Neoteny may affect only one sex: the female glow-worm is neotenous while the male is normal. On the other hand, in the crustacean *Hapalocarcinus marsupialis* it is the male that is neotenous while the female is normal, as Fize has discovered. It should be noted also that the neoteny need not affect all the structures of the body: it may affect only some of them, so giving rise to partial neoteny. Schulze showed this to occur in the acarine family Eriophyidae in which the two hinder pairs of legs do not develop ('merostasis'), and Vandel in Isopoda where appendages may remain juvenile in the adult.

It is clear that paedogenesis involving acceleration of sexual maturity leads to specialization and degeneration, and is of little importance for phylogeny. On the other hand, it is easy to see that a condition of neoteny will be achieved if there is no acceleration of the rate of development of the reproductive organs, but a relatively greater retardation in the rate of development of the body. Such cases are of great interest from the point of view of phylogeny.

The evolution of some invertebrate groups

The evolutionary history of Siphonophora is obscure, and attempts have been made to explain it by suggesting that they were descended either from highly developed medusae complicated by budding, or from colonies of hydroid polyps that had become free-swimming. Neither of these views, which would derive Siphonophora from other fully developed types of Coelenterates, is satisfactory, and Leloup has suggested that the Disconanth Siphonophora *Velella* and *Porpita* were evolved from larval forms of solitary Hydrozoa such as *Tubularia*. The conaria larva of *Velella* is very similar to the actinula larva of *Tubularia*. Both are floating structures, but whereas the actinula settles on the bottom and produces the sessile polyp of *Tubularia*, the conaria remains floating and gives rise to the similarly free *Velella* or *Porpita*. An indication of how the float of *Velella* may have evolved is provided by Hydrozoa such as *Margellopsis* where the aboral stalk of the actinula develops vacuolated cells. The most satisfactory explanation of the evolution of Disconanth Siphonophora is therefore that they are persistent larvae or neotenous Hydrozoa. These views have been extended by Garstang (1946), and by Totton who has demonstrated many cases of neoteny within the Siphonophora. For example, the Calycophore *Nectopyramis diomedeae* is a neotenous form resembling the post-larva of *Vogtia glabra*. Among Physonectae, *Athorybia* is a neotenous form which never develops nectophores, representing the larval stage of *Agalma*; *Melophysa* is similar but less markedly neotenous and corresponds to a larval stage in which the

nectophores have begun to develop. Totton (1960) derives
Siphonophora (including *Physalia*), *Pelagohydra*, and margellopsid
Hydrozoa from actinula-like larvae by neoteny.

The similarity between the Ctenophora with their eight
ciliated plates and Müller's larva of Polyclad Turbellaria with
its eight ciliated lobes has long been known. The resemblance
between them goes further, for they each have a pharynx and
tentacles, aboral sense-organs, statoliths, epidermal gland-cells,
and during their development the method of formation of
the gastrula, mesoderm, mouth, pharynx, and gut-cavity is the
same. These resemblances were taken by MacBride to mean
that the Polyclad Turbellaria were evolved from the Ctenophora, and that Müller's larva recapitulates the ctenophore
stage in the development of Polyclad Turbellaria. Hadži, on the
other hand, has shown that it is much more likely that the Ctenophora are neotenous Polyclad Turbellaria which have retained
in their adult stage many of the features of Müller's larva.

It has commonly been held that the so-called 'Mysis' stage of
development in decapod Crustacea represents an adult ancestral
form and that therefore the Decapoda were evolved from the
Mysidacea. The fallacy of this view was exposed by Foxon who
wrote that 'the larvae of the Decapoda do not in their ontogeny
pass through either a typical Euphausid or Mysid stage, and
neither their structure nor their function is recapitulated.'

The real significance of the decapod larval forms is very
different. Instead of representing any ancestral adult form, the
protozoea larva was almost certainly the starting-point of the
evolution of the Copepoda which have retained many larval
features. As Beurlen wrote: 'the Copepoda are representatives
of the Pygocephalomorpha [fossil Mysidacea of the Carboni-
ferous period] which have remained in the larval condition,
degenerate and neotenous. A comparison between Copepods
and larval stages of Schizopods [Euphausiacea and Mysidacea]
demonstrates this very clearly.' This view was adopted by Gurney
who brought forward much additional evidence in its support.
The protozoea larva of Decapoda has a setose antenna, three
pairs of thoracic appendages, an unsegmented abdomen, and a
caudal fork bearing six setae, all of which features are characteristic of the first copepodid stage of Copepoda. The hypothesis
that the Copepoda are neotenous Decapoda was accepted by

W. T. Calman who had long ago recognized the possibility that 'the Copepoda are persistently larval rather than phylogenetically primitive'.

Margalef has shown that neoteny occurs in several groups of Crustacea. It is accompanied by the reduction in the number of joints in the antennae and the limbs, often found in the copepods *Diacyclops* and *Megacyclops*, and in the smaller size and reduced number of joints in the antennae of the brackish-water subspecies (*aequicauda*) of the marine amphipod *Gammarus locusta*. The most striking example in the Crustacea of what can only be regarded as a case of neoteny is that of the Cladocera. These are Crustacea characterized by shortening of the body, reduction in the number of segments, and reduction in the number of cells which they contain, as compared with the other groups of the Sub-Class Branchiopoda to which they belong. Grobben, Eriksson, and Margalef have suggested that the Cladocera are really neotenous Conchostraca. The latter possess a larval form termed a heilophore which resembles a Cladoceran, and a series can be made out of existing families, leading from the Conchostraca to the Cladocera, viz.: Limnadiidae, Imnadiidae, Caenestheriidae, Leptestheriidae, and Cyclestheriidae.

The pteropods are gastropods which have become adapted to a pelagic mode of life, and H. Lemche has suggested that 'it seems reasonable to regard the Spiratellidae (and to some degree, other pteropods also) as opisthobranch larvae growing large without metamorphosing, reaching maturity in a greatly enlarged larval stage, whereas most other opisthobranchs alter their organization with age and metamorphose from pelagic into benthonic animals.' In other words, pteropods are neotenous opisthobranch larvae.

The evolution of man

Bolk pointed out that many of the features of the adult structure of man show resemblances to those of the embryonic structure of the anthropoid apes, and the same point of view has been expressed by Devaux. These features include the relatively high brain-weight, the position of the foramen magnum and the cranial flexure, the retarded closure of the sutures between the bones of the skull, the dentition, the flatness of the face (orthognathy), the position of the vagina, the big toe, the hairlessness of the body, the light colour of the skin, and a number of other features.

The axis passing through the front and back of the head forms a right angle with that of the trunk in the embryo of all mammals (and of nearly all vertebrates, for that matter), and this bend is

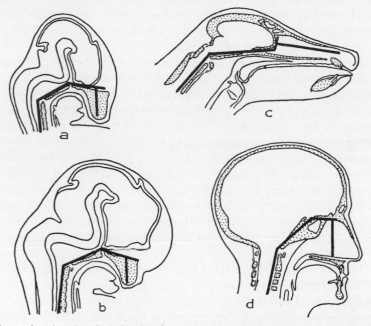

FIG. 9. A series of sections showing the angle which the head makes with the trunk in *a*, embryo dog; *b*, embryo human being; *c*, adult dog; *d*, adult human being. The embryonic curvature is preserved in adult man. (From Bolk.)

known as the cranial flexure. Whereas in mammals other than man the axis of the head is rotated during later development so that the animal's head points in a direction which is a continuation of the line of its backbone, in man the cranial flexure is retained so that his head points in a direction at right angles to the axis of his body. This is a consequence of the fact that in adult man the cribriform plate remains horizontal and parallel with the line of sight, whereas in the adult dog the cribriform plate is tilted backwards so that it is nearly vertical and lies more or less at right angles to the line of sight. The foetal condition of the cribriform plate is retained unchanged in adult man. Since the direction in which man's head points, i.e. his line of sight, is horizontal, the position of the body will be vertical; and so man's erect attitude is associated with the retention during ontogeny of a condition which in other mammals is embryonic and temporary, as it must have been in man's ancestors. At the same time, the flexure of the base of man's skull in the adult is accentuated by changes in the plane of the occipital bone, as Kummer has shown. The erect posture of man is, in Bolk's view, a consequence of neoteny of the shape of the head.

The retention of the cranial flexure accounts for the position of the foramen magnum, or hole in the skull through which the spinal cord enters, which position resembles that which is found in the embryos of the apes. The retention of the embryonic condition also accounts for the flatness of the human face, as compared with the elongated muzzle which is found in other mammals. This feature is of importance, for a muzzle separates the eyes, and, when it is not formed and the face is flat, the two eyes can come to the front of the face and let their fields of vision overlap. This enables both eyes to be focused on one object, and Elliot Smith pointed out that this development of the power of accurate vision has played an important part in the evolution of man.

The retention of the cranial flexure in adult man is paralleled by his retention of what may be called the pubic flexure. In the hind region of the body in embryos of all mammals including man, the orientation of the urogenital sinus and rectum is such that the axis of these structures is directed ventrally. In mammals other than man this condition is changed in the adult, by the rotation of the axis of these structures which comes to lie parallel with the backbone, with the result that the aperture of the vagina is directed backwards. In adult man, on the other hand, the embryonic orientation of these structures is retained, with the result that the aperture of the vagina is directed ventrally. The human mode of copulation is therefore associated with the neotenous condition of the pubic region of the body.

The sutures between the bones of the human skull do not close until the age of nearly thirty years. In apes and other mammals these sutures close much sooner after birth, and when that has happened the skull cannot increase in size any more. The human skull, on the other hand, can increase in size for a very long time after birth, and this enables it to provide accommodation for the large volume of the human brain.

Another interesting feature is the absence of large brow-ridges (such as characterize the skulls of *adult* apes, Australopithecines, *Pithecanthropus*, and Neanderthal man) in adult man and in foetal apes. These brow-ridges are subsequent developments in the apes, and A. Thomson showed that they fulfil a mechanical function in buttressing the upper jaw against a heavy lower jaw. Man is neotenous in not having developed them, the buttressing function being performed by the vertical wall of the forehead, and the necessity for this function having been reduced by the diminished size of the lower jaw.

It is because it has no brow-ridges that the fossil Fontéchevade skull is regarded as close to the line of modern man's descent, and Keith pointed out that the occipital region of the Swanscombe skull bears resemblances to that of a young ape. In this respect young Neanderthal man presents features of great interest and similarity with adult modern man, because the young Neanderthal skulls from Devil's Tower (Gibraltar), La Quina, Mount Carmel, and Uzbekistan had no brow-ridges. Similarly, the young *Pithecanthropus* skull from Modjokerto, and the skull of *Australopithecus*, which was that of a young individual, lacked brow-ridges.

Drennan, and also Buxton and de Beer suggested that modern man may be related to a neanderthaloid type, if he can be regarded as descended by neoteny from a *juvenile* form of the latter. If the human ancestors were similar to Neanderthal, *Pithecanthropus* or *Australopithecus*, modern man would have descended from them by retention of features in the juvenile forms of their skulls, which is exactly what is meant by neoteny.

With regard to the brain, Coupin has shown that the newborn chimpanzee resembles man more closely than does the adult chimpanzee, in respect of the relative preponderance of the different lobes of the cerebral hemispheres.

Man's big toe provides another example of neoteny, for there is reason to believe that the foot in the ancestor of man had a big toe, which, as in the lower primates, was capable of opposition. This feature has been retained and perfected in the great apes, but lost in man whose foot is particularly adapted for walking erect on firm ground. This loss of power of opposability in man

is, however, an example of neoteny, for his foot retains throughout life the simple condition of the toes found in early foetal apes
where it is only transient, as A. H. Schultz (1950) has shown.

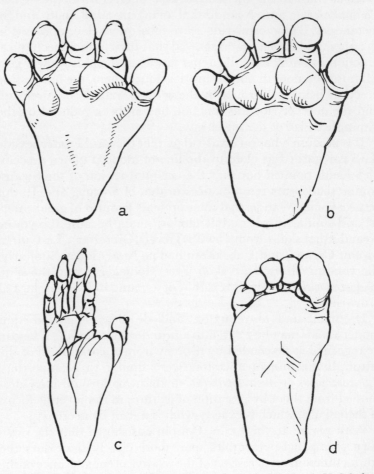

FIG. 10. The foot in foetal and adult macaque and man. Partly after A. H. Schultz,
Proceedings of the American Philosophical Society, **94,** 1950. *a.* macaque foetus of 23 mm.
length; *b.* human foetus of 24 mm. length; *c.* macaque adult; *d.* human adult.

The rosy lips of man were probably evolved in the young as
an adaptation to prolonged suckling, and have persisted in the
adult, possibly under the influence of sexual selection.

Apes when new-born have very much lighter skins than adults;

additional pigment becomes deposited during later development, and the same is true of the negro. In this respect the
white races are neotenous, for they retain the embryonic condition of other forms. One of the most interesting cases of this kind
is that of the hair, for Bolk has shown that a progressive series in
reduction can be made out in the monkeys, apes, and man:

1. the monkey is born with a complete covering of hair;
2. the gibbon is born with the head and back covered with
   hair, and the other regions are covered later;
3. the gorilla is born with the head covered with hair, and
   the other regions are partially covered later;
4. man is born with the head covered with hair, and the
   other regions are scarcely covered at all later.

It is to be noted that the lanugo, which forms a very fine
covering to the unborn infant before being lost, is also present in
the unborn apes. Further, the lanugo is retarded in man, for he
has not completely shed it by the time of birth.

This series shows that the neoteny of man as regards hair is
associated with a progressive retardation in the rate of its development. This retardation in the rate of development of the
body, it will be remembered, is what is required to produce
the other human features mentioned above. It therefore becomes
interesting to inquire whether the rate of human somatic development is really slow as compared with that of other mammals.

A comparison of the average ages at which corresponding
stages of development are reached in lower primates, great apes,
and man, has been made by A. H. Schultz (1949), extracts from
whose results are shown in Table I (p. 74). From this it will be
seen that man takes a longer time than do his nearest relatives
among the mammals. It must, of course, be remembered that
there can be no question of man having evolved from the present
apes, and that the proper terms of comparison are modern man
and the human ancestor. Nevertheless, it does appear to be true
that man's development is retarded as compared with the other
primates, and that both man's and the primates' developments
are retarded as compared with other mammals. There is therefore an objective basis for Bolk's thesis that the foetalization of
certain features in man is associated with a retardation of
development. Slijper has contended that there is no real connexion between foetalization and retardation since there are

cases of foetalization without retardation of development, as in Cetacea and Sirenia, and cases of retardation of development without foetalization, as in the elephant. Slijper gives figures for the ages at which corresponding stages of development are reached which differ from those of Schultz, and he considers that it is an error to include foetalization under the same heading as neoteny. He is nevertheless obliged to admit that 'in the production of neotenous individuals or species, very many characters develop with foetalization', which is all that is contended here.

TABLE I

Comparative Table of Average Ages at which Corresponding Stages are Reached in Lower Primates, Great Apes, and Man. (From A. H. Schultz, 1949.)

Character	Lower Primates	Great Apes	Man
Gestation	5 months	8 or 9 months	9 months
Postnatal growth . .	3 years	11 years	20 years
Life-span	14 years	35 years	75 years
Milk-teeth begin to erupt at	birth	3-4 months	8 months
Permanent teeth begin to erupt	1 year	3 years	6 years
Female fertility . . .	3 years	9 years	18 years
Ossification of skeleton at birth	advanced	comparatively retarded	very retarded

Further information on the relative rates of development in apes and man has been obtained by Bolk and by Schultz from a study of the times of eruption of teeth and the sequence in which they are replaced.

In the apes the milk-teeth are cut directly after birth, the 1st molar is cut soon after the 2nd premolar, and the replacement of the milk-teeth then takes place, accompanied by the cutting of the 2nd and 3rd molars. The sequence of eruption of the permanent teeth is therefore as follows: 1st molar, incisors, 2nd molar, premolars, canine, 3rd molar. Essentially the same sequence is found in *Pithecanthropus* and Neanderthal man. In man, the cutting of the milk-teeth is only finished two years after birth, and this is followed by a pause until at five or six the 1st molar is cut, and the milk-teeth are replaced; not until this is done does the 2nd molar appear. The 3rd molar may be cut after the 2nd, but its development is often so retarded that it is not cut at all. The sequence of eruption of the permanent teeth reflects the evolutionary trend tending towards the replacement of milk-teeth before the eruption of the permanent molars. Spuhler has shown that the milk-teeth of *Australopithecus* resemble those of man, the permanent teeth those of the gorilla.

Retardation characterizes the development of the human dentition as a whole. Associated with this retardation, as Bolk pointed out, is the prominence of the human chin for there is plenty of room for the retarded and smaller teeth, and there is no necessity for the line of their sockets to protrude over the point of the chin. It is interesting to note that *Pithecanthropus* and Neanderthal man had the simian mode of tooth-development and lacked a prominent chin. In very young apes indications of a chin may be present as Selenka showed for the gorilla and Weidenreich for the orang. It is the adult ape and Neanderthal man that have lost the foetal chin which modern man has retained in the adult and accentuated.

It may then be safely concluded that the rate of development of the human body has been retarded. On the other hand, the reproductive glands have probably not varied their rate of development, for the human ovary reaches full size at the age of about five, and this is about the time of sexual maturity of the apes, and presumably of man's ancestors. The human body is, however, not ready for the reproductive glands to function until several years later. The retardation is due to the action of hormones, which play an important part in regulating the speed of development.

The retardation in the development of man is also associated with higher energy requirements. Rubner has calculated that in the duplication of the weight of new-born mammals of all species investigated, 4,808 calories are required for every kg. of body produced, except in the case of man, who requires 6 times as much. These figures will probably have to be corrected when experimental evidence becomes available.

Haldane (1932 A) has pointed out a fact which has had a great importance in the evolution of man by paedomorphosis: the rarity of human twins. If there is more than one embryo in a uterus, they will inevitably compete for space and maternal blood-supply, and advantage will automatically accrue to the embryo which develops fastest. The result, as in all other mammals, will be the conferment of survival value on speed of development and precociousness. This is the exact reverse of the conditions required for the retardation of development in man, which only became possible by the abolition of intra-uterine competition as a result of the reduction of the normal number of young in a litter to one.

It has to be concluded therefore that in the evolution of man from his ancestors, neoteny has taken place in respect of several features which show foetalization. At the same time, of course, in other directions, the evolution of man has involved progressive change of vast importance, some of which, however, might not have been possible (e.g. the development of the brain) had it not been for certain features of neoteny (e.g. the delay in closing the sutures of the skull).

This case has been described fairly fully to serve as an example of the phylogenetic effect which heterochrony can produce by allowing characters which had been juvenile in the ancestor to become adult in the descendant. Some more cases will now be considered, from other kinds of animals.

The evolution of chordates

Garstang (1894, 1928 B) was the first to look for the trace of the ancestors of chordates and therefore of the vertebrates in early instead of adult stages of invertebrates; and he focused his attention on the larvae of echinoderms (star-fish, sea-urchins, sea-cucumbers, &c). He showed that if the ciliated bands on the larva (auricularia) of a sea-cucumber were to become accentuated and rise up as ridges leaving a groove between them, and if these ridges were to fuse, converting the groove into a tube, a structure would be produced which has all the relations of the vertebrate nervous system, including such details as the neurenteric canal. Not only this, but the two modifications of the vertebrate nervous system which are found in *Amphioxus* and all higher forms on the one hand, and in ascidians on the other, can be based on differences which are found in the disposition of the ciliated bands on different kinds of echinoderm larvae. This theory of the origin of the vertebrate nervous system has several advantages. In the first place, it avoids the difficulties which beset any attempt to derive it from the existing nervous systems of any other invertebrate. It also agrees with the principle of neurobiotaxis, according to which a concentration of nervous tissue takes place in the region of greatest stimulation. If the ancestors of the vertebrates had crawled about on their ventral surfaces like most invertebrates, one would expect their nervous

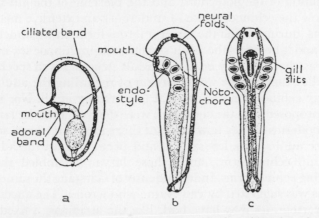

FIG. 11. A comparison between the larva of an echinoderm (*a*) and the form of a typical primitive chordate (*b* and *c*). The bands of cilia of the former correspond exactly to the neural folds of the latter, as do the adoral band and the endostyle. *a* and *b*, side view; *c*, dorsal view. (After Garstang.)

system to be ventral, like that of most invertebrates. But the nervous system of vertebrates is dorsal, and it is precisely the dorsal side of the body which would receive the greatest stimulation in a form swimming freely in the sea, the stimuli being the rays of light penetrating through from the surface. Not only is the auricularia free-swimming, but it bears an unmistakable resemblance to the tornaria larva of *Balanoglossus*, and *Balanoglossus* is an undoubted relative of *Amphioxus* and the early vertebrates or chordates as they may more correctly be termed.

The resemblance between the echinoderm larva and the chordate goes farther still, for the former has an adoral ciliated band formed partly from the inner layer of the body; and in a corresponding position the chordates have a ciliated band called the endostyle, which is looped in the same peculiar manner as the other. The middle layer of the body arises in three tiers or

segments in the echinoderm larva and in *Balanoglossus*, and
indications of this tripartite arrangement are present in *Amphioxus*. Further, the body-cavity of the echinoderm larva is in
communication with the outside by a pore, as in *Balanoglossus*,
Amphioxus, and several other chordates. In fact, if the nervous
system and endostyle are formed in the way suggested, all that
is required to turn the echinoderm larva into a chordate is the
formation of the notochord and the piercing of the gill-slits.

Now the echinoderm larva undergoes an extensive metamorphosis, during which the general larval form and symmetry are
lost, and it becomes the adult starfish, sea-urchin, or sea-cucumber, as the case may be. Their adult structure is so special and
peculiar that no one would dream of regarding the adult form
of any echinoderm as ancestral to anything at all. Nor indeed
is it proposed that the chordates were derived from the larvae of
echinoderms as they now are. But there must have been animals
whose adults were less special and peculiar than the adults of
existing echinoderms, and whose larvae resembled those of
existing echinoderms. Independently of Garstang the same hypothesis was suggested by van Name who wrote: 'The ancestors of
the vertebrates may have had, like the ascidians, a fixed adult
stage . . .; the existing vertebrates may be a development of the
free-swimming larvae of such organisms, not of the fixed stage.'

This view of the origin of chordates has also been accepted by
W. K. Gregory (1946) and J. Z. Young. If, then, the larval form
of these animals persisted and they became sexually mature in
this state, such neotenous forms would provide exactly the necessary material for the evolution of the chordates on the lines
suggested. Indeed, the general form and symmetry of the tornaria
do persist when this larva develops into the adult *Balanoglossus*.

The larva of the ascidians, the 'ascidian tadpole', is of particular importance in this respect, for with its notochord, dorsal
nervous system, and gill-slits it already has all the essential
features of chordate structure, and it is from larvae similar to the
ascidian tadpole that it may be imagined that the chordates
were evolved.

As for the phylogenetic significance of the ascidian tadpole,
the view held on the theory of recapitulation was that it represented the adult ancestral chordate. But if that were so, it would
be necessary to believe that the Appendicularia or Larvacea,

which retain the type of structure of the ascidian tadpole throughout life, were the most primitive tunicates. Garstang (1928 A)
showed that they can only be regarded as paedogenetic or
neotenous forms, and he gave reasons for thinking that the
Larvacea were evolved from larvae of Doliolids, ascidians which
in the adult have become specialized for a pelagic mode of life.

If, as Garstang and Grave have shown, the ascidian tadpole
represents no ancestral adult form, it can only represent a larval
form, and the question arises whether it reflects the larva of the
ancestors of the ascidians or was evolved by the ascidians. Garstang, Berrill, and van Name have pointed out that the latter
interpretation is correct. The ascidians were primitively sessile
and their original larvae must have been something like the
auricularia or tornaria, in which the introduction of caenogenetic
novelties produced the ascidian tadpole. As Berrill has expressed
it, 'ascidians have their tadpoles for their own sakes and not out
of any sentimental though unconscious regard for the past'. The
sensory and motor equipment of the ascidian tadpole are adaptations to the modes of life of the ascidians.

Realization of the fact that extreme simplicity of structure in
animals that are closely related to highly organized forms is a
suspicious sign of secondary simplification by neoteny and not
of a phylogenetically primitive condition, invites consideration
of the cases of other lower chordates, the Enteropneusta and
Amphioxus.

From his studies of the development of the nervous system in
Saccoglossus, Knight-Jones has been led to the view that the
Enteropneusta show retention of larval features in that the enclosure of the neural tube is not complete, leaving open anterior
and posterior neuropores without ever enclosing the blastopore
as in all other chordates.

Amphioxus presents a case of exceptional interest because it has
always been hailed as representative of the most primitive type
of chordate, pointing the way to the evolution of the craniates and
all vertebrates. The first published recognition of the possibility
that *Amphioxus* may be the permanent larva of some other more
highly developed chordate was made by A. S. Romer (1949:
20), but similar views were held by Garstang and published
after his death (1954). Holmgren and Stensiö had drawn attention to the similarity between *Amphioxus* and the Cephalaspida;

and Garstang stressed the point of special correspondence between *Amphioxus* and the ammocoete larva of cyclostomes, chief among which are the endostyle and ciliary method of feeding, and the velum. The 'finray' boxes of *Amphioxus* which are arranged in a single row in the midline dorsally and two rows ventrally, are comparable with the pockets in which dermal scutes are developed in Ostracoderms and fishes. The metapleural folds of *Amphioxus* prior to the enclosure of the atrial cavity have the same relation to the gill-slits as the edges of the head-shield have in Cephalaspida and are for a time bordered by sense-organs.

That *Amphioxus* shows simplification is probable from the fact that the sense-organs in the central nervous system are not nearly so well developed as in the tadpole larva of ascidians with its statolith and eye provided with a lens. There are also the uninterrupted segmentation of the myotomes and the separate dorsal and ventral roots of the segmental nerves. It is therefore possible that *Amphioxus* may owe some of its simplification to neotenous descent from a more highly organized type; but the evidence in favour of such a view is not yet sufficient, and some of the features of *Amphioxus* such as the nephridia are undoubtedly primitive. It is also possible that it may be a representative of the Silurian *Jamoytius*.

However that may be, it is remarkable that neotenous tendencies are traceable in so many of the lowest chordates and in the original ancestor which gave rise to the chordates as a whole.

The evolution of insects

Next, we may turn to the comparison which may be drawn between the adult form of the insects and the larval form of certain Myriapoda such as *Glomeris*, a millipede. The body of the adult insect consists of a head which is made up of six or seven segments, some of which bear jaws; a thoracic region of three segments each of which bears a pair of legs; and an abdominal region of eleven segments which usually do not bear any legs. The larva of *Glomeris* hatches as a little animal with a head which seems to be composed of the same number of segments as that of the insect, and a body of roughly a dozen segments of which the first three each bear a pair of legs. The 4th and following segments of the body are not devoid of legs but they are

retarded in development and so small that they do not protrude far, as Metschnikoff showed. The six-legged larva of *Glomeris*
eventually develops into an elongated adult form composed of
several segments and bearing many legs. Now, if the retardation
in the development of the legs behind the first three pairs were
increased, and the larval number of about a dozen body-seg-
ments persisted into the adult stage, there would be formed an
animal like an insect with the legs behind the first three pairs

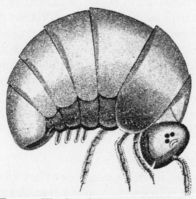

Fig. 12. The larval form of a Myriapod
soon after hatching, showing its great resemblance to an insect. (From vom Rath.)

either reduced to vestiges or vanished altogether. It is therefore
of interest to find that there actually are insects in which vestigial
legs are present on the abdominal segments (*Campodea, Iapyx,
Machilis*). These insects have no wings, and, on the other hand,
have preserved features which the other insects have lost (such
as the segmental arrangement of the reproductive glands), and
they may therefore be regarded as an intermediate stage in the
process of heterochrony and of the evolution of the insects from
neotenous larvae like those of some Myriapoda.

The derivation of insects from forms like Myriapoda is sup-
ported by many other considerations. To start with, the insects
must have been derived from forms which possessed longer
bodies with more segments and legs than the insects now have,
for, in common with Myriapoda, Crustacea (lobsters), Arach-
nida (spiders), and the Peripatoidea, the insects must ultimately
have been derived from worms. Of all animals with long bodies

and many legs, the Myriapoda are the most likely to have been the ancestors, or closely related to the ancestors, of the insects, for they have several features in common. Such, for instance, are the tracheal tubes and Malpighian tubes of the respiratory and excretory systems respectively. At the same time, insects could not have been derived from adult Myriapoda for the structure of the latter is too specialized and peculiar.

Support for the view that insects evolved from Myriapoda is provided by Imms, Tiegs (1947), and also by Manton's (1953) studies on the methods of walking in different groups of arthropods. She has shown that there is a basic similarity between the gaits of the insects and of the Symphyla, and that 'the insectan condition would result from that of the Symphyla by a reduction in the number of legs, together with their increase in length, the gaits remaining almost unaltered'. She concludes that 'overwhelming support is accordingly provided for a supposed common origin of Symphyla and Insects'.

The neoteny of flightless birds

As we have seen, neoteny need not affect all structures of the body and may be restricted to only a few. A case of this kind is provided by the plumage of the ostrich and other flightless birds and penguins, which resembles the nestling down of young flying birds. Far from meaning that the ostrich is primitive and that its plumage is 'recapitulated' in the 'chick' stage of the ontogeny of a bird like a fowl, this series must be read exactly the other way. Steiner's morphological researches establish beyond doubt that the nestling down feathers are derived from quill feathers, and Hosker's embryological studies show that the former are merely the precociously formed and fluffed-out tips of the latter. It is clear therefore that the ostrich, in retaining in the adult a type of plumage characteristic of the young of other birds, is neotenous. This accords perfectly with the now generally accepted view that the flightless birds were evolved from birds with well-developed power of flight and have therefore lost their flight feathers.

The ostriches show other neotenous features besides the plumage. In flying birds the bones of the skull become fused to one another at an early age giving rise to a strong and compact brain-case. In the ostrich the fusion of the skull bones is delayed and the sutures remain open, which is a neotenous feature.

It has long been thought that the palate of ostriches and other ratites was primitive in that the pterygoid bones extend forward and meet the prevomers. This type of palate is called dromoeognathous or palaeognathous and is contrasted with the neognathous palate of carinate birds where the palatine bones separate the pterygoids from the prevomers. But Pycraft, and de Beer (1956), showed that in many carinates the palate during its development passes through a palaeognathous stage in which the pterygoids touch the prevomers. The tips of the pterygoids then become detached and fuse with the palatines, thereby producing the neognathous condition. Adherents of the theory of recapitulation might be tempted to see here a proof of the primitive nature of the palaeognathous type of palate of the ratites. Fortunately, the palate of *Archaeopteryx* appears to be of the neognathous (schizognathous) type, and the only possible conclusion is that the palaeognathous palate has been evolved from the neognathous type by neoteny and retention of the juvenile condition of the ancestor. This is further confirmed by the fact that the palaeognathous palate is found in Tinamus which are carinate birds. The ratites therefore, without doubt, are neotenous carinates that have secondarily lost the power of flight.

The evolution of flying fishes

The needle-fish *Belone* in the adult has very elongated jaws of equal length. In the young its jaws are equal and short; then the lower jaw lengthens, and finally the upper jaw catches it up. For this reason Sewertzow considered that the young stages of *Belone* passed through conditions corresponding to those of the adult in *Exocoetus* (the flying fish in which the jaws are short and equal) and *Hemirhamphus* (in which the lower jaw is much longer than the upper). He therefore regarded *Belone* as a case of 'overstepping' (described below in Chapter XII). But unfortunately for this view it is quite clear, as Schlesinger and Regan have shown, that *Belone* is more primitive than *Exocoetus* and *Hemirhamphus*, and the series must be read the other way. Nichols and Breder find that 'instances are not lacking where . . . specialised larval forms become established as the adult form, making an evolutionary step upward, and it is just this which seems to have taken place in the transition from needle-fish to half-beak'. In other words, *Hemirhamphus* has been derived from *Belone* by

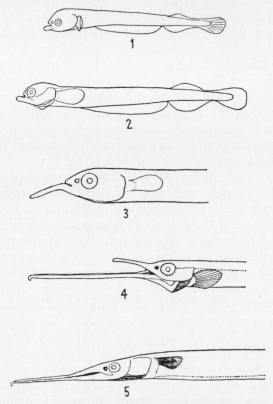

FIG. 13. Development of *Belone acus*. 1 and 2, young stages showing a condition of the jaws retained in adult *Exocoetus*; 3 and 4, intermediate stages showing a condition of the jaws retained in adult *Hemiramphus*; 5, adult *Belone*. From A. N. Sewertzow, *Jena Z. Naturwiss.* **63**, 1927.

neoteny. Nichols and Breder go on to show how *Exocoetus* and the flying fishes were derived from forms like *Hemirhamphus* by shortening the lower jaw in the adult. The key to this interpretation is the realization that the elongated jaw of the larva is an adaptive feature, masked in adult *Belone* by the subsequent lengthening of the upper jaw, retained in the adult *Hemirhamphus* and lost in the adult *Exocoetus*.

The evolution of some fossil groups

From the living animals so far considered attention may now be turned to the evolution of certain fossil groups. In many cases the nature of the organisms concerned was such that the whole of the life-history was recorded in the growth and accretions effected during life, with the result that preservation and fossilization have made possible the drawing of definite conclusions regarding the relations of the ontogenies of these organisms to their phylogeny.

The ammonites call for special mention here, for A. P. Pavlov found that characters may make their first appearance in phylogeny at early stages of development and subsequently extend into adult stages.

Cardioceras alternoides has inner whorls bearing ribs continuous with those of the opposite side which resemble the adult whorls of its successor *C. alternans*. *Kepplerites* has inner whorls which are flattened and resemble the outer whorls of *Kosmoceras*: it is impossible to say that *Kepplerites* passed in ontogeny through a '*Kosmoceras*' stage because *Kepplerites* is earlier than *Kosmoceras*; instead of *Kepplerites* having been evolved from *Kosmoceras*, *Kosmoceras* has been evolved from *Kepplerites*.

Simberskites versicolor has inner whorls marked with tubercles which resemble the outer whorls of *S. elatus*; the inner whorls of *S. elatus* resemble the outer of *S. decheni*. This cannot be interpreted to mean that *S. versicolor* passed through an '*elatus*' stage, nor that *S. elatus* similarly passed through a '*decheni*' stage, because the stratigraphical order in which these species are found shows that *S. versicolor* is the oldest and is followed by *S. elatus* which in turn is followed by *S. decheni*.

To this phenomenon Pavlov gave the names of 'phylogenetic acceleration' and 'precession of characters'. Since it involves the retention in the adult stage of the descendant of characters which were juvenile in the ancestor, it is a further example of neoteny.

Independently of Pavlov, the same principle was discovered by Spath (1938: 12) who showed that *Whaeneroceras* has a grooved periphery only on the young inner whorls of the shell, the older outer whorls being ungrooved; yet it is the undoubted ancestor of *Schlotheimia* in which the grooving persists into the outer whorls. Similarly, in *Asteroceras* the spines first appear on the inner whorls and only extend on to the outer whorls in the later species of this genus. In Cretaceous genera the uncoiling of the shell began in the inner whorls and later also affected the outer whorls. In a precisely similar way Schindewolf has shown that in *Prorasenia* trifid ribs make their appearance in the inner whorls and extend on to the outer whorls in *Rasenia*. Further examples were found by Mazenot in the Palaeohoplitidae: in *Beriasella ciliata* the marginal groove appears only in the inner whorls; in the later form *B. oppeli* it is present in both inner and outer whorls. Yet others have been reported by J. P. Smith and by Kieslinger.

Pavlov found that his principle of precession of characters also applied to the belemnites. The young form of *Belemnites kirghisiensis* is short and flattened on the ventral side, and resembles the adult of *B. roulleri* which succeeds it. The young form of *B. roulleri* is even more flattened and resembles the adult of its successor *B. russiensis*. A comparable series is provided by the appearance of the ventral groove in the young of *B. spicularis* and in the adult of its successor *B. oweni*, and in the young of *B. magnificus* and in the adult of its successor *B. absolutus*. In each case, the evolutionary novelty first appeared in the young; there is no recapitulation, but instead, a retention by the adult descendant of a juvenile ancestral character, thus providing further examples of neoteny.

FIG. 14. Introduction of an evolutionary novelty (reflexed theca) in the first-formed members of the graptolite *Monograptus argenteus*. Arrows indicate the directions of the thecal apertures. (From O. M. Bulman, *Biol. Rec.* **8**, 1933.)

In Mollusca, Pavlov also found that the young forms of *Turritella montensis* show characters which resemble those of the adult of the more recent *T. biserialis*.

In graptolites Elles (1924) and Bulman (1933) found that it is the initial thecae which exhibit the first signs of incoming developments. That is to say, these evolutionary novelties appear first in early stages of colony-formation and become prolonged into later stages in subsequent phylogeny; this notwithstanding the fact that in some other characters (change of direction of growth, delayed bud formation) the evolutionary novelty first affects the terminal parts of the stalks on which the thecae are borne. This is a case of 'colonial neoteny'.

In the trilobites, Jaekel and Stubblefield showed that the Proparia, which were later forms, were probably neotenous descendants of the earlier Opisthoparia. The latter during their ontogenetic development passed through a stage showing a condition of the facial suture which persisted throughout life in the Proparia. Størmer has confirmed and extended these conclusions and shown that the development of the preantennal segment is retarded or arrested to an ever-increasing extent in the more advanced forms. 'Among the trilobites . . . [the partial neoteny] has not only caused a differentiation into species and genera, but even into separate orders.'

In a similar way there appears to have been a progressive reduction in the number of the hinder segments. Hupé has shown that the Meraspis larvae of Silurian trilobites have fewer segments than those of Cambrian forms of similar size. This implies the retardation and retention in the descendant of a youthful character of the ancestor.

In Brachiopoda some examples of neoteny were described by Beecher as occurring in the Terebratellidae in which some genera 'did not go through the complete series of metamorphoses'.

Finally, to give examples from among coelenterates, the Rugosa or tetracorallid corals of the Palaeozoic era were characterized in their adult state by the possession of four septa. In their ontogeny, however, they passed through a stage in which they had six septa. The Tetracorallia went extinct at the end of the Permian, and in the Triassic period there appeared the Hexacorallia, with a system of septa based on six primary septa. Cloud has therefore suggested that the Hexacorallia were the neotenous descendants of the Tetracorallia, and this view receives valuable support from the fact that some of the latest Palaeozoic Tetracorallia (such as *Polycoelia*, *Plerophyllum*, *Hapsiphyllum*, and *Lophophyllidium*) show a prolongation into later stages of ontogeny of the hexamerous arrangement of the septa.

Neoteny in the placenta

The various orders of mammals are characterized by the type

of structure of their placenta. In the simplest form, as shown by pigs and lemurs, the maternal uterine epithelium is preserved and the embryonic membranes are apposed to it. Such a condition is called epithelio-chorial.

In other mammals such as the rodents, primates, and insectivores, the uterine epithelium and underlying tissues are eroded and invaded by the embryonic membranes which develop spaces in which the maternal blood flows. This condition is known as haemo-chorial.

In one insectivore, however, *Scalopus*, Mossman has found that the placenta is epithelio-chorial. Since this cannot mean that *Scalopus* is the most primitive insectivore, or that the other insectivores, rodents, and primates have evolved the haemo-chorial placenta independently, it follows that *Scalopus* must have secondarily retained an 'embryonic' condition of the placenta (epithelio-chorial), through which its relatives pass in the formation of their haemo-chorial placenta.

Adult cartilage, a neotenous tissue

Under the old and fallacious argument that because cartilage develops before bone in ontogeny, cartilage must have evolved before bone in phylogeny, the ancestors of the chordates would have had to pass through a stage when they had cartilage but no bone. It is, however, a remarkable fact that those forms such as cyclostomes and selachians, which today have cartilage but no bone, can be shown to have been derived from groups such as the ostracoderms and the acanthodians in which bone was extremely well developed. It therefore seems probable, as de Beer (1937) and Romer (1942) have suggested, that cartilage first arose caenogenetically as a youthful adaptation to skeletal necessities, and that its retention and extension in the adult, as in cyclostomes, selachians, or sturgeons, is a case of neoteny.

The evolution of some mammalian teeth

In mammals the permanent teeth of the adult are preceded by the milk-teeth of the young, and in accordance with the theory of recapitulation Rütimeyer thought that he could make out a resemblance between the milk-teeth of descendants and the permanent teeth of their ancestors. The examples which he chose (*Equus* and *Hipparion*) were unfortunate because it is now known that *Hipparion* was not ancestral to *Equus* and that its teeth were highly complicated. Milk-premolars are frequently found to be more complicated in structure than the permanent premolars which replace them in the same species. This is true of *Equus*, and the similarity between its milk-premolars and the permanent teeth of *Hipparion* is spurious.

Marie Pavlov claimed to show that in the evolutionary series of fossil horses, the milk-premolars resemble the permanent teeth of descendant species. Through *Pachynolophus* (Eocene), *Anchilophus* (Upper Eocene), *Miohippus*, and *Merychippus* (Miocene) this relation is found between each form and the next.

Marie Pavlov also claimed the same principle to apply to the evolutionary series of rhinoceroses: to *Aceratherium lemanense* (Upper Oligocene) and *Rhinoceros sansaniensis* (Lower Miocene), to *Rh. hemitoechus* (Upper Pliocene) and *Rh. tichorhinus* (Lower Pleistocene), and to *Rh. sivalensis* (Upper Miocene) and *Rh. (Diceros) simus* (recent). Some of the early members of Marie Pavlov's sequence of fossil horses would not have been admitted by Matthew to be on the direct line of evolution of the horses, but the later members seem to be unexceptionable. If this be accepted, it follows that the milk-premolars in these forms do not recapitulate the permanent premolars of their ancestors but are prophetic of the permanent premolars of their descendants.

A similar conclusion emerges from Butler's (1951) studies on the molarization of the premolars, in which he has shown that this process is the result of two components: the making of milk-premolars to resemble molars, and the attainment by the permanent premolars of a degree of development equivalent to that of the milk-premolars.

The evolutionary novelties in the structure of the premolar teeth would thus make their first appearance in the young and subsequently persist into the adult stage of the descendants. At their first appearance in the milk-teeth, these novelties are caenogenetic, and it is probable that the greater complexity of structure in these teeth as compared with their successors of the permanent dentition may be adaptive. The milk-premolars are the only functional grinding teeth until they are replaced, and the permanent teeth which replace them (premolars and molars) are more numerous. It may be supposed therefore that in order to provide adequate function the milk-premolars make up in *quality* what they lack in *quantity* and are correspondingly better developed.

Be that as it may, the retention in the adult descendant of a character which was juvenile in the ancestor is an example of neoteny.

Neoteny in plants

It was realized by Nicoloff that the theory of recapitulation could not be generally applied to plants because the structure of young forms is so often found to be useless in the search for the affinities of a species. Guillaumin pointed out that the young foliage leaves of a plant frequently are more specialized than those formed later on, which means that evolutionary novelties make their first appearance in young stages. These observations have been extended by Gaussen and by de Ferré who have shown that in conifers the characters of young stages of plants that are believed to be ancestral are found in the fully formed stages of their descendants. Of the series *Pinus*, *Cedrus*, and *Abies*, *Pinus* is held to be the most primitive and *Abies* the most specialized on morphological and palaeontological grounds. The fully formed leaves of *Pinus* are clustered on dwarf shoots, but the young leaves are single and borne on long shoots and resemble the definitive leaves of *Abies*. Comparable observations have been made on cones and other structures. These cases where 'the young form shows the way of future evolution' are examples of neoteny.

Conclusion

On looking back over this chapter we may say that there are a number of cases in which the adult structure of an animal resembles the embryonic or larval structure of another animal, and in each case there are good reasons for regarding the former as having been derived from the latter: i.e. the adult descendant resembles the young stage of the ancestor, which is precisely the reverse and opposite of that which would be required under the theory of recapitulation. If the neotenous condition is achieved by accelerating the rate of development of the reproductive glands and hastening the time of maturity, the phylogeny usually results in a simplification often associated with parasitism. But if the neoteny is brought about by a slowing down of the rate of development of the body relatively to that of the reproductive glands, then changes are brought about which may have considerable importance in phylogeny. Many of the characters which have been introduced into the adult stage of descendants in this manner must have been neanic in origin in the ancestors.

VESTIGIAL STRUCTURES DUE TO REDUCTION

W E shall deal in this chapter with those cases in which a character, which in the ancestor was present in both young and adult, comes in the descendant to be either very reduced or absent in the adult and therefore present only in the young stages. These cases really constitute the other side of the picture presented by deviation. In deviation, as we have seen, a character appears in the ontogeny and often substitutes itself for a previously existing character. The latter character thus becomes suppressed, reduced, and vestigial. In this way we may say, reverting to the example of intersexuality in the gipsy moth, that the female characters become vestigial in the adult of a female moth which during its early stages of development has been switched over to maleness. This, as we have seen, is due to the relatively lower rate of action of the female-producing genes.

Consequently, we may ascribe the cause of the reduction of structures to vestiges to a quantitative decrease in the intensity and capacity of the internal factors controlling the formation of those structures. If the structures are related to the size of the body and are positively allometric (p. 32), then, if the size of the body decreases during phylogeny, the structure in question will be reduced. The case of the tail of the fish *Xiphophorus* described in Chapter IV (p. 33), is an example of this type of reduction. Conversely, if the structures are negatively allometric, they will be relatively reduced if body-size increases.

Examples of reduction

The frog tadpole possesses a tail, which is a characteristic chordate structure, of universal occurrence in the young, but whereas most chordates preserve their tails in the adult state, the adult frog is tailless.

The young oyster has a foot, like the young of other shell-fish, but whereas the latter preserve the foot in the adult state, the oyster loses it. The abdominal limbs, which in the larval stage of the myriapod *Glomeris* are small but become fully developed in the

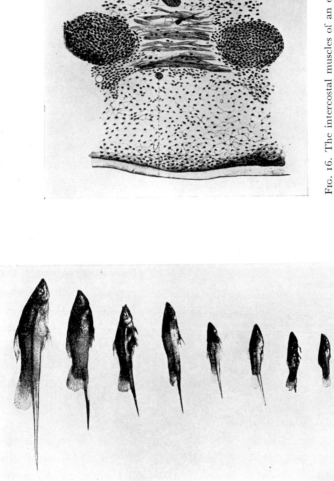

Fig. 16. The intercostal muscles of an embryo of *Emys lutaria* prior to their reduction. From A. N. Sewertzow, *Zool. Jahrb. Abt. Anat.* **53**, 1931.

Fig. 15. Reduction of an allometric structure—the tail of *Xiphophorus helleri*—accompanying reduction in body-size. From C. Champy, *Sexualité et hormones* (G. Doin, Paris, 1924).

adult, remain small in the adult *Campodea*, *Iapyx*, and *Machilis*, as vestiges, and in other insects they are reduced altogether. In early stages of development, the slow-worm (*Anguis*) has tiny vestiges of the hind limbs, and so has the early stage of the lizard. But whereas in the latter these limbs go on developing and are present in the adult, in the slow-worm they do not develop any further and eventually disappear, so that the adult is limbless. This reduction goes still further in snakes, where, with the exception of Typhlopidae, Leptotyphlopidae, Anilidae, Pythonidae, and Boidae, which still show a trace, the limbs never arise at all.

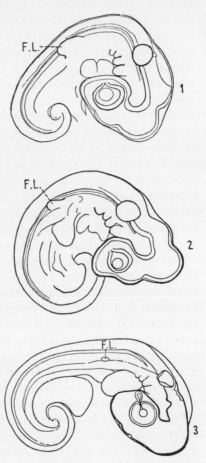

The notochord (primitive spine) arises in early stages of development of all chordates, but while in *Amphioxus*, lampreys, some fish, and newts it persists more or less into the adult, in reptiles, birds, and mammals it is reduced and replaced in the adult by the vertebral column. Franz has emphasized the fact that the notochord of the embryo of these higher vertebrates does not resemble that of the adult *Amphioxus* or sturgeon, but rather the notochord of

FIG. 17. Embryos of 1, *Ascalabotes fascicularis*; 2, *Seps chalcides*; 3, *Ophisaurus apus*, showing reduction of the rudiment of the forelimb, F.L. (From A. N. Sewertzow, *Zool. Jahrb. Abt. Anat.* **53**, 1931.)

the early stages of development of these animals. The possession of these vestiges is therefore no evidence of the pressing back of adult ancestral characters into the young stages of the descendant. The same is true of the tooth-band and small teeth which are found in the embryos of the whale-bone whales. These animals are toothless in the adult, and their embryonic teeth represent the embryonic condition of other mammals. Other examples are the 3rd toe of the young ostrich, while its adult has only two, the 3rd toe persisting in the adult stages of other birds; the rudiments of the intercostal muscles which the chelonian *Emys lutaria* has in its embryo but loses in the adult, while adult non-chelonian amniotes retain them; the rudiment of Jacobson's organ in embryonic man who loses it in the adult stage, while it is present in other adult mammals; and the rudiment of the head-kidney or pronephros which is formed in the embryonic stages of all chordates, persists in the adult of some fish, but is lost in the adult of all other forms.

Sewertzow (1931) analysed the processes of reduction and claimed that they can be referred to one of two types. In the first, 'rudimentation', the embryonic rudiment of the organ in question is smaller throughout ontogeny as compared with the corresponding organ in more normal forms. The rudiment is not retarded in its development, but some of its constituent parts, such as phalanges of the digits, may be absent from the start. In Sewertzow's view the parts which are completely abolished in this way are those which normally develop latest. Examples are provided by the lizards *Seps chalcides* and *Ophisaurus apus*. In these cases when reduction has reached a certain stage the vestigial organs are functionless.

In the second type of reduction, 'aphanisia', the organ in question develops as in more normal forms up to a certain point and is then rapidly destroyed. Examples are the tail of the frog tadpole and the intercostal muscles of *Emys*. In these cases the organs are functional up to the time of their loss. 'Rudimentation' seems to involve reduction in size of the presumptive organ-forming regions and negative allometry; 'aphanisia' is brought about by phagocytosis, humorally controlled involution, and histological degeneration.

To Sewertzow's two types of reduction Steiner and Anders have added a third which they call 'adaptive reduction'. This is characterized by the reduction of only some specified parts of a structure, brought about in adaptation to a change in function of the structure as a whole. Thus in the skinks, which are lizards that have adopted a snake-like form and a burrowing mode of life, the function of the limbs has changed from being organs of propulsion and locomotion to being organs of digging. The 3rd finger has lost its 2nd phalanx while the 4th and 5th fingers have been completely reduced. In the geckos, which are adapted to climbing by means of their adhesive pads, the formula of reduction is quite different and affects the 2nd phalanx of the 3rd digit, the 2nd and 3rd phalanges of the 4th digit, and the 2nd phalanx of the 5th digit.

The phylogenetic significance of reduced structures

The effect of a reduction from the point of view of phylogeny will usually be to produce changes of relatively small systematic importance. This is, however, not always the case, and, as Goldschmidt (1923) pointed out, the reduction of the hyomandibula of the fish to form the columella auris or stapes of higher vertebrates was an evolutionary change of great importance. The same may be said of the reduction of the quadrate and articular of reptiles to the incus and malleus of mammals. This change represented one of the most important steps in the evolution of the mammals.

J. S. Huxley (1932) has drawn attention to the importance of allometric growth-studies in connexion with the reduction of structures. If, as appears to be the case, the initial steps in the reduction of a structure involve decreases in the activity-rates of growth-controlling genes resulting in negative allometry, the mere fact of the existence of limb rudiments in the embryo slow-worm is no evidence of any recapitulation of adult ancestral characters; it is evidence of the repetition of embryonic characters which the organism is going to get rid of by what may perhaps be the only means at its disposal: negative allometry.

Further, it may be noted that as the size of an allometric organ is related to that of the body, the absurd degree of reduction of some organs, such as the hind limbs of whales, can be accounted for quite independently of the question of the function that such organs could possibly perform.

The complete reduction of a structure, resulting in its absence even from the earliest stages of development, illustrates an important principle: the absence of such a structure in the embryo of a descendant does not mean that the structure in question was not present in the ancestral adult. The limbs of the ancestors of snakes are a case in point. Nor can the time at which a structure disappears in the ontogenetic development of a descendant be held to represent the stage in the phylogeny of the ancestors at which the structure in question was lost in the adult ancestor.

In man the suture between the premaxillary and maxillary bones disappears at a very early stage of ontogenetic development, and this fact was held by Wood Jones (1941) to imply that in the phylogenetic series of man's ancestors the obliteration of this suture occurred in very early times. Because it shows a persistent suture between the premaxilla and the maxilla, he excluded *Australopithecus* (the Taungs skull) altogether from the line of man's ancestry. There is, however, no necessity for this conclusion, as de Beer has pointed out (1948). The stage of development at which the suture is obliterated is correlated with the size of the premaxilla as Ashley-Montagu has shown. The smaller the premaxilla, the sooner is the suture between it and the maxilla obliterated. The evolution of man has been accompanied by a progressive reduction in the size of the premaxilla, and there is no reason why this bone may not have been of fair size, with a persistent suture between it and the maxilla, in comparatively recent ancestors of man.

Some vestigial structures show reduction not from the adult but from the embryonic ancestral condition. Such are the remnants of the egg-tooth and caruncle found by Hill and de Beer (1950) in some marsupial embryos. It is more than 70 million years since their ancestors used these structures to hatch out of egg-shells.

We see also that, as in the case of deviation, the instances in which structures are reduced to vestiges obey von Baer's law of the greater degree of resemblance that exists between young stages of different animals than between young and adult stages or between adult stages *inter se*.

X

ADULT VARIATION

U NDE R this heading we include what is really only a special case of the phenomenon which was described under the term deviation. As has been stressed before, the reactions which result in the appearance of characters are set going some time before those characters appear. The adult form is being prepared during the earlier stages of development. We cannot draw any hard and fast line between the characters which, substituting themselves for others in phylogeny, appear early in ontogeny, and those which appear late. However, the later a character appears in ontogeny, the smaller as a rule is the change which it produces by its presence. On the other hand, a character which appears early in ontogeny has time to produce more important changes. So, while under the heading of deviation we include variations which have produced fairly large phylogenetic effects (such as the divergence in evolution between different families, orders, and classes of animals), adult variation deals with the differences between individuals, varieties, races, and, probably, species. Darwin himself drew attention to the fact that 'slight variations generally appear at a not very early period of life'.

It is of course not denied that some trivial characters may appear early in ontogeny. For instance, right- or left-handedness in the asymmetry of snails is determined in the ovary of the previous generation and manifested at the first cleavage division of the fertilized egg, but the results do not even confer specific distinction. Cope cited cases in which the appearance of specific characters precedes that of generic characters. What is contended, however, is that characters of major systematic categories do not arise late in ontogeny.

To this chapter, then, belong the slight differences between animals, and genetic research tends increasingly to show that these differences are controlled by Mendelian factors or genes, and that they may concern any and every feature of an animal. No useful purpose would be served by going more fully into them. The substitution of one character for another in the adult does not usually involve heterochrony and produces only small phylogenetic effects. Just as, however, caenogenetic variations may become phylogenetically important by undergoing heterochrony, attention must be paid to the possible results of heterochrony if applied to adult variation, and this will form the subject of the following chapters.

XI

VESTIGIAL STRUCTURES DUE TO RETARDATION

WHEN, as in neoteny, characters which had been larval or embryonic in the ancestor become adult in the descendant, the original adult characters of the ancestor tend, as it were, to be pushed off from the end of ontogeny. They arise too late to be fully formed by the time maturity is reached in those animals which have a definite adult form, and, in consequence, such characters become reduced and vestigial. Retardation of structures to vestiges is therefore the other side of the picture presented by the phenomenon of neoteny. Hair is vestigial on the body of man, as are the molars, especially the last, which are often not cut at all. The bones are vestigial in the skull of the axolotl, and the maxillary bone, which is present in the newts that undergo metamorphosis into the terrestrial adult form, is absent in those urodeles that are permanently neotenous.

A very instructive case of retardation is that of the bands on snail shells investigated by Diver. These bands vary considerably in the time in ontogeny at which they make their appearance on the shell. Some may be so late as to appear as a mere dot just behind the terminal lip of the shell. 'Others may even be, as it were, pushed off the shell altogether, that is they fail to appear at all because their time of appearance has been so retarded in relation to general development that growth is terminated before they are due.'

It is possible to interpret these cases in terms of the phenomenon of intersexuality in the gipsy moth by noting that, in a normal female moth, the male-producing genes are too slow to produce the appearance of any male characters before the time of maturity arrives and development ceases. Characters may become vestigial by the over-retardation of the rate of action of the factors which control them. The effects of such heterochrony will not in themselves be important in phylogeny, but they will be associated with neoteny, and this, as we have seen, may and often does have important results in evolution.

XII

HYPERMORPHOSIS

IF those characters which only appear in the adult stage of the ancestor are retarded so that they do not appear in the descendant by the time development ceases, they will become vestigial, as shown in the previous chapter. But if the time when development stops is *relatively* delayed, it will be possible for the descendant to add characters on to the adult ancestral stage. Referring again to the example of intersexuality in moths, male characters do not normally appear by the time development ceases; but if the time of maturity is postponed, these male characters can and do make their appearance. This additional development, or *hypermorphosis*, may then be expected in cases where the evolution has resulted in progressive increase in size, or where the time of maturity is delayed relatively to the body-characters. The cases to be considered here conform to the principle of 'overstepping' of Müller, of 'prolongation' as suggested by Franz, and partly to the principle of 'anaboly' as enunciated by Sewertzow.

The best example of hypermorphosis is that of the Pteraspida of the Lower Devonian described by E. I. White. In *Poraspis* the dorsal shield of the adult is characterized by the pattern of the lateral-line canals which extend over the whole of it. In the later species, *Pteraspis leathensis*, *P. rostrata*, and *Rhinopteraspis dunensis*, the dorsal shield is formed of the same size as in *Poraspis*, but to its edges is added a peripheral extension which increases in size in the successive species. The adult form of the ancestor is therefore repeated in the descendants and is 'overstepped' by the addition of new structures and an increase in size. But the adult ancestral form is not pressed back into earlier stages of development in the descendants, and there has therefore been no abbreviation or recapitulation. The whole ancestral ontogeny has been repeated in full, and full-size.

Other examples are given by J. S. Huxley (1932). The limbs of lambs of domestic breeds pass through stages in which their proportions correspond to those of adult wild (and therefore presumably ancestral) sheep. Schultz's demonstration of the

lengthening of the arm of the gibbon during ontogenetic development reflects the lengthening that must have occurred in the
phylogeny of gibbons from anthropoids whose arms were of more
normal length.

This case is particularly interesting, because the same phenomenon, the lengthening of the arms during human ontogenetic
development, clearly does not reflect man's phylogenetic evolution from brachiating ancestors, during which the length of his
arms has been reduced.

The apparently recapitulatory effect in the cases of the sheep's
limbs and the gibbon's arm are simple consequences of the
values of the growth-constants. A change in these values immediately produces a very different state of affairs. For instance,
in the horse the growth-rate in ontogeny of the splint bones does
not reflect the changes in size of the lateral digits of the 3-toed
horses in phylogeny, as Robb has shown. This case and that of
man's arm show caenogenesis, producing an anti-recapitulatory
effect.

The caution needed in interpreting these cases is well illustrated in the evolution of gryphaean oysters. Trueman pointed
out that the hinge of the left valve of the shell undergoes progressive spiral coiling in phylogeny. The descendants show not
only additions to the coils of the ancestors, i.e. hypermorphosis,
but the coil itself becomes tighter. Thus the angle of the coil in
Gryphaea obliquata increases in ontogeny to a value of 60° in late
stages. In the descendant *G. incurva*, this is the value of the angle
at early stages, rising to 80° at late stages. Here, therefore, we
have hypermorphosis combined with acceleration, producing a
recapitulatory effect.

Sewertzow's principle of anaboly is a modification of that of
'overstepping'. In the ontogeny Sewertzow distinguished an
earlier period of morphogenesis during which the various structural characters of the developing animal are moulded, and a
later period of growth in which the animal increases in size until
it reaches the adult state without undergoing further modification. He regarded it as possible for a descendant to add a new
stage on to the last stage of morphogenesis of the ancestor. As an
illustration of this principle Sewertzow cited the development of
the long-snouted fish *Belone*. But as we have already seen (Chapter VIII), the evolutionary series of these forms must be read

exactly the other way and constitutes a very good case of neoteny.

It will be noticed that Sewertzow's anaboly differs from 'over-stepping' only in that it is the final stage of morphogenesis instead of the definite adult stage of the ancestor which is passed through in the ontogeny of the descendant. But in either case the stage which the descendant passes through is the final stage of 'development' of the ancestor, for development, i.e. structural alteration, does not take place during Sewertzow's period of growth.

At all events, both Franz and Sewertzow laid stress on the fact that the adult stage or final stage of morphogenesis of the ancestor is not pressed back into earlier stages of development in the descendant, but the ontogeny or morphogenesis of the latter is prolonged. The adult condition or final stage of morphogenesis of the ancestor is present unreduced in the development of the descendant, but it is no longer the terminal stage of ontogeny or morphogenesis. With this reservation, cases of hypermorphosis may be said to conform to Haeckel's principle of the recapitulation of adult (or final morphogenetic) stages in the ontogeny of the descendant. It is to be noted that such recapitulation is not as its name would imply an abbreviated (i.e. accelerated) repetition, but a simple repetition.

Here we may draw attention to the possibility that hypermorphosis may provide an explanation of some cases of the widespread phenomenon which J. Barcroft called 'anticipation', i.e. the formation of a structure in anticipation of its use. The haemoglobin of a mammalian foetus is adapted to placental intra-uterine respiration, and differs from the haemoglobin of a post-natal mammal, adapted to pulmonary atmospheric respiration. The transition from one type of haemoglobin to the other takes place at birth in man, but before birth in the sheep. If the period of gestation of the sheep has been prolonged, as is not improbable in view of its well-developed state at birth, but the time of transition of the haemoglobins remained unaltered, this 'anticipation' in the sheep would be explained. But even the case of man and other mammals which change their haemoglobins at birth is anticipatory in the sense that it is the result of processes antecedent in time to the realization of the adaptive value of the change. It might be expected that in the ancestors of the mammals the change in haemoglobins took place after birth or hatching, and it is therefore of great interest to note that in the chick, Hall found that the change is not completed until 6 weeks after hatching.

In a sense, of course, the problem of 'anticipation' is that of all embryology during the prefunctional period, when organs are formed, apparently purposefully, 'in order to function' later. It would be more than rash to conclude that all cases can be explained as the one above, especially as so many developmental processes can be proved to be caenogenetic innovations which cannot have any ancestral adaptive significance. Nevertheless, there are probably many cases of physiological anticipation which might well repay comparative study from the point of view of hypermorphosis.

Repetition by hypermorphosis is apparently possible as the result of heterochrony and prolongation of the period of development, as the other cases mentioned in this chapter seem to show. While they appear to support Haeckel's theory of recapitulation, it must be remembered that the adult ancestral characters are not compressed into earlier stages of the development of the descendants in hypermorphosis. It may also be noticed that the phylogenetic effect that hypermorphosis may produce is not great.

XIII

ACCELERATION

W E have now to consider the last of the possible results
that heterochrony may produce. By acceleration of the
rate of action of the internal factors which control its
formation, a character which appeared in the late stages of
ontogeny of an ancestor may appear early in the development of
a descendant. Swinnerton's term 'deuterogenesis' applies to those
cases in which the character in the adult descendant is farther
developed than in the adult ancestor, owing to its acceleration. In other cases the accelerated character may no longer
appear in the adult stage of the descendant. The embryonic or
larval features of the descendant may then resemble the adult
stage of the ancestor. The conditions required for Haeckel's
theory of recapitulation will then be fulfilled, but again with the
remark that accelerated repetition of a character in the ontogeny
of the descendant does not constitute a pressing back of a complete ancestral adult stage into an earlier period of ontogeny.
The following examples of acceleration may now be considered.

It is not always easy to be certain that a case which appears to
show acceleration is not really one of hypermorphosis. This is
especially true when the character in question is associated with
a shell formed by successive increments. Acceleration and hypermorphosis are, of course, not mutually exclusive, for in the
evolution of *Gryphaea*, as we have seen (p. 101), the angle of the
coil of the older part of the shell of the ancestor is reproduced in
the younger part of the shell of the descendant.

A case in many ways analogous is provided by the Foraminifera. The inner whorls of the coiled shell of *Cycloclypeus*
repeat the formation of chambers characteristic of the probably
ancestral form *Heterostegina*, as Tan Sin Hok has shown. But the
number of these heterostegine chambers diminishes in successive species of *Cycloclypeus* from 38 in the Oligocene to 3 in the
Pleistocene.

It had been thought by Schindewolf and others that the series
of Foraminifera represented by *Nubecularia*, *Ophthalmidium*, *Spiro-
phthalmidium*, and *Spiroculina* presented an example of neoteny,

winding, first affecting only the earliest stages of
eventually involving the entire life-history of *Spiro-*
...ut Wood and Barnard have shown that a critical study
of the stratigraphy of these forms requires a reversal of this
view, and that the series should be read the other way. It would
then provide an example of acceleration.

The corals of the genus *Zaphrentis* provide a phylogenetic
series of which the later stages of ontogeny are also known. The
series runs from *Z. delanouei* through *Z. parallela* and *Z. constricta*
to *Z. disjuncta*. It is found that the penultimate stages of ontogeny
of each of these species resemble the ultimate stages of the
immediately preceding species in each case. If hypermorphosis
is not at work here, *Zaphrentis* can be taken as a good example of
acceleration. At all events, the effect is recapitulatory, although,
as Swinnerton pointed out, other characters of *Zaphrentis* show
deviation.

Although the protaspis stage of trilobites appears to be caenogenetic, the later stages of their ontogeny may show acceleration,
for Raw claims that these stages in *Leptoplastus salteri* recapitulate the conditions in *Ctenopyge*, *Parabolina*, and other presumed
adult ancestors.

Acceleration was claimed to occur in ammonites by Hyatt and
Würtenberger and by J. P. Smith. In fact, these cases do not
show recapitulation at all, as already explained (p. 85). In
brachiopods, acceleration has been described by Fenton among
other authors. Beecher, in particular, contended that *Lingula*
has ontogenetic stages corresponding successively to the adult
stages of the older genera *Paterina* and *Obolella*. 'Progressively
through each series, the adult structure of any genus forms the
last immature stage of the next higher, until the highest member
in its ontogeny represents serially, in its stages of growth, all the
adult structures, with the larval and immature stages of the simpler genera.' But unfortunately for this view, more recent research has made it necessary to conclude that *Lingula* is more
primitive than *Paterina* and *Obolella*, and this series cannot be
claimed as representing a case of recapitulation at all. But even
in the other cases in which such a claim is made, it is not always
clear that the ancestral characters repeated were those of ancestral
adult rather than young forms (i.e. cases of deviation), while
some examples appear to conform to hypermorphosis.

One of the most interesting features of the very e
of development of the chick is the precocious forma
heart. Indeed, the heart may almost be said to arise ar
upon its functions before the embr
there. In the development of lo
such as the frog, for instance, the general
form and architectural plan of the embryo is
fully marked out by the time the heart appears. There can, then, be no doubt that in
the chick the formation of the heart has been
accelerated relatively to the rest of the body.
The 'reason' for this precocity in the formation of the heart is not far to seek. The chick
embryo is provided with an enormous quantity of yolk which cannot be made use of without a system of transportation, which conveys
the yolk to the embryo. This system is the
vascular system, and the heart is the pump
which provides the mechanical energy for the
transportation. In the frog, on the other hand,
the yolk, which is present in much smaller
quantity, is enclosed inside the embryo from
the earliest stages of development, and there
is no need for a precocious system of transportation.

FIG. 18. Hypermor-
phosis and accelera-
tion in the lineage of
Gryphaea incurva, 4. 1,
Ostraea irregularis; 2,
Gryphaea dumortieri; 3,
Gryphaea obliquata. At-
tached area shaded.
(From A. E. True-
man, *Geol. Mag.* **59,**
1922.)

The chick provides another example of
acceleration in the precocious formation of
the inner layer of cells (endoderm, yolk-epi-
thelium) which precedes the appearance of a
structure known as the blastopore (primitive
streak), instead of resulting from it as in the
frog. In primitive mammals, the amnion,
extra-embryonic coelom, and allantoic mesoderm are formed after the embryo itself. But in
man, these structures precede the formation of the embryo and
show acceleration. Alternatively, this case may be regarded as
one in which the human embryo is retarded relatively to its
membranes.

Another example of acceleration may be obtained from a
consideration of the tubes which grow out from the middle layer

of cells of an animal (mesoderm) and place the space of the body-cavity (coelomic cavity) in communication with the exterior. These tubes are called coelomoducts, and Goodrich (1895) emphasized that originally they served to free the reproductive cells which are formed in the body-cavity. As the reproductive cells are not freed until they are ripe, and they are not ripe until the animal is adult and has completed its development, the coelomoducts must originally have been formed in the last stages of ontogeny, as indeed they are in many worms. In other animals, however, and especially in the chordates, the coelomoducts make their appearance in the early stages of development, long before the reproductive cells are ripe, or even formed. In such animals, then, the formation of the coelomoducts has been accelerated, and the precocity of their appearance has made it possible for them to take on another function, viz. excretion or the getting rid of waste products. This function of excretion must be served from the earliest stages of development, and in those forms in which the coelomoducts only appear late, it is served by a different system of tubes altogether (the nephridia), which arise from the outer layer of cells. This latter system of tubes is, in general, not formed in the animals in which the coelomoducts arise in early stages of development.

The egg-teeth found in lacertilia, snakes, and monotremes, by means of which the embryos hatch out of their egg-shells, are precociously developed and enlarged teeth of the normal dentition, and may therefore be regarded as presenting a case of acceleration. But this condition is obviously functional and does not mean that these embryos are recapitulating any adult ancestral stage.

According to Osborn (1915), horns were present only in the late stages of development in the early members of the titanotheres, whereas, in the later evolved members of this family, the horns were present before birth. This case has already been alluded to in Chapter IV, where the principle of allometric growth was mentioned. It was shown that the greater size of the allometric organ, and, consequently, the more rapid rate of action of the internal factors controlling it, were associated with an increase in the size of the body. It would seem, then, that in the case of the titanotheres the accelerated rate of action of the factors causes the allometric organ to arise earlier in ontogeny, just as in the case of the eye of *Gammarus* the stronger the factor the earlier the eye becomes black. Mehnert (1898) also drew attention to the fact that progressive structures, i.e. those which have become enlarged during phylogeny, tend to appear at earlier stages of ontogeny, and to develop faster than they did in ancestral forms. Here, therefore, acceleration is the result of developmental mechanisms and does not imply any recapitulation of adult ancestral conditions in young stages of descendant.

These examples show that it is possible for characters which appeared late in the ontogeny of the ancestor to undergo heterochrony and to appear early in the ontogeny of the descendant. In these cases the young stages of the descendant show greater similarity with the old stages than with the young stages of the ancestor in respect of the character in question. But the acceleration of these characters does not justify the conclusion that the early stages in the ontogeny of the descendant represent in miniature the complete adult ancestor. We cannot claim to obtain information as to the form of the adult in an ancestor from a study of the young stages in the development of a descendant unless acceleration has occurred, and, as we have seen, it may be that a few characters here and there are accelerated, but that is all.

It may be pointed out that those who believe in Haeckel's theory of recapitulation are accustomed to treat the repetition of the early ontogenetic stages of the ancestor in the early ontogenetic stages of the descendant as if these repeated stages represented an adult ancestor. They would, therefore, include in this chapter all the examples which we have used to illustrate progressive deviation. It may be recalled that we were in some cases able actually to show that the early stages of a descendant did not bear as great a resemblance to the adult as to the early ontogenetic stages of the ancestor. There are also many cases in which our knowledge is insufficient to decide whether we have to do with deviation or acceleration. For example, starfish pass through a stage in which the larva becomes attached to its substratum and presents an appearance similar in form to that of the adult *Aristocystis*. But until we know what the young *Aristocystis* was like, no conclusions can be drawn from this case.

Many recapitulationists would also be disposed to ascribe the resemblance between young descendant and adult ancestor

(which admittedly can sometimes occur, as shown by the examples given in this chapter) to the 'inheritance of acquired
characters'. We have already seen that this implies the conversion of an external factor, which originally caused a modification
in a character of the body, into an internal factor, which being
transmitted by inheritance produces that same modification in
the absence of that external factor. We
may also repeat that satisfactory evidence of the occurrence of this phenomenon has never been produced, and
we may conclude this chapter with a
description of cases which illustrate the
care which is required in interpreting
such evidence.

In mammals, teeth are formed beneath the gums and they may be cut
before the young animal is born. Such
teeth show unworn conical cusps or
ridges, and it is only after birth that
these cusps or ridges are worn down to
flat surfaces in the molars, as a result
of the wear and tear of grinding.

a   b

FIG. 19. View of the crowns of
the upper molars of embryos of
the dugong. In the younger
embryo (a, 42 mm. long) the
cusps are conical, while in the
later embryo (b, 62 mm. long)
flat surfaces are present, as if
they had been formed by wear-
ing down. (From Kükenthal.)

Kükenthal discovered that in the early
unborn embryo of the dugong the
grinding teeth have unworn cusps, as
one would expect. But in a later embryo, still unborn, he found that the
teeth showed flat surfaces, as if they
had been worn down by friction. Here,
then, is a case in which the young
animal presents a feature which is definitely characteristic of
the effects of use in adult animals; the embryo 'recapitulates'
the ground surfaces of the teeth of its adult ancestors. An effect
has been produced in the absence of the external cause which
normally produces it, for Kükenthal showed that even if the
embryo had the habit of grinding its teeth before it was born, they
would not wear one another down, for the teeth of the opposite
jaws do not yet touch. How, then, are these flat surfaces produced? The teeth of the dugong are peculiar in that they are
penetrated by canals through which blood-vessels pass, and it

appears that the flat surfaces are due to removal of the tooth-substance by living cells, which were brought and are nourished by these blood-vessels. It is obvious that the internal factor which controls the formation of the flat surfaces in the unborn embryo is totally different from the external factor (friction) which produces the same result in the adult. Nobody can suppose that friction in the adult has had anything to do with the origin of the internal factor which controls the resorption of the tooth in the unborn embryo. To accept such a conclusion would be to fall into the trap of the 'post hoc, ergo propter hoc' type of argument.

Conclusion

If Haeckel's theory of recapitulation had been correct, this chapter would be the longest and most important in this book. Instead, only a few scrappy instances can be found, and this mode has only played a minor part in evolution.

XIV

PAEDOMORPHOSIS AND GERONTOMORPHOSIS

THE aim of the last eight chapters has been to show that each of the theoretically possible effects of heterochrony in producing phylogeny has actually occurred in the evolution of different animals. Not only that, but the different characters of one and the same organism may have evolved by different modes. Thus in graptolites, thecal elaboration shows neoteny, changes in direction of growth show acceleration; in the horse, skull dimensions show deviation, splint-bones show caenogenesis. The evolution of the hinge of *Gryphaea* shows combined hypermorphosis and acceleration. The following conclusions may therefore be drawn:

1. Qualitative evolutionary novelties can and do appear at all stages in ontogeny, and not solely in the adult.
2. Characters can and do change the time and order of their appearance in the ontogeny of the descendant as compared with that of the ancestor.
3. Quantitative differences between characters, resulting in heterochrony, play a part in phylogeny in addition to the introduction of qualitative novelties.
4. The different characters of an organism do not necessarily all evolve by the same mode.

The magnitude of evolutionary effects

It now becomes necessary to consider the magnitudes of the phylogenetic effects which are associated with the different types of heterochrony; the magnitude being estimated by the value of the classificatory groups which contain the forms in question. This is by no means easy, as it is in many cases impossible to assess the phylogenetic effect of changes in a small number of characters of an organism. Such as they are, however, the conclusions arrived at in previous chapters present the following picture, expressed in tabular form:

Associated with	The degree of divergence in phylogeny between the following:	Is of the value of a
Caenogenesis	*Lineus gesserensis*, larval dimorphism	race
	Chironomus salinarius, larval dimorphism	race
	Peripatopsis capensis and *P. balfouri*	species
	Polygordius lacteus and *P. neapolitanus*	species
	Acronycta tridens and *A. psi*	species
	Culex, Chironomus, and *Corethra*	genus
	Unio and other Lamellibranchs	family
	Sitaris and other Coleoptera	family
	Haemocera and other Copepoda	family
	Amniota and other Chordata	class
Deviation	*Portunion* and other Isopoda	family
	Entoconcha and other Gastropoda	family
	Hermit-crab and other Crustacea	family
	Flat-fish and other Teleostei	order
	Antedon and other Echinodermata	order
	Gastropoda and other Mollusca	order
	Monocotyledons and Dicotyledons	sub-class
Neoteny	*Amblystoma* and axolotl	species
	Polystomum integerrimum and *P. ocellatum*	species
	Exocoetus and *Belone*	sub-family
	Pteropods and Opisthobranchs	family
	Homo and other Primates	family
	Siphonophora and Hydrozoa	order
	Copepoda and Decapoda	order
	Cladocera and Conchostraca	order
	Hexacorallia and Tetracorallia	order
	Appendicularia and other Tunicata	order
	Proparia and other Trilobita	order
	Ctenophora and Polyclada	class
	Insecta and Myriapoda	class
	Chordata and Echinodermata	phylum
Adult variation	mutants	race
Hypermorphosis	*Poraspis* and *Pteraspis*	genus
	Gryphaea and *Ostrea*	genus
Acceleration	*Zaphrentis delanovei* and *Z. parallela*	species
	Titanotherium with and without horns	genus
	Cycloclypeus and *Heterostegina*	genus
	Leptoplastus and *Ctenopyge*	genus

Characters rendered vestigial: (i) by reduction are associated with deviation, (ii) by retardation are associated with neoteny.

The table given above has no pretensions to completeness, being composed merely of such examples as I have been able to collect. On consideration, however, it does appear that the largest phylogenetic effects are produced in association with caenogenesis, deviation, and neoteny, which are to be regarded as having played a part in the evolution of Amniota, Gastropoda, insects, and chordates. Caenogenesis, deviation, and neoteny, of course, also produce small phylogenetic changes, as do adult variation, hypermorphosis, and acceleration. But it seems that a big change in evolution is more likely to occur if ancestral youthful characters become those of adult descendants, than if ancestral adult characters become youthful characters of the descendants. The correlation between early ontogenetic appearance of the evolutionary novelty and possible systematic importance of the resulting new type has also been recognized by Schindewolf. It is probably not without significance that the groups which provide the best examples of recapitulatory effects are the Foraminifera and Lamellibranchiata, which are precisely those that have made the least progress during evolution.

Caenogenesis, deviation, and neoteny may then be grouped together since they are concerned with characters which appear early in the ontogeny, and they may be contrasted with adult variation, hypermorphosis, and acceleration, which are concerned with characters that appear late in ontogeny. The production of phylogenetic change by the introduction into the adult descendant of characters which were youthful (caenogenetic) in the ancestor, by means of deviation and neoteny, may be termed *paedomorphosis*. Phylogenetic change as a result of modification of characters which were already adult, by means of adult variation, hypermorphosis, and acceleration, may be termed *gerontomorphosis*.

A position in many respects similar to this had been reached by Sewertzow who distinguished between evolution along broad lines, termed by him 'aromorphosis', and evolution of small details, 'idio-adaptation'. The former has been responsible for large changes, such as the production of the chordate brain, heart, jaws, and appendages. These are all innovations which do not restrict the possible habitats in which the organisms may live. On the other hand, idio-adaptation has restricted the modes of life of organisms by introducing specializations which fit them for some habitats and disqualify them from others. Such evolution has produced rays and skates, flat-fish, snakes, flightless birds, and countless other highly adapted forms. Sewertzow's terms aromorphosis and idio-adaptation are therefore in some measure the ecological equivalents of our paedomorphosis and gerontomorphosis, but with stress laid on the importance of the evolutionary novelty rather than on the stage in ontogeny at which it appeared. The latter aspect of the problem is covered by Sewertzow's terms 'archallaxis', 'deviation', and 'anaboly', for the appearance of novelties at early, middle, or late stages of development. Major novelties are likely to result from 'archallaxis', while 'anaboly' leads to modification and specialization of structures already present.

It may be noted that Sewertzow's 'idio-adaptation' is practically the equivalent of Osborn's (1902) 'adaptive radiation'.

'Large' and 'small' evolution

It should be made clear that although the expressions 'large' and 'small' evolution are frequently used, there is no basis for any distinction between so-called large evolution and small evolution as regards the mechanism by which evolution is brought about. But it is a matter of common observation that some groups of organisms represented by the higher systematic categories (phyla, classes, orders) have undergone more modification in their descent than other groups represented by the lower systematic categories (species, varieties). From this point of view it is legitimate to speak of 'large' and 'small' evolution as descriptive terms relating to the evolutionary histories of the groups in question.

Magnitude in evolutionary change is measured by the taxonomic rank of the group of organisms that show it. As Mayr and Simpson have pointed out, the recognition of higher categories is *ex post facto*. 'If pterodactyls had persisted to become the dominant flying vertebrates and as richly various as birds, they would not be reptiles, but a separate class; and if birds had stopped short with *Archaeopteryx*, they would be reptiles and not a separate class.' What distinguishes the originators of lineages which have led to the production of groups of high systematic value is the appearance of evolutionary novelties which enabled their possessors to spread into new ecological zones. These adaptive characters, or 'key characters', seem to have been associated with paedomorphosis, and examples of the groups in which this is believed to have occurred were described in Chapters VII and VIII.

While some evolutionary novelties had a greater potential

taxonomic importance than others, this does not mean that there is any difference in principle between 'small' evolution and 'large' evolution. All evolution must have taken place by the action of selection on variation resulting from mutation and recombination of genes. The only difference was that the lineages destined to give rise to higher categories (phyla, classes, &c.) began as species and rose from that rank; while others, associated with gerontomorphosis, did not earn high promotion.

If it be true that big evolutionary changes, and therefore the large groups of the animal kingdom, are due to paedomorphosis, it should be possible to correlate the characteristics of large groups with the essential feature of paedomorphosis, viz. the appearance of characters in early stages of the ontogeny of the ancestor. Now, the large groups of the animal kingdom such as phyla and classes have two characteristics. In the first place, the animals in any phylum or class differ considerably from animals in other phyla or classes, i.e. there has been considerable phylogenetic structural change between the different phyla and classes. Next, the large groups, phyla or classes, contain more numerous different types within them than do the smaller groups such as families, genera, or species. This means that the changes which gave rise to the large groups have enabled the animals in these groups to go on evolving further and in more numerous directions than the animals in the small groups. The potentiality of evolving further is called *phylogenetic* or *evolutionary plasticity*, and so it becomes necessary to show that paedomorphosis is capable of producing large changes in phylogeny without sacrificing plasticity, and that gerontomorphosis is not capable of this.

First, as to the amount of structural change effected, we know that the adult form is the result of ontogeny, and also that the earlier a character appears in ontogeny, the longer it has to proceed with its development. Experiments on the gipsy moth have proved that the earlier the male characters appear in would-be females, the greater is the change that results in the adult form, viz. intersexuality. That the degree of divergence should be greater the earlier the divergence sets in, is only another way of expressing von Baer's law of the greater resemblance between young forms, and we have seen that in phylogeny this has been brought about by deviation. On the other hand, characters which appear late in ontogeny have as a rule not much time to produce much effect before development ceases. The large amount of structural change affected in evolution by paedomorphosis is therefore based on the principle of deviation, as is illustrated by the supposed evolution of the whole class Gastropoda as a result of a variation in the young.

Deviation and neoteny combined may also play a part in producing large structural changes. In animals in which the young stages have to undergo considerable change before the adult form is reached, a retention of the form of the young stage will produce a phylogenetic change as big as (but in opposite direction to) the difference between young and adult. This is illustrated by the supposed evolution of chordates from forms like larval echinoderms. The adult chordate differs as much from the adult echinoderm as the latter does from the larval echinoderm.

The question of the part which neoteny or deviation may be expected to have played in the retention or increase of evolutionary plasticity is very difficult to answer, largely because of the lack of direct evidence bearing upon it. A difficulty also arises from the fact that the term 'plasticity' has been used in many different senses.

Plasticity

Evolutionary or *phylogenetic plasticity* is the quality attributed to stocks which during their phylogeny have evolved and radiated widely. It is, however, by no means certain that the individuals of such groups were superior in their genetic plasticity to those of slowly evolving groups.

Genetic plasticity is the ability of individuals of a species to show a high degree of variance, and this condition obtains when the number of individuals carrying genes in the heterozygous condition, and the number of those genes, is large. In such species the possibilities of recombination of genes are numerous, and there is a reserve of recessive genes which may come into play, in one way or another, in the new conditions which recombinations and permutations provide.

A species undergoing paedomorphosis will find itself in possession of a number of genes whose functions were to control characters which no longer appear, since the old adult characters will be lost in neoteny, and old structures will be replaced by new ones in deviation. It is, therefore, possible to imagine that these 'unemployed' genes are available for new variation, and that paedomorphosis may contribute directly to an increase of genetic plasticity in this way. Whether such genetic plasticity would result in evolutionary plasticity appears to depend on the conditions of selection to which the organisms are exposed.

Yet another sense in which the term plasticity has been used relates to the ability of a tissue to undergo further or other differentiations. This is *histogenetic plasticity*. Experiments on regeneration and tissue-culture have shown that there exists an antagonism between the degree of specialization of a tissue and its power to grow and become specialized in other directions. At the outset of ontogeny, all the cells to which the fertilized egg has given rise are more or less similar, and devoid of any specialization or differentiation. Such cells are described as being in the *embryonic* or undifferentiated condition. Experiments have shown that embryonic cells are capable of rapid growth, and that their eventual fate is not yet irrevocably determined. A cell which would normally have undergone specialization to form part of the skin, for instance, can be made to turn into part of muscle, or stomach, or nervous system, as O. Mangold showed. As development proceeds, however, the cells and tissues become irreversibly committed to specialization and differentiation, each along its own line, and can no longer alter their prospective fate. In other words, the histogenetic plasticity of the tissues which characterizes the young stages of development is lost at the older stages. Now, since phylogeny is the result of changes in successive ontogenies, it is impossible to expect much alteration to take place when the animal has reached the later stages of its development. This is presumably why gerontomorphosis can only result in the production of small groups of animals, which become more and more specialized and incapable of evolving further. But paedomorphosis is concerned with the young stages of development, and the question arises whether, if the more or less embryonic condition of the tissues at these young stages can be preserved into later stages, these tissues will still be capable of undergoing a considerable degree of further alteration. The question might therefore be asked whether prolonged histogenetic plasticity could play any part in increasing evolutionary plasticity, but the answer is almost certainly not.

The loss and gain of evolutionary capacity

We may conclude, then, that evolution by gerontomorphosis produces relatively small changes which reduce the organism's power of changing further and re-adapting itself, and that paedomorphosis produces large changes which do not sacrifice that power. If gerontomorphosis were the only possible method of evolution, as Haeckel's theory of recapitulation would suggest, phylogeny would gradually slow down and become stationary. The race would not be able to evolve any further and would be in a condition to which the term 'racial senescence' has been applied. It would be difficult to see how evolution was able to produce as much phylogenetic change in the animal kingdom as it has, and it would lead to the dismal conclusion that the evolutionary clock is running down. In fact, such a state of affairs would present a dilemma analogous to that which follows from the view that in the universe energy is always degraded. If this were true, we should have to conclude that the universe had been wound up once and that its store of free energy was irremediably becoming exhausted. We do not know how energy is built up again in the physical universe; but the analogous process in the domain of organic evolution would seem to be paedomorphosis. A race may become rejuvenated by pushing the adult stage of its individuals off from the end of their ontogenies, and such a race may then radiate out in all directions by specializing any of the stages in the ontogenies of its individuals until racial senescence due to gerontomorphosis sets in again. It is, however, to be noted that if a race has become excessively over-specialized, even the younger stages of the ontogenies of its individuals may have lost their plasticity. In this way excessive adaptation may prevent the possibility of paedomorphosis.

When Conklin (1922) wrote that 'in every well-tried path of evolution progress has practically come to an end', he expressed the results of gerontomorphosis. And if we look round to try to see which of the species of animals living today are the ancestors of the leading evolutionary novelties of, say ten million years hence, focusing our attention only on adult forms we find it impossible to point out any such ancestor. If any new orders, classes, or phyla of animals are to arise by evolution in the future, it is to the early stages of animals alive today that we must look for their characterizations. In this connexion a remark by Haldane (1932 B) is significant: 'If human evolution is to continue along the same lines as in the past, it will probably involve a still greater prolongation of childhood and retardation of maturity. Some of the characters distinguishing adult man will be lost.' Not only physical characters but types of behaviour and mental traits may be susceptible of paedomorphosis and gerontomorphosis.

We may, then, picture the evolution of a race as a series of revolutions; periods of gerontomorphosis alternating with bouts of paedomorphosis. Such a possibility has also been envisaged by Sewertzow, who imagined an alternation between periods of 'aromorphosis' and of 'idio-adaptation' (see p. 113), by Wedekind, and by Beurlen, who accept the view that bouts of 'large' and of 'small' evolution have alternated.

Broom and Schepers interpreted the evolution of man in terms of the alternate trends of paedomorphosis and gerontomorphosis. While modern man has for some time followed a paedomorphic trend, at different levels from his ancestral stem twigs have come off and, by gerontomorphic specialization, given rise to the adult forms of the anthropoid apes, australopithecines, *Pithecanthropus*, Neanderthal, and Rhodesian man.

The terms gerontomorphosis and paedomorphosis, therefore, express not only the stage in the life-history of an animal with which they are concerned, but they also convey the meaning of racial senescence and rejuvenescence. It is interesting to note that as a result of considerations based on a different line of thought, Child (1915 : 464) had been led to express similar views. 'If evolution is in some degree a secular differentiation and senescence of protoplasm, the possibility of evolutionary rejuvenescence must not be overlooked. Perhaps the relatively rapid rise and increase of certain forms here and there in the course of evolution may be the expression of changes of this sort.'

Primitive and specialized forms

If two animals in a series are compared, one animal may be regarded as antecedent to the other in that it either does not possess, or possesses only partially developed, a character which the other animal possesses fully developed; or, it still possesses a structure which the other animal has lost. The antecedent animal in such a case is called *primitive*, and the other *specialized* or *secondary*. These words can only be used to describe members of a phylogenetic series, and one member in terms of another: for an animal which is primitive in respect of one may be specialized in respect of another animal. For instance, a reptile is more primitive than a mammal because the reptile's heart has only three chambers to the mammal's four. But a reptile is more specialized than a fish, because the heart of the latter has only two chambers.

Now, it is often said that the structural changes which take place in evolution are irreversible, and that no case is known in which a race of animals after having lost a character acquires that *identical* character again. The problem is, however, not quite so simple, for the 'loss' of a character may be due to fairly recent changes in the hereditary factors, changes which may still be reversed, resulting in a reconstitution of the original conditions. Or the loss of a character may be due to long-standing hereditary changes incapable of being reversed. Guinea-pigs have lost the thumb and the little toe; dogs have lost the big toe. But these digits can be redeveloped under certain genetic conditions, as Stockard (1930) showed. By particular recombinations of genes, the original conditions are reconstituted under which all the digits are developed. It looks as if the 'loss' of the digits was due to the acquisition of genes and genetic conditions resulting in their suppression. The phylogenetic history of the horses has involved the reduction and loss of all fingers and toes except the third. In some very exceptional cases horses may have extra fingers or toes besides the third. Here it is unlikely that the original ancestral conditions are exactly reproduced; for some unknown reason the rudiments of the extra digits grow large instead of being reduced to vestiges. But whatever the cause, the result is the redevelopment of lost structures. However, it is impossible to imagine that any descendants of the horses may reacquire all five fingers and toes and evolve further on those lines. The horses are committed to their phylogenetic line and cannot reacquire all the genetic factors which they have lost.

As L. Dollo put it, the past is indestructible. But while a character once lost is lost for ever if the genetic factors and conditions controlling its formation are irretrievably lost or irrevocably changed, a substitute character may appear which fulfils the same function as the old character, but is always structurally distinct and easily recognizable. As an example we may take the tendency which is observable in the phylogeny of the colonial hydroids for the originally free-swimming medusa to become more and more reduced to the condition of a sac which never becomes detached and therefore has lost its freedom. In some cases, however (e.g. in *Dicoryne*), such a sac may become detached and regain its mobility, but it cannot be mistaken for a medusa. The muscles which served for the locomotion of the medusa have gone and are not replaced, and for its locomotion the sac has to have recourse to a different system altogether, viz. cilia. Thus, while structural reversibility appears never to have taken place in evolution, functional return to a previous condition, using other instruments, is not uncommon.

The result of these considerations is to put a new interpretation on the hitherto accepted view that it is not possible to derive one form in phylogeny from another if the latter is specialized. Crow has expressed this view in the following words: 'As one higher class succeeds another, so the higher members of the lower class may disappear, the lower ones remaining. It is from the latter alone, the more undifferentiated species of the older class, that the new class type can arise.' But the reason why these lower (? primitive) members of the class were more undifferentiated is either that they have retained the plasticity which their previous paedomorphosis gave them and have not undergone extensive gerontomorphosis; or that they have reacquired fresh plasticity by a bout of paedomorphosis, if the previous gerontomorphosis was not too excessive.

But since paedomorphosis allows 'an escape from specialization', as Hardy has put it, there is the possibility that groups may have evolved from others which hitherto have been regarded as disqualified because of the specialized condition of their adult stage.

It is probable that ecological factors were not inactive in favouring the evolution of groups by paedomorphosis. The correlation between paedomorphosis and increased power of evolution may be due to an effect to which attention was first called by Young. He showed that some environments in which organisms live may be regarded as 'difficult' and others as 'easy'.

In general, the environments in which adult animals live are more 'difficult', specialized, and restricted than the environments of larvae. It is possible therefore that the significance of paedomorphosis lies in the withdrawal of a species from its 'difficult' adult environment to the 'easier' environment of its youthful condition, and that this opens up new ecological avenues of evolutionary possibilities.

The results of gerontomorphosis, on the other hand, are progressive specialization of the adult structure, usually in adaptation to some more or less restricted mode of life. Such adaptation entails either the development or loss of characters which handicap the animal in any walk of life other than its own. If, then, climatic or other external factors arise or change, upsetting this mode of life, the animal being unable to evolve further will have no alternative to extinction. But primitive animals are not committed to any particularly restricted mode of life; they are generalized instead of being specialized, and they will be less likely to undergo extinction as a result of environmental change, for they possess plasticity. And we have just seen that the primitive nature of an animal is associated with the plasticity which we believe is the result of paedomorphosis.

It is worth noticing that man, whose phylogeny we have seen to be characterized by paedomorphosis, largely owes his success to the fact that he is not adapted to any particularly restricted mode of life at all. Instead, he is fitted for all sorts of habits, climates, and circumstances. Man himself is generalized, not specialized, and, as Wood Jones (1916) and Elliot Smith (1927) emphasized, his body has retained a large number of primitive features which other mammals have lost.

A word may be said in connexion with the bearing of paedomorphosis on the construction of phylogenetic trees or pedigrees. We have seen (p. 113) that characters conferring important systematic distinction are more likely to arise by means of paedomorphosis than gerontomorphosis. We have also seen that early phylogenetic stages are called primitive, late ones specialized or secondary. We may call the early ontogenetic stages (embryonic or larval) young, and the late ones adult. Now, if the theory of recapitulation were of universal application, it would follow that an animal which in its adult stage possesses characters which are present only in the young stages of development in other animals, would always be regarded as phylogenetically primitive. But this would lead to absurd conclusions, as, for instance, that the human stock gave rise to apes, that the so called flightless birds gave rise to flying birds, or that the neotenous urodeles gave rise to the other newts, instead of vice versa.

The possession of embryonic or larval characters in the adult does not necessarily prove that the possessor is primitive, for it is equally if not more likely to be due to neoteny, and therefore to be phylogenetically secondary. P. R. Lowe revealed the most interesting fact that the plumage of the ostrich and of the penguin remains throughout life in the condition of the down plumage of the chicks of flying birds. Since the wings of the ostrich and other so-called flightless birds and of penguins must have been derived by degeneration from those of flying birds, it is to be concluded that these embryonic and larval features have been secondarily prolonged and retarded by neoteny in the evolution of flightless birds and penguins from flying birds. (See p. 82.)

Lastly, we may draw attention to a small but not unimportant point of terminology. For Haeckel (1875 A: 490) a caenogenetic character was necessarily originally youthful, a palingenetic character originally adult. But as the essential feature of Haeckel's palingenetic characters was that they were ancestral, and as we have seen that ancestral characters may originally have been adult or youthful, it is best to discard the term palingenetic in favour of Garstang's (1922) term *palaeomorphic*. A palaeomorphic character may of course have been originally caenogenetic, i.e. have made its first appearance in early stages of ontogeny or it may have appeared first in late stages. Conversely, characters of more recent origin, to which Garstang applies the term *neomorphic*, may have originated in early or in terminal ontogenetic or adult stages.

Paedomorphosis and the fossil record

It has been mentioned in the chapter on Phylogeny (p. 30) that neoteny following on the evolution of caenogenetic characters may result in the sudden appearance of new characters in the phylogenetic series of adults; a condition described as 'clandestine' evolution. It follows that paedomorphosis will also be associated with this type of phenomenon; and as the characters undergoing clandestine evolution will not appear in the phylogeny of adults for some time, not only will such characters make their appearance in phylogeny suddenly, but, before they do so, the fossil record will show a gap.

It is to be expected, therefore, that in those cases where paedomorphosis has occurred by means of neoteny, resulting in the production of markedly new types such as the chordates, much of this evolution will have been clandestine, and there will be a gap in the record of fossil ancestors of the new type. *Jamoytius* is about as primitive a chordate as is ever likely to be found fossil, and no transitional forms between any adult echinoderm-like ancestor and it are to be expected. In other words, the theory of paedomorphosis not only explains the gaps in the fossil record, but also supplies the reason why such gaps must be expected.

In cases where paedomorphosis has been brought about by means of deviation as in the evolution of gastropod molluscs, the fossil record would be expected to show a sudden change. As explained on page 57, the appearance of torsion may have occurred between the genera *Helcionella* and *Oelandia* as an abrupt novelty.

XV

REPETITION

WE have now come nearly to the end of our review of the relations which ontogeny and phylogeny bear to one another, and we have seen that the characters which appeared in the ontogeny of the ancestor tend to reappear in the ontogeny of that descendant, either at a corresponding stage of development, or earlier, or later.

That the reappearance of characters mostly takes place at corresponding stages was clear to Darwin when he wrote 'at whatever age a variation first appears in the parent, it tends to reappear at a corresponding age in the offspring.' The possibility of change in the time-relations was also clear to him, for he continued: 'variations, which, for all we can see might have first appeared either earlier or later in life, likewise tend to reappear at a corresponding age in the offspring and parent. I am far from meaning that this is invariably the case.'

We have seen that that which is repeated in the ontogeny of the descendant may represent the embryonic or larval just as well as the adult characters of the ancestor, and that the retarded repetition of youthful ancestral stages is of particular importance because of the part which it plays in paedomorphosis. The appearance of new characters in the early stages of development is caenogenesis, and these characters which loom so largely in neoteny and deviation are flies in the Haeckelian ointment of recapitulation, for this theory was bound to treat them as exceptions to his rule of evolution. It is because these early-developed characters are not exceptions in phylogeny, together with the fact that phylogeny is the result of ontogeny instead of being its cause, that we reject Haeckel's theory of recapitulation.

We have also seen that the accelerated appearance of a character in the ontogeny of a descendant cannot be construed as the pressing back of a complete adult ancestral stage into earlier stages of development, especially as, accompanying the acceleration of some characters, there may be neoteny of others (example: graptolites). Evolution does not take place by the addition or deletion of 'stages' to or from successive ontogenies.

It takes place by changes in organs, parts, proportions, and characters.

There is, then, no recapitulation in the Haeckelian sense of accelerated repetition of complete adult stages, although this may apply to some isolated characters. But there *is* repetition, or *palaeogenesis*.

This useful term was introduced by Garstang to replace Haeckel's palingenesis with its unacceptable connotations, and to designate primitive and repeated processes of development. Characters which appeared in the ancestor do tend to appear in the descendant, and, whatever stage these characters may 'represent', it is clear that the enthusiasm of the recapitulationists is really based on this obvious fact of repetition. If only the recapitulationists would abandon the assertion that that which is repeated is always the *adult* condition of the ancestor, there would be no reason to disagree with them.

Berrill (1953: 91) has stressed that the 'historical quality' in development is a fact. It is true that repetition of palaeogenetic characters may have far-reaching effects in the ontogenetic development of an animal if these characters are concerned with the plan of structure of the organism. The pattern imposed on the morphology of all vertebrates from the presence of visceral pouches in the embryo may go deep and affect many organ-systems. This example is one of many that impress the observer with the importance of the 'historic principle' in the ontogenetic development of organisms. It is necessary, however, to realise that the act of repetition shown by the formation of visceral pouches in the embryos of vertebrates does not mean that the visceral pouch of the mammalian embryo represents the gill-slit of the adult fish.

There is no *a priori* reason why it should be supposed that what is repeated in the development of the descendant must be the adult of the ancestor as Haeckel insisted, and it seems to have been the enthusiasm to spin phylogenies, kindled by the recognition of the fact of evolution, that was responsible for the uncritical adoption of such a view.

All that can be said regarding the information which onto-genetic stages of the development of descendants provide concerning the structure of the adults of their ancestors is, that since that ancestor gave rise to this descendant, that ancestor was more primitive. It is probable that in its ontogenetic development the ancestor did not depart so much from its own youthful form as the adult of the descendant departs from its youthful form. If the young form of the descendant repeats the young form of the ancestor, and if that young form laid down the main lines of the plan of structure of the ancestor, features of the structure of the adult of the ancestor *may* sometimes be inferred, but not demonstrated, from the study of the embryology of the descendants. This is possible in vertebrates but not in insects.

The word *recapitulation* means the condensed and abbreviated repetition of the main events of a *whole story*, and Haeckel used it to denote the repetition in the ontogeny of the descendant of the whole series of its adult ancestors. It is better therefore to drop the word recapitulation and to substitute *repetition* for the manifestation of the 'historic principle' in ontogenetic development, since it does not prejudice the significance or the extent of what is repeated.

Recapitulatory parallelism

A word of caution is necessary here. Repetition of characters interests us as a reflection of events which were manifested in the ontogenies of the ancestors and are continued in those of the descendants. But there are cases of repetition which clearly call for a special explanation. For instance, Needham has drawn attention to the fact that the nitrogen excreted by adult invertebrates, fishes, and birds takes the form of ammonia, urea, and uric acid respectively. The chick embryo starts by excreting ammonia, then urea, and lastly uric acid, thus apparently providing a case of recapitulatory repetition of adult ancestral characters. But even apart from the fact that the chemistry of urea-production in the chick embryo (involving the arginine-arginase system) is not the same as that of adult fishes (which takes place by means of the ornithine cycle), this case is instructive in bringing out the principle of parallelism of processes showing increasing degrees of complexity, exemplified by the series ammonia–urea–uric acid. Many other such sequences are cited by Needham, and there is apparently a natural order in which things can be done: a necessitation which affects all ontogenies alike. Repetition of such sequences is evidence, therefore, not of any influence of phylogeny on ontogeny, but of the limitations of physico-chemical possibilities in the transition from the simple to the more complex.

The same argument applies to cases of repetition involving allometric growth. As is shown by the case of the gibbon's and sheep's limbs (p. 100), the constants and coefficients of growth have been unchanged during evolution, with the result that the descendants in their ontogenetic development pass through and beyond the final stages of ontogeny reached by the series of their ancestors in respect of the length of their limbs. As J. S. Huxley pointed out (1926) 'recapitulation of growth-stages may be only recapitulatory as an accident, the essential fact being the convenience of differential growth as a developmental mechanism'.

That changes due to differential growth need have no phylogenetic significance at all is shown by the development of the urino-genital organs in the two sexes in mammals from a common embryonic type, by positive allometric growth of some parts and negative allometry of others. 'If these changes were recapitulatory we ought to assert that the ancestral mammal was hermaphrodite.'

Repetition of vestigial structures

Attention may now be turned to the repetition of vestigial structures. Why does the snake embryo repeat the development of its pharyngeal pouches and not that of its limbs? One answer to this question has been given by Needham: the structures whose development is repeated are in some way or other essential. The fact that the pharyngeal pouches of an amniote embryo will never become gill-slits is no evidence that these pouches are useless. On the contrary, they play an essential part in providing the rudiments of a host of structures, e.g. tympanic cavity, tonsils, thymus, and parathyroid glands. In other words, these vestigial structures are functional and preserved by natural selection.

Kleinenberg's principle of substitution is relevant here, for it holds that the ontogenetic development of an evolutionary novelty is dependent in some way on the presence of the old structure for which the novelty is substituted. The notochord may perhaps be 'necessary' for the development of the vertebrae that replace it, though this has not been proved by direct experiment. On the other hand, the result of the experiments of

Spemann and his school have revealed the indispensable nature of the notochord which induces the overlying ectoderm to differentiate into a neural tube. They have also shown that similar embryonic 'necessities', now known as inductors or 'organizers', are plentiful. It is therefore not surprising that the development of such structures which have inducing properties should be repeated in every ontogeny, even if such rudiments no longer give rise to the same structures as in the ancestors, or, indeed, to any structures at all. The functional significance of the repetition of structures has also been stressed by Lehmann.

The real answer to the wider question, Why are characters repeated? is so simple that it and its implications have often been overlooked. It was most aptly formulated by Morgan (1916) and by Broman. Characters are repeated when the groups of factors or genes which controlled their appearance in the ancestors have been transmitted to the descendants, and the appropriate environmental conditions persist. Repetition is, therefore, evidence of *affinity* between ancestor and descendant, which might not always be obvious by a comparison between the structures of the adult forms, and this is the real value of embryology in the interpretation of evolution. It is the sense in which Darwin appealed to embryology as evidence for evolution: 'community in embryonic structure reveals community of descent', and he was able to illustrate this point with the help of the cirripedes whose larvae show that they are Crustacea.

If it were true, as Haeckel contended, that the embryonic stages of the descendant represented the adult stages of the ancestors, 'atavism' and structural reversion would take place in every ontogeny. It is recognized that evolution takes place by the action of selection on the mutations and recombinations of genes. The result of this process is that the gene-complexes of species are constantly undergoing change. The genes in any species are no longer the same as those which existed in the parent species. It is therefore absurd to expect that the embryonic stages of a descendant can reproduce the adult stage of a remote ancestor of which its species no longer possesses the genes. On the other hand, the genes controlling the development of the embryonic and young stages of the life-history are likely to be preserved and retained in the gene-complex, and this is why embryonic and young stages are often repeated, and why these stages are evidence of affinity between the organisms that show them.

Atavism depends on the possibility of re-production of the gene-complex that controlled the character in question.

'*Atavism*'

The nature of the repetition of characters in successive onto-genies throws an interesting light on the phenomena which are usually included under the term atavism, which means the re-appearance in the descendant of characters that were present in the ancestor and have since been lost.

In the horse, all the fingers and toes have been lost except the third on each limb. When, as very occasionally happens, a horse has an extra finger or toe in addition to the third, it presents a certain resemblance to a more primitive phylogenetic condition in which the reduction of fingers and toes had not proceeded as far as it has in the normal structure of the modern horse. But does this mean that the abnormal horse with extra fingers has 'gone back' to an ancestral type? Gegenbaur showed some time ago that this could not be affirmed, and indeed each case must be considered on its merits. In some cases there can be no question of atavism, for the extra digit is merely a product of the subdivision of the originally undivided rudiment. Thus a horse may have a sub-divided third digit which is not at all the same thing as having a third and fourth digit. In other cases, as in those of the guinea-pigs and dog mentioned in the previous chapter, an ancestral condition is reproduced. As Stockard has shown, these atavistic phenomena must be regarded as due to the reconstitution of the original genetic conditions by suitable recombinations of genes.

In the more primitive insects *Iapyx* and *Machilis*, the female reproductive organs are repeated in each of seven segments of the abdomen. That this is a primitive feature is most probable, for the essence of the segmentation of the body is the repetition of the reproductive glands, as in many worms. In the higher insects, of which the gipsy moth is an example, the reproductive glands are localized in one abdominal segment only and are not repeated. Goldschmidt (1923) found, in the course of experimental breeding of races which differ in the relative speeds of development, that gipsy moths can be obtained in which the reproductive glands are segmentally repeated. This condition is to be explained by the different rates of actions of the factors which control the processes of segmentation and of formation of the reproductive glands, respectively. Normally, the latter are quick enough to form the reproductive gland before the processes of segmentation can divide it up between several segments. But if these processes are relatively delayed, the processes of segmentation will effect a partitioning of the reproductive gland before the latter is definitely formed, and so 'reproduce' the ancestral condition. 'Atavism' here is, therefore, due to the fortuitous reintroduction of a set of conditions (a definite system of reaction-speeds) which obtained in the ancestor and is in no way a primitive condition.

To a case such as that just described, in which the formation of a structure is relatively delayed, Schulze's (1922) term *hysterotely* is applied. The converse condition known as *prothetely*, in which the development of a structure is relatively accelerated, has, curiously enough, also provided cases which have been regarded as atavistic. For instance, the occasional presence of wings in caterpillars has been held to reflect a primitive ancestral condition of insects in which development is progressive and gradual without the abrupt metamorphosis which characterizes the higher forms. But here again R. Goldschmidt (1923) showed that the condition is merely the result of changes in the rates of activity of different processes, and has no phylogenetic significance at all.

Analogous results of an 'atavistic' nature were also obtained by Runnström in the course of his investigations on experimental embryology in echinoderms. The larvae of echinoderms are characterized generally by the possession of three pairs of body-cavities, but in the larva of *Antedon* the first and second cavities on the right side are normally not formed. If, however, a larva of *Antedon* is cut into two by a transverse cut, the posterior half develops these cavities, thereby differing from a normal *Antedon* larva and resembling the larvae of other echinoderms. This case of 'atavism' is to be explained by the re-establishment of an ancestral set of conditions brought about by the removal of an inhibiting factor which was eliminated when the anterior half of the larva was cut off. A number of other 'atavistic' appearances can be produced in the same way, but they are devoid of any phylogenetic significance.

Lastly, we may consider some atavistic phenomena in man. It was shown in Chapter VIII that the evolution of man was in a large measure due to ncoteny and retardation, and we saw in Chapter III that the rate of development in mammals is under the control of the ductless glands which secrete hormones. During human phylogeny, therefore, the rate of development of the body must have been progressively retarded by the action of the ductless glands. Suppose now that, for some pathological reason, one or other of the ductless glands ceases to exert this retarding function, the result will be the production of a man with so-called pithecoid characters: the hair will be over-developed, or the skin dark, or the brow-ridges accentuated, or the jaws larger, or the length of the bones will be increased, or sexuality will be precocious, or the sutures between the bones of the skull will close up prematurely. These features are atavistic in that they result from a reversion to the set of circumstances under which development took place in the ancestor.

Atavism is, therefore, based on an inheritance of similar genetic factors by the descendant from the ancestor, and the reconstitution of similar conditions. But, like normal development, atavism is actually brought about by that new creation of an animal which constitutes ontogeny. The atavistic feature is not directly inherited from the ancestor as such, for nothing is solely inherited without also being acquired.

The opposite condition to repetition or palaeogenesis is seen in those cases in which the primitive processes of development of a character in an ancestor have been discarded in the descendant and replaced by modified processes which Garstang (1922) termed *neogenetic*. Neogenesis will be the result of caenogenetic modifications of development, such as those mentioned on page 37. It is important to note that the terms palaeogenetic and neogenetic refer to processes of development, old and recapitulatory or new and anti-capitulatory, respectively. On the other hand, the terms *palaeomorphic* and *neomorphic* denote the phylogenetic age of characters, regardless of the stage of ontogeny in which they originated in the ancestor, or of the manner in which they develop in the descendant.

The neural tube in chordates is a palaeomorphic structure, but its method of development in Teleostei as a solid rod of cells is neogenetic. The mammalian incus and malleus as auditory ossicles are neomorphic structures, but their development is palaeogenetic. Torsion in gastropods is palaeomorphic and palaeogenetic, but it was neanic and caenogenetic in origin. The horns of titanotheres were neomorphic structures, but they were probably palaeogenetic in their method of development, and in origin they must have been ephebic (adult).

XVI

EMBRYOLOGY AND TAXONOMY

THE evolutionary history of all organisms should, ideally, be reflected in the scheme of classification in which they are placed. And since ontogeny has so important a bearing on phylogeny, it becomes of interest to inquire into the significance of embryology for the principles of classification or taxonomy.

The taxonomic value of embryonic and larval characters

Reference has already been made to von Baer's dilemma, quoted by Darwin: 'In my possession are two little embryos in spirit, whose names I have omitted to attach, and at present I am quite unable to say to what class they belong. They may be lizards or small birds, or very young mammalia, so complete is the similarity in the mode of formation of the head and trunk in these animals.' It was, of course, on the basis of experiences such as this that von Baer was led to formulate his famous principle that 'embryos of different members of the same group are more alike than their adults, and that the resemblances are greater the younger the embryos examined', as Sedgwick has epitomized it.

The bearing of von Baer's generalization on systematics was also seen by Sedgwick (1894), for it might mean 'that whereas the differences between the adults are large and important differences of class value, the differences between the embryos are slighter and unimportant, and of less than class value'. If von Baer's principle were of universal or even of general application, it is clear that the outlook for the possible contributions which embryology might make to minor taxonomy would be unpromising, although its importance in establishing affinities between large groups (e.g. annelids and molluscs, both of which groups have a trochosphere larva) may be great. Embryology enabled Thompson to recognize the crustacean nature of cirripedes from their nauplius larva, and to establish the systematic position of *Sacculina* from its cypris larva, and Baur to recognize the molluscan nature of *Entoconcha* from its veliger. Embryological studies can often supply evidence of affinity in a general way between groups, but can only rarely provide material for the establishment of divergences between small groups.

However, with the progress of embryology and increasing familiarity with embryonic and larval material, it becomes more and more clear, as Sedgwick was among the first to show, that (in his words) 'a species is distinct and distinguishable from its allies from the very earliest stages all through the development, although these embryonic differences do not necessarily implicate the same organs as do the adult differences'. In whatever way the 'value' of differences may be determined, it must be held to apply to the whole life-history of an organism and not merely to a time-section through it.

Even if the important systematic differences of the adult are imperfectly or incompletely developed in the young, this would provide no justification for degrading the value of these differences from that of one systematic group to that of another of lower rank. The principle enunciated by von Baer is merely a rough formulation, without detailed analysis, of the phenomena of development as presented by most organisms; and there are no grounds for the view that an organism as it develops passes through systematic categories of differing 'values', or of differing degrees of estrangement from organisms of other groups.

These considerations do not, however, conflict with the fact that there are, occasionally, marked similarities between young forms not exhibited by their adults, largely because the differentiations which characterize the adults have not yet appeared. This is especially the case with groups which possess characteristic larval forms. For a considerable time the study of this question was obscured and obstructed by the desire to see in larval forms the adult form of the ancestors, as the theory of recapitulation tried to make out. On the contrary, it is now accepted that the various larvae, trochosphere, veliger, pilidium, nauplius, pluteus, &c., represent adaptive modifications to a pelagic habit of life, fulfilling the function of securing the dispersal of the species. The wealth of larval forms found in insects are likewise adaptations to their very various modes of life. It is a corollary of such adaptations that the better the larva is suited for its mode of life, the greater will be the difference between it and its adult, and the more violent will be the metamorphosis by which the adult is produced. But although it can

in many cases be shown that these larval forms could not represent the adult ancestral forms, this does not detract from their
value as evidence of affinity between the organisms which possess
any particular type. Thus, annelids are related to molluscs
because of their trochosphere larva; the tornaria larva of *Balanoglossus* relates it to echinoderms. In the same way, the phenomenon of spiral cleavage exhibited by Polyclad Turbellaria,
Nemertini, Polychaeta, and Mollusca may be regarded as having been inherited from a common ancestor, but itself gives no
information as to what that ancestor was like. A pretty indication of the common descent of Scaphopod Mollusca and Polychaeta is provided by the fact that the method of cleavage, with
formation of a polar lobe containing the organ-forming substances for the apical organ and the post-trochal region, is
identical in *Dentalium* and in *Sabellaria*, as E. B. Wilson (1904)
and P. Hatt (1932) showed. Their common ancestor may not
actually have possessed a polar lobe, but they must have inherited
from it the prerequisite conditions for its development.

From the point of view of evolutionary studies, something
very valuable is gained by the grouping together of the above-
mentioned phyla and classes which possess the method of spiral
cleavage; and it is satisfactory that reptiles, birds, and mammals
agree in the possession (though not necessarily in the method of
formation) of an amnion by their embryos; the structure of the
placenta has enabled Hill to make a valuable contribution to
the phylogeny of primates. On the other hand, there are many
cases in which developmental phenomena by themselves have
proved a very insecure foundation upon which to build systematic categories, as a consideration of a few examples will reveal.

The idea of classifying Insecta according to whether they
undergo metamorphosis or not can be traced back to Swammerdam and Ray, while Leach introduced the terms Ametabolia
and Metabolia. Since then there have been numerous other
attempts, for an account of which the reader is referred to
Handlirsch. But such a subdivision of the class in no way reflects
the structural resemblances between the adults of the various
orders, and is clearly artificial.

The same is true of Latreille's classification of Urodela into
Caducibranchiata and Perennibranchiata. Here it can be demonstrated beyond question that neoteny and the retention of

larval characters has occurred independently in each of the five orders of the sub-class: in Cryptobranchoidea, *Cryptobranchus alleghaniensis* (Daudin); in Amblystomoidea, *Amblystoma tigrinum* (Green); in Salamandroidea, *Amphiuma means* Garden and *Typhlomolge rathbuni* Stejneger; in Proteidae, *Necturus maculatus* Rafin. and *Proteus anguineus* Laur.; and in Sirenoidea, *Siren lacertina* L. It may be added that perennibranchiate forms also occurred among labyrinthodonts such as *Dvinosaurus*, quite unrelated to urodeles.

Attempts to base systematic groups of high rank on developmental phenomena may, therefore, present serious dangers. As to groups of lesser rank, as will be seen below, the value of embryological studies to systematics lies not so much in the establishment of groups on this or that larval character, as in the recognition that groups of different rank vary in the extent of the discrepancies that they may show when classified according to adult or larval characters.

Congruent and incongruent classifications

A study of the relations between development and sytematics must consider the difficult problems presented by those cases in which the larval forms of groups of related organisms lend themselves to schemes of classification which disagree with schemes on which the adults are classified.

The condition most usually found is that in which differences between the adults of related groups are reflected in corresponding but less well-marked differences between their larval or youthful forms. This simple condition, in which classification-schemes built upon adult and larval characters would coincide, is, however, by no means universal, and Weismann (1876) considered the possibilities of larval and adult classification-schemes being 'congruent' and 'incongruent'. The problem has been reinvestigated by van Emden (1929), who has shown that many situations are possible. The first is the congruent condition: group-definitions based on larval and on adult characters coincide. The last is the incongruent condition: classification based on larval structure is at odds with that based on adult structure. Between these extremes, however, there are other possibilities, including cases in which indistinguishable or very similar larvae give rise to different adult types, and others in which distinguishable larvae give rise to very similar adult types. It will be useful, then, to consider in turn the conditions of: I, congruence; II, adult divergence; III, larval divergence; and IV, incongruence; and to find examples for each of these, as van Emden has done in respect of: *a*. species of a genus (or closely related genera); *b*, subspecies of a species; and *c*, mutants. (The last category in van Emden's work is 'varieties', but it is preferable to restrict attention to varieties whose genetic basis has been established.)

I*a*. The congruent condition is the most usual. It is necessary to bear in mind the fact that in all these cases, which follow von Baer's principle of progressive specialization during development, the differences between young forms will be less marked than between adults, though nevertheless of specific value. An example given by van Emden is that of *Carabus clathratus* L., *C. granulatus* L., and *C. cancellatus* Illig., in which, although very similar, differences of specific value are found between larvae as well as between the adult beetles.

I*b*. Less common is the congruence between larval and adult characters in subspecies of a species. *Haliplus fulvus* F. has a Pyrenean subspecies *carlitensis* Règ., the larva of which is also distinguishable by a difference of subspecific value in mandible form.

I*c*. The occurrence of mutations which visibly affect both larva and adult is rare. This, as Ford (1937) has pointed out, is to be expected, as larval and adult organisms usually possess different habits of life entailing different adaptive requirements. An example is that of *Colias philodice* Godt. in which the larva and the eye of the butterfly are grass-green in colour owing to the presence of chlorophyll-α and xanthophyll. A recessive mutation studied by Gerould inhibits the extraction of xanthophyll from the food and results in blue-green larvae and imagines with eyes of similar colour. Another mutation has been discovered which reddens the xanthophyll pigments, so that larvae and imaginal eyes are olive-green.

II*a*. Examples of different species in which the larval forms are apparently indistinguishable, or very similar, are provided by *Bematistes macarista* (E. M. Sharpe) and *B. poggei* Dewitz, where the larvae are 'of identically the same appearance' as described by Hale Carpenter, who also observed great similarity between the larvae of *Acraea alciope* Hew. and *A. humilis* E. M. Sharpe, and between those of *Acraea terpsichore* L. and *A. alicia*

E. M. Sharpe. Other examples are supplied by species of *Chiro-nomus* as described by Lenz. *Smerinthus populi* L. and *S. ocellata* L. provide a case where the larvae are much more similar than the adults, and, among Anura, Boulenger could find only a trivial colour-difference between the tadpoles of *Megalophrys montana* Kuhl and those of *M. parva* Boulenger.

II*b*. *Pieris napi bryoniae* O. has been regarded as a subspecies of *Pieris napi*, and its larva is similar to that of the type. However, L. Müller has produced evidence tending to show that *bryoniae* is a distinct species of *Pieris*, in which case this example should be included under II *a*. Boulenger was unable to find any differ-ences wherewith to distinguish between the tadpoles of the various races of *Rana esculenta* L. which he had diagnosed.

II *c*. The greatest number of mutant genes known affect the adult and not the larva, and so fall into this category. For examples the reader is referred to monographs such as that of Morgan, Bridges, and Sturtevant on the genetics of *Drosophila*.

III *a*. Cases in which young forms of different species differ greatly while their adults are very similar, are widely scattered. Sedgwick states that he was in doubt whether *Peripatopsis capensis* (Grube) and *P. balfouri* (Sedgwick) were distinct species until he studied their development; for while the adults differ in trivial characters, the ovum of *P. capensis* is 0·6 mm. long and the embryo contracts and shortens when touched, but the ovum of *P. balfouri* is 0·4 mm. long and the embryo when touched coils into a spiral.

Another example is provided by the worms *Polygordius lacteus* and *P. neapolitanus* whose larvae develop very differently although the adults, according to Woltereck (1904), are indistinguishable.

The best example of this category is, however, that of the moths *Acronycta tridens* Schiff. and *A. psi* L. So similar are the adults of these species that South states: 'I am unable to indicate any character that will serve to distinguish between this moth [*A. tridens*] and the Grey Dagger [*A. psi*].' In fact, the distinction as based on the genitalia is given by Pierce and amounts practically to little more than the bifurcation of the clasper in the male in *psi* and its trifurcation in *tridens*. But the larva of *tridens* has a white stripe with orange spots down the back and a blunt black hump on the fourth ring, whereas that of *psi* has a yellowish stripe and a slender tall hump on the fourth ring which is easily distinguishable.

Russell has shown that the polyps of *Amphinema dinema* P. & L. and *A. rugosum* (Mayer) are indistinguishable, but the medusae are distinct in colour and size. In sponges, *Halichondria panicea* can only be distinguished from *H. bowerbanki* by the structure of the larva and spawning-time. In ascidians, Grave noted that the larvae of different species differ more than the adults.

Among Amphibia, Annandale discovered that two closely allied species of frog, *Rana tigrina* Daudin and *R. cancrivora* Gravenhorst, have tadpoles which differ widely in their buccal armature. Other examples in which the larvae differ more than the adults are provided by *Rana jerboa* Günther and *R. whiteheadi* Boulenger, described by Boulenger, and by *Rana beddomei* Günther and *R. semipalmata* Boulenger, described by Annandale. Lastly, there are those cases like *Salamandra salamandra* [L.], and *S. atra* Laurenti, in which related and similar adults differ in their development, which is in one case of the larval and in the other of the embryonic type. Chapter VI gives other examples.

III *b*. Of subspecies of a species in which the larval forms differ more than the adults, an example given by van Emden is *Acronycta auricoma* F., the larva of which has yellowish-red tubercles on each ring, while that of subspecies *alpina* Frr. has the tubercles a brilliant white. According to Lenz, *Chironomus salinarius* Kieff has two larval forms differing in the degree of reduction of the gills.

Schmidt described a very remarkable developmental dimorphism in the nemertine *Lineus gesserensis-ruber* O. F. Müll. It has long been known that this species develops by means of an embryo of the Desor type; the eggs, 0·5 mm. in diameter, are laid, six in a soft-membraned capsule, in flexible masses of spawn. All eggs develop into inert embryos with small blastopore and thick epidermis. But occasionally spawn is found in sausage-shaped masses of capsules with thick membranes, each containing about fifteen eggs 0·25 mm. in diameter. Only 30 per cent. of these eggs develop into very mobile embryos with thin epidermis and large blastopores which engulf the other eggs. The adult *Lineus* shows colour variations ranging from red to green, and Schmidt observed that red or reddish adults laid eggs which developed solely according to the newly discovered type, while green or greenish adults laid eggs which developed along the lines of the Desor type.

III *c*. Several examples were given by Cockayne of larval variation in insects and by Ford (1937) of larval mutants. The larva of *Lasiocampa quercus* var. *sicula* Stgr. has red fur; that of var. *meridionalis* Tutt has white fur; the difference is due to a single pair of genes. In *Lymantria dispar* L., Goldschmidt (1924, 1933) found that a single pair of genes is responsible for the fact that the larvae of Eurasian races are dark, while those of south-west Japan are light in colour. Races of *Lymantria* may also differ in the number of moults which they undergo, without affecting size at pupation, and Goldschmidt also produced evidence to show that moulting is controlled by a system of three multiple allelomorphs. Many mutant genes of *Bombyx mori* belong here.

IV. Incongruence of classification based on larval and adult characters provides problems of great interest. These are cases where in three species *A*, *B*, and *C*, *A* and *B* resemble one another in the young stages more than they resemble *C*, and *B* and *C* resemble one another in the adult form more than they resemble *A*. The problem of classification here, as always, is to distinguish the resemblances due to affinity from the resemblances due to other cases.

Van Emden cites the case of *Smerinthus ocellata*, whose adult resembles that of *Calasymbolus excaecata* (Abb. and Smith), while its larva resembles that of *S. populi* and differs considerably in colour from that of *C. excaecata*. In this case, a classification based on adults would group *ocellata* with *excaecata*, while a classification based on larvae would dissociate them and group *ocellata* with *populi*.

Perhaps the best example of incongruence is that provided by the Hydrozoa in which there is an alternation of generations between medusae and polyps. A classification of these animals based on the structure of the polyps was made by Hincks and Allman; another classification based on the structure of the medusae was made by Haeckel. The present state of knowledge of the structure, development, and life-histories of the Hydrozoa is sufficiently advanced for it to be possible to marry the two schemes of classification, as Rees (1957) has shown. In some cases, classifications based only on the polyps or only on the medusae would place in different genera what are really phases of one and the same species. Under the dual classification, the

following hydroids and their medusae of the family Corynidae
would be classified as follows:

By the Hydroid polyp.	By the Medusa
Coryne (*Syncoryne*) *sarsi* Lovén	*Sarsia tubulosa* (M. Sars)
Coryne (*Syncoryne*) sp.	*Dipurena halterata* (Forbes)
Stauridiosarsia sp.	*Dipurena ophiogaster* (Haeckel)

This incongruence has been shown by Rees to be due to
failure to consider the species throughout its life-history as a
whole and to base the classification on the sum of the characters
of each hydroid and its medusa. It so happens that in this particular example, these species fit into an integrated classification
under the names in the column under the heading Medusa. In
other words, the resemblance between *Coryne* (*Syncoryne*) *sarsi* and
other species of *Coryne* (*Syncoryne*) in the hydroid are fortuitous
and do not represent the true affinities of the species. Similarly,
the differences between these other species of *Coryne* (*Syncoryne*)
and species of *Stauridiosarsia* in the hydroid are fortuitous and
outweighed by the resemblances of more fundamental characters in their medusae.

For the practical purposes of taxonomy the adult scheme of
classification is usually regarded as the more important, though
it is not always easy to see how the larval scheme is to be brought
into line with it. This task, however, was attempted for the
apparently incongruent species of *Carabus* by Bengtsson (1927).
While it is clear, as Noble showed for Amphibia and Mortensen for echinoderms, that group-characteristics can be recognized in the larvae of the majority of groups as characterized by
adult structure, exceptions occur which transcend the classification widely.

The remarkable case of the Echinoidea and their plutei was
studied by von Ubisch (1933). The structure of the skeleton
of the four-armed pluteus is practically identical in *Sphaerechinus
granularis* A.Ag. and *Echinocyamus pusillus* Gray, although the
families (Strongylocentrotidae and Fibulariidae) to which they
belong are in different sub-classes (Regularia Ectobranchiata
and Irregularia). Similarly, the four-armed pluteus of *Arbacia
lixula* (L.) (sub-order Arbacina) is practically indistinguishable
from that of *Strongylocentrotus franciscanus* A.Ag. (sub-order Echi-
nina); and the eight-armed pluteus of *Arbacia punctulata* Gray is
very similar to that of *Echinocardium cordatum* Penn. On the other

hand, the plutei of *Lytechinus variegatus* Lamk. and of *L. verruculatus* Ltk. differ markedly, owing to the trellis-work of the postoral arms and the aboral 'basket' of the latter. Mortensen was even inclined to create a separate genus for *verruculatus*.

The incongruent distribution of the characters of the plutei was interpreted by von Ubisch on morphogenetic grounds. There is evidence in the larva of a gradient of skeleton-forming activity, with its high point at the vegetative pole. Skeletal pieces near the vegetative pole of the larva tend to be more complex in structure, to show trellis-work instead of simple rods, and to be massive instead of slender. Alterations in intensity of the skeleton-forming gradient might occur for reasons totally unconnected with common descent, and might occur independently in different groups. This would go far to explain the similarities between distantly related and the differences between closely related plutei.

A crude case of incongruence is provided by the Ophiuroidea, for whereas their adult structure relates them much more closely to the Asteroidea than to the Echinoidea, the ophiopluteus larva bears a closer resemblance to the echinopluteus than to the brachiolaria. Such resemblance is, however, spurious and due to the adaptive needs of flotation.

Having now considered the various modes of congruence and incongruence between larval and adult characters, it remains to see whether conclusions may be drawn of importance from the point of view of systematics. It will have been noted that in all the categories the material chosen for the demonstration of examples, whether nemertine, insect, echinoderm, or amphibian, is uniformly characterized by extensive metamorphosis. This is, of course, a necessary condition for the emphasizing of larval structures, which in forms with direct development are harder to differentiate. It must also be remembered that such conclusions as can be drawn are subject to the manner in which the species and subspecies in question have been defined by the systematists. Nevertheless, the following points emerge and are probably valid.

The systematic unit in which the limits as defined by larval and adult characters coincide most frequently is the species; i.e. in the preceding analysis, category I *a* is commoner than I *b* or I *c*. In other words, when the whole life-cycle is taken into

	a. Species of a Genus	b. Subspecies	c. Mutants
I. Congruence	Most species	Haliplus fulvus and var. carlitensis	Colias philodice
II. Adult divergence	Bematistes macarista and poggei Acraea alciope and humilis Acraea terpsichore and alicia Chironomus sp. Smerinthus populi and ocellata Megalophrys montana and parva	Pieris napi and var. bryoniae Rana esculenta	Most mutants
III. Larval divergence	Peripatopsis capensis and balfouri Polygordius lacteus and neapolitanus Nematus miliaris and fagi Lytechinus variegatus and verruculatus Acronycta tridens and psi Rana tigrina and cancrivora Rana jerboa and whiteheadi Rana beddomei and semipalmata	Acronycta auricoma and var. alpina Chironomus salinarius Lineus gesserensis-ruber Palaeocimbex quadrimaculata	Lasiocampa quercus vars. sicula and meridionalis Bombyx mori Lymantria dispar and very many larval variations not yet genetically analysed

IV. Incongruence

Species of related genera

Larval similarity   Adult similarity

     { Smerinthus populi
     { Smerinthus ocellata .   .   .   .   .   }
       Calasymbolus excaecata .   .   .   .   }
     { Echinocyamus pusillus
     { Sphaerechinus granularis .   .   .   .   }
     { Strongylocentrotus franciscanus .   .   .   }
     { Arbacia lixula   .   .   .   .   .   }
     { Arbacia punctulata .   .   .   .   .   }
     { Echinocardium cordatum
       Sarsia tubulosa = Coryne (Syncoryne) sarsi .   .   }
     { Dipurena halterata = Coryne (Syncoryne) sp..   .   }
     { Dipurena ophiogaster = Stauridiosarsia (Stauridium) sp.

consideration, the species has more clearly defined limits than the subspecies or the mutant. Conversely, it can be seen that the systematic unit in which the categories of adult and larval divergence are most rarely found is again the species; categories II *c* and III *c* are much commoner than II *a* or III *a*. In other words, adult divergence and larval divergence are most frequently found in subspecies and mutants. The unit which systematists call the species appears, therefore, to be in a slightly different position as compared with the subspecies and the mutant. This conclusion is not only of interest and importance in itself, but it also suggests a reason for the difference between the species and the lower categories. For during the time that the differences between mutants and subspecies have widened into the value of interspecific differences, the now distinct species, ceasing to resemble one another sufficiently closely in either larval or adult state, no longer fall into any other category of the preceding analysis than I *a*.

As pointed out by van Emden, in respect of possibilities of incongruence, the species agrees in general with the lesser systematic categories of subspecies and mutant, for they are too 'small' to show incongruence; and all three differ from the family and higher ranks of classification. The genus appears to occupy an intermediate position in this respect.

These matters can be profitably expressed in the form of a table (p. 144).

XVII
EMBRYOLOGY AND HOMOLOGY

An important concept in biology to which modern embryology has a contribution to make is that of homology. The recently accepted view of homology between structures based the resemblance between them on the genetic affinity underlying them as structures descended, however modified, from a representative in a common ancestor. This concept is at the root of all phylogenetic schemes, for it is by means of their homologous structures and the modifications which they have undergone that the ancestry and affinities of organisms are determined. The essential notion of homology as thus conceived is the continuity of structures in phylogeny and not the resemblance between homologous structures, for structures undoubtedly homologous may be very different anatomically and histologically (e.g. the pineal eye in reptiles and the pineal gland in mammals).

This concept of homology, in its strictest sense, held that structures must have been present and visible all along the phylogenetic lines leading back to the point of divergence from the common ancestor if they were to be regarded as homologous. In other words, the concept is one of homology of phenotypes, i.e. of types determined by their appearance regardless of their genetic constitution.

It is now clear that in requiring the visible presence of structures as far back as the point of divergence from the common ancestor, the theory of homology was over-exacting. There seem to be cases (e.g. horns in titanotheres) in which the independent appearance of closely comparable characters in related but divergent stocks is more satisfactorily explained, as by J. S. Huxley (1932), on lines which admit of genetic affinity; the manifestation of the character in the common ancestor having been obscured or delayed for developmental reasons, involving questions of growth and magnitude. Such cases are covered by the expression 'latent homology'.

Homology and genetics

It is, of course, obvious that, in so far as homology implies a common descent, it must involve genetic affinity. But the results of recent advances in genetics have shown that genes are not restricted in their sphere of influence to the characters which they have been found to control in a normal environment and a normal gene-complex. Further, under varied conditions of the gene-complex, a gene may cease to control the formation of one particular character, and, instead, may control another completely different character. Thus in poultry, as Fisher showed, a gene controlling the formation of a crest of feathers also produces cerebral hernia. In the wild type, the gene behaves as a dominant in respect of crest, but as a recessive for hernia. The action of the gene on hernia can be entirely suppressed in certain gene-complexes (such as that of the Japanese silky fowl), while the production of crest is unaffected. There is no homology between crest and hernia, and therefore it is clear that characters controlled by identical genes are not necessarily homologous.

There is another sense in which this statement is also true. Even where a character in two related organisms can be shown to be under the control of a single gene, and this gene can (by crossing) be proved to be identical in each, the characters may nevertheless not be homologous in the recently accepted sense. For it is possible that the common ancestor may not have possessed these characters, and their appearance may have been due (as in the case of 'white eye' in *Drosophila*) to independent and parallel mutation in the two stocks. Such cases would perhaps fall under the heading of 'latent homology', since the fact of mutation at the same locus may reflect an inherited common tendency.

A case of homologous genes controlling characters which were independently evolved and therefore not homologous has been demonstrated by Ford in *Triphaena comes*. This is a moth which is grey in colour on the mainland of Great Britain. Dark races have been evolved in the Orkneys and in the Hebrides, and they are under the control of a gene which has been proved by crossing to be identical in both. But crossing also shows that the manner in which these genes have come to determine the dark colour is quite different in the two races, for subsequent offspring from hybrids between them show a complete break-down in the gene-balance by which the gene in question exerts its effect in the two races. Each race has therefore built up its gene-complex by selection in its own way, differently from the other. Although the gene is the same in both races and its effects apparently the same in both, these effects are not homologous in any sense.

On the other hand, the control of a character normally effected by one gene may come to be assumed by other quite different genes. A good example of this possibility is provided by the gene controlling the formation of the eyes in *Drosophila*, the recessive allelomorph of which produces the eyeless condition. Nevertheless, in homozygous eyeless stocks, the other members of the gene-complex can by breeding be reshuffled and recombined in such a way that they 'deputize' for the absent normal allelomorph to the 'eyeless' gene, and eyes reappear in the stock. Such eyes must be regarded as homologous with the eyes of the normal wild stock, and therefore it is clear that homologous characters need not be controlled by identical genes. Since this may be the case even when the homologous characters are identical, it is likely that when homologous characters do not resemble one another closely, the genes controlling them may be very diverse.

Another sense in which this statement is also true concerns the action of 'mimic' genes—different genes with identical effects. Examples of these are provided by many cases of albinism in animals, and in plants Harland has drawn attention to the existence of three different ways in which homologous characters may be produced genetically. He has summed up the position very aptly by stating that 'a character or organ is not genetically in a static but is in a dynamic condition. The genes, as a manifestation of which the character develops must be continually changing, according to whether their allelomorphs are selected to strengthen other physiological processes. There must be continual competition between different organs or functions for one or the other member of a pair of allelomorphs. On the dynamic view of organs and functions we are able to see how organs such as the eye, which are common to all vertebrate animals, preserve their essential similarity in structure or function, though the genes responsible for the organ must have become wholly altered during the evolutionary process.' To this it may be added that the evolution of the genetic control of a character must be regarded as having involved not only the substitution of allelomorphs for genes already concerned, but also the introduction of other genes to the control.

The genetic link between homologous structures cannot be analysed down to individual genes, but must be based on the gene-complex or such portions of it, or groups of genes, which control the structure in question. The individual members of these groups of genes may, during phylogeny, become changed by substitution, addition, or loss, so that, on the analogy of the two new blades and the new handle of the penknife, the groups may come to contain few or none of their original members. In other words, the homology of phenotypes does not imply the similarity of genotypes, i.e. of types determined by their genetic constitution regardless of their appearance.

The analysis of the concept of homology in terms of single genes therefore breaks down. It is of great interest to find that an analysis of homology in terms of cellular or precellular correspondence of position in ontogenetic development likewise fails.

Homology and embryology

The study of homologous structures has hitherto tended to consider them as structures fully formed, or, when their development was considered, as structures arising simply out of the tissues which supply their substance. But the necessity for a consideration of morphogenesis in addition to morphology is becoming increasingly apparent. For instance, in gastrulation, as Pasteels (1937) has shown, the forms of gastrulae can only be compared very unsatisfactorily, whereas the tissue-movements involved in gastrulation (extension of ectoderm, convergence and epiboly of chorda-mesoderm, invagination of endoderm) show some fundamental similarities, though differing in extent and in time-relations.

Another aspect of the importance of morphogenesis is shown by the fact that many structures owe their existence to a process of induction by special regions of the embryo. To give a familiar example, the neural tubes have been regarded in themselves as homologous throughout the chordates, as no doubt they are. But in addition to the correspondence between those portions of ectoderm forming the neural tubes, there is a more deep-seated correspondence between their inductors, the primitive gut-roofs which have been shown in lampreys, fishes, amphibia, birds, and mammals to be active in inducing the formation of the neural tubes out of the ectoderm overlying them, and without which no neural tubes would have been formed at all.

Clearly, the homology between the neural tubes in these classes of chordates is partly a result of the homology between the gut-roofs. An interesting attempt has been made by von Ubisch (1928) to show an analogy between the primitive gut-roof of chordates, which possesses such remarkable inducing powers, and the hydrocoel of echinoid larvae, which is likewise a derivative of the wall of the archenteron, and induces the formation of the echinus rudiment, as MacBride (1918) showed. At all events, there seems to be a common property of inducing-power in the region of the blastopore, i.e. the opening of the archenteron in coelenterates, echinoids, and the chordates enumerated above. In addition, a large number of secondary inductors are now known.

It might seem, then, that in considering the homology of any given structures it is necessary to consider not only the tissues from which they arose, but the inductors which have induced their formation. This does not mean, however, that the homology between structures is nothing but the homology between their inductors, and it would be a fatal mistake to deny any significance to the reacting tissue from the point of view of homology. A warning against this danger is provided by experiments in which the blastomeres of developing ascidians are disarranged. It appears from Tung's results that the neural tube of the ascidian tadpole is not dependent for its formation on the activity of an underlying inductor; but this does not invalidate the homology of the ascidian tadpole's neural tube with that of other chordates in which it is so dependent. However, in the ascidian tadpole it is interesting to note that the formation of the sense-organs in the neural tube is dependent on the presence of the underlying notochord, which brings the ascidian partially into line with higher chordates.

Other experiments which point in the same direction are those in which urodele belly epidermis is grafted over the mouth-region of anuran embryos, and reciprocally. In each case the underlying host-tissue induces the graft to differentiate into mouth epidermis with lips. But on the anuran host the urodele epidermis produces enamel-organs for proper teeth, and balancers, both of which anuran embryos lack; while on the urodele host, the anuran epidermis produces horny teeth and suckers, both of which urodele embryos lack.

The grafted tissues have thus responded in a general way to the inductors in the host and have given rise to buccal epidermis. But as the inductors in the hosts can hardly be regarded as capable of inducing structures which the sub-class of vertebrates to which they belong do not possess, these results must be taken to mean that within each group both inductor and reacting tissue are active in controlling the type of structure produced. Holtfreter (1936) suggests that there is a distant homology between the horny teeth of anura and the true teeth of urodela. But as Baltzer says, only the inductors are partially homologous.

It is important to refer again to the case of the lens of the eye in the two species of *Rana*, for the lenses are clearly homologous, although in *R. esculenta* the lens is determined *in situ* via the gradient-field co-ordinates of the whole embryo, and in *R. fusca* the lens is induced by the optic cup. This case represents a stage in the substitution of one inducing mechanism for another. But the important point to notice is that structures can owe their origin to different methods of induction without forfeiting their homology.

The question next arises whether the reacting tissues which are induced to form a structure must also be 'the same' if the structures formed out of them are to be regarded as homologous. If by 'similarity' of tissues is meant similarity of position in the fertilized egg or early embryo, then clearly homologous organs can arise from material of dissimilar original location. Organ-forming substances for corresponding structures may be found in different places. Larval mesenchyme arises from different quadrants of the cleaving egg in Platyhelmia, Nemertina, and Annelida; the presumptive mesoderm lines the ventral lip of the blastopore in tunicates, but the sides of the dorsal lip in craniates. Often, as in *Dentalium* and in tunicates, there is evidence of extensive translocation and rearrangement of organ-forming substances. It was pointed out by Jenkinson (1913: 150) that structures as obviously homologous throughout the chordates as the gut might be formed from the roof of the archenteron (Selachii, Teleostei), from the floor of the archenteron (Cyclostomata, *Ceratodus*, Urodela), from both roof and floor of the archenteron (*Lepidosiren*, Anura), from yolk-cells in the floor of the cleavage cavity (Gymnophiona), or from the lower layer of the blastoderm (Amniota). If these sources are plotted back into the places whence they came in the egg, it will be seen that they occupy very different positions.

The ganglion of the trigeminal nerve contains neurons belonging to the general cutaneous functional component, and these arise typically from the cells of the neural crest. But in the frog, as Knouff showed, these neurons arise from an epidermal placode and not from the neural crest. In the course of phylogeny there has thus been an alteration in the site of origin of these structures in ontongeny. It may further be remembered that homologous structures need not arise from the same segments of the body; the arm in the newt is formed from segments 9 to 11; in man, segments 13 to 18. In other words, the site of origin of a structure may vary along the antero-posterior axis of an organism, as Goodrich (1913) proved.

The reacting tissue need not be the 'same' for structures to be homologous. For these reasons it is impossible to agree with Holtfreter's (1936) proposal to restrict homology solely to those structures which develop under similar inductive influences.

Homology and comparative anatomy

The fact is that correspondence between homologous structures cannot be pressed back to similarity of position of the cells in the embryo, or of the parts of the egg out of which the structures are ultimately composed, or of developmental mechanisms by which they are formed. As E. B. Wilson (1894) pointed out, 'Embryological development does not in itself afford at present any absolute criterion whatever for the determination of homology . . . comparative anatomy, not comparative embryology, is the primary standard for the study of homologies.' It is still necessary to hold, as did Geoffroy St. Hilaire (1818: xxv) more than a century ago: 'the only general principle which can be applied is given by the position, the relations, and the dependencies of the parts, that is to say, by what I name and include under the term of *connexions*'. These are now more usually referred to as morphological relations, and it is their general constancy which gives them their value. Variation in morphological relations of homologous structures sometimes occurs, as, for instance, in the skull. But in these cases it is usually possible to find some special reason for the departure from type. In any case it should be noted that, since the developmental mechanisms of homologous structures can become changed, the wonder is not that morphological relations sometimes may vary, but that they are usually so remarkably constant. From these morphological correspondences presumptions of community of descent may be obtained, and the probability of their correctness rises with the increasing number and refinement of the correspondences. But the interesting paradox remains that, while continuity of homologous structures implies affinity between organisms in phylogeny, it does not necessarily imply similarity of genetic factors or of ontogenetic processes in the production of homologous structures.

XVIII

THE GERM LAYERS

The germ-layer theory

I T is inevitable that the results of the present discussion should
lead to a re-examination of the whole question of the status
of the germ-layer theory. In its essentials this theory claims
two things: first, that in normal development from the egg, the
materials out of which the primary organ systems arise are
arranged simply in layers—the serous (ectodermal), mucous
(endodermal), and vascular (mesodermal) layers of Pander,
and, secondly, that homologous structures in all types of animals
are consistently found to arise from corresponding layers. By
this latter contention von Baer (1828) initiated comparative
embryology. The germ-layer theory is therefore a morphological
concept and has nothing to do with developmental potencies of
embryonic tissues. It belongs to the historic-descriptive aspect
of biological studies, not to the causal-analytic aspect, and it is
designed to systematize the derivation of organ systems during
embryonic development. This it attempts to do by projecting
the concept of homology to early stages of development and
by giving names to the layers found in such stages.

Many misapprehensions surround the germ-layer theory.
First of all, it must be realized that it is only legitimate to speak
of the separate germ layers when their segregation from one
another is complete. This is particularly important in the case of
forms which develop by means of a blastoderm which, although
it is external and superficial, should not be designated ectoderm
until the endoderm, mesoderm, and notochord have been separated from it.

Next, it must be emphasized that if in asexual reproduction
(as in Polyzoa or Tunicata), in regeneration, and in experimentally modified or operated embryos (as shown by Mangold),
structures are formed from tissue which was derived from a
layer which would not have given rise to such structures in
normal embryonic development, this fact does not invalidate
the germ-layer theory's claim to represent a topographic and
descriptive generalization covering the events of normal develop-

ment from the egg. What asexual reproduction, regeneration, and experimental embryology prove is that the segregation of the germ layers is not necessarily accompanied by any determination or fixation of fates or restriction of potencies.

The germ-layer theory and homology

The first proposition of the germ-layer theory given above, viz. that in embryos of different groups of animals certain layers are constantly found, has a validity of its own as a generalization covering the structure of embryos. It is when the second proposition is added, that homologous structures consistently arise from corresponding layers, that difficulties appear.

It might be argued that in cases of non-correspondence, it is the concept of homology that is at fault, and that the germ-layer theory is the true guide. But we have examined the concept of homology (p. 147) and shown that the similarity to which the term homology is applied in comparative anatomy is independent of identity of genes controlling the structure, independent of the developmental mechanism evoking the formation of the structure, and independent of the position in the egg of the material out of which the structure is formed. The value of homology lies therefore in the fact that it is the only concept which relates the structures of organisms through their phylogenetic histories.

For the purposes of this argument, therefore, the concept of homology will be retained, and attention will be turned to the problems presented by the formation of homologous structures from 'wrong', i.e. atypical germ layers.

Apparent exceptions to the germ-layer theory

In the Metazoa, muscles have generally been regarded as having been derived from the mesoderm, but Cannon has shown that in certain Crustacea, some muscles are derived from the ectoderm: the sphincter muscles of the maxillary gland of Cypridae, and the dorso-ventral, proctodaeal dilator, and proctodaeal circular muscles of *Chirocephalus*. Similarly, Manton (1928, 1934) has demonstrated the ectodermal origin of the extensor, flexor, and carapace muscles in *Mysis*, and of muscles formed at the intersegments in *Nebalia*. At first sight this would appear to invalidate the entire conception of the germ-layer theory as a consistent system, if it were to claim that all muscles must be derived from the mesoderm. But this would not be the case if it could be shown that in addition to mesodermal muscles, there were ectodermal muscles which the Crustacea had inherited from their ancestors. It is therefore of great interest that Staff was able to recognize the ectodermal nature of certain muscles in an annelid—*Criodrilus*; and it must not be forgotten that in the Coelenterata nearly all the muscular tissue is in the outer layer. In fact, it is quite probable that the ectodermal muscles of the Crustacea and Annelida may be phylogenetically older than the mesodermal musculature. The deduction to be made with regard to the germ-layer theory is, therefore, that it is not impossible for structures and tissues apparently similar histologically to be formed from different layers, but that when this occurs it is not necessarily the result of sheer inconstancy, but may be the reflexion of ordinary processes with a phylogenetic history behind them. In other words, it might still be true that homologous structures are formed from the same germ layer.

The development of the cartilages of the visceral arches out of cells derived from the neural crest has been shown to occur in Amphibia by numerous authors as a result of their experiments, and confirmed by de Beer (1947) in normal development. This anomalous fact may perhaps receive an explanation on the same lines as that suggested for the ectodermal crustacean muscles, viz. that throughout phylogeny these cartilages have always been formed in this way. It has, indeed, been claimed by many workers that in the various groups of vertebrates this is in fact the case. If it should turn out that in these forms also the visceral arch cartilages are formed from the neural crest, the position would be quite clear. The neural crest, which also gives rise to many neural elements, has always been regarded as a part of the ectoderm. Since the cartilages other than those of the visceral arches are known to arise from mesoderm, it would have to be realized that cartilage can arise from cells derived from two different layers. Perhaps the same thing might have to be said of bone, since Wagner has proved that in Amphibia the osteoblasts which form some of the dermal bones are derived from the neural crest. Long ago Kölliker (1884) concluded that the germ-layer theory is of little value to histology.

The 'mesenchyme' problem

It cannot be denied that the origin of structures of such close identity of histological, structural, and functional character as axial cartilages and visceral arch cartilages from germ layers as distinct as the mesoderm and ectoderm, is difficult to fit into a satisfactory concept. The question therefore arises whether it is really justifiable to regard cartilage as a derivative of either mesoderm or ectoderm in the same sense as coelomic epithelium or epidermis are derived from those respective layers. This is a problem which, by another and different approach, confronted the classical embryologists of the nineteenth century, foremost among whom was Wilhelm His. Criticizing Remak's concept of the mesoderm as a layer from which *all* tissues and organs other than those derived from ectoderm or endoderm are formed, he says: 'You are up against a problem to which neither Remak nor his supporters are able to give a satisfactory answer consistent with the facts, the solution of which can, however, only be found in a clarification of the germ-layer theory. Whence come the rudiments of the blood-vessels, the connective tissue, and cartilage?'

The reason why His was dissatisfied with Remak's concept was because in the material which he studied, viz. the chick, blood vessels, connective tissue, cartilage and bone, are formed not by the conversion and differentiation of any layer of cells at all, but from wandering cells which come to occupy the spaces between the true germ layers and differentiate there. To such tissues and structures he gave the name of 'parablastic', to distinguish them from the 'archiblastic' structures derived directly from the layers: epidermis, nervous system, coelomic epithelium, kidney tubules, and muscles, gut and associated glands.

It is true that His was to a certain extent mistaken in claiming that his parablastic structures were all of extra-embryonic origin and formed from the germ wall. That is to say that he did not recognize the origin of cells from the sclerotomes, but his general criticism of the idea that connective tissue, blood, cartilage and bone are 'mesodermal' in the same sense as coelomic epithelium or muscle, forms the basis of O. and R. Hertwig's theory of mesenchyme. The term mesenchyme was applied by these authors to 'cells which wander singly out of the germ layers here

and there and give rise to the connective tissue where such is
present, and also to blood, between the layers of the body'. Had
the Hertwigs been aware of the origin of visceral-arch-cartilage
cells, of osteoblasts, and of odontoblasts from the neural crest
when they formulated their theory of mesenchyme, it is probable
that they would have considered these facts to provide additional support for their view.

As the result of an even deeper analysis, Hadži (1949) has
questioned the equivalence of 'mesoderm' in different groups
(see p. 168) and has proposed the term mesohyle for it.

However, there is one awkward fact which invalidates any
attempt to make a formal distinction between those structures
which arise as modifications of layers and those which arise from
single cells which have wandered out of those layers. In *Amphioxus*
E. S. Goodrich (1930) showed that the sclerotome arises as a hollow outgrowth of coelomic epithelium, enclosing a cavity (the
sclerocoel) bounded by a layer of cells. It is therefore clear
that the origin of mesenchyme cells from the sclerotome (and
other parts of the coelomic epithelium) as isolated wanderers in
the vertebrates is an equivalent of the condition in *Amphioxus*,
and that mesenchyme cells derived from the sclerotomes cannot
be denied the same right to the appellation mesoderm as muscle
or kidney-tubules. There is therefore no logical basis for the
distinction of mesenchyme from mesoderm as a separate category of embryonic elements, and no escape from the conclusion
that some cartilages are mesodermal and others are formed
from the ectoderm.

Real exceptions to the germ-layer theory

The formation of the midgut of animals from the endoderm is
a fundamental tenet of the germ-layer theory. In some insects
such as *Calandra*, however, it has been shown by Mansour and
by Tiegs that the midgut arises from cells budded off from the
stomodaeum and proctodaeum, which are ectodermal in origin.
Attempts have been made to salvage the germ-layer theory by
pretending that these cells are 'latent endoderm', retarded in its
formation and displaced into the ectodermal territories of the
stomodaeum and proctodaeum. Since the essence of the germ-
layer theory is the formation of the primary layers of the embryo
at a very early stage, as Tiegs has put it, this attempt to force

the conditions in *Calandra* into the framework of the germ-layer theory means that 'the germ-layer nomenclature is then retained at the expense of the theory'.

With regard to the odontoblasts which, in the Amphibia, have been shown by several authors, including Landacre and de Beer (1947), to arise in normal development from the neural crest, it is difficult to say much at this stage; for whereas they have previously been presumed to arise from 'mensenchyme' and therefore from a mesodermal source, this has not been proved by modern methods in any other group of animals, and it would be premature to assert that they have a dual possible origin. With regard to the enamel organ, however, the position in so far as Urodela are concerned is quite clear. As was stated by Adams, the enamel organ of the tooth rudiments which will become attached to the maxillary, prevomer, and dentary bones is derived from the stomodaeal collar, or ectodermal tissue, which extends back round the foregut. In this region the gut cavity is lined by a double layer of cells of which the stomodaeal ectodermal layer is the farther away from the cavity and therefore lies between the endodermal gut wall and the mesenchyme. The presumptive odontoblasts therefore come into contact with enamel organs formed out of this ectodermal stomodaeal layer. Farther back, however, the enamel organs of the tooth rudiments which will become attached to the palatine and splenial bones are formed from the endodermal gut wall, behind the hindmost limit to which the stomodaeal collar extends. In one and the same animal, as de Beer has confirmed, it is possible to observe enamel organs composed of yolk-free, pigment-containing cells, and of yolk-filled, pigment-free cells, and of both types of cell. No demonstration could be clearer that the enamel organ can be formed from either ectodermal or endodermal tissue, and this fact lends probability to the view that it is the accumulation of ectomesenchyme cells forming the odontoblasts of the future tooth pulp which is the primary factor in inducing the formation of the enamel organ as an ingrowth of whatever layer of cells is present, i.e. the superficial epidermis, the stomodaeal ectoderm, or the endoderm. The recognition of the fact that the enamel organ can be formed from the endoderm in Urodela facilitates the solution of the problem presented by the pharyngeal placoid scales of Selachii and the pharyngeal teeth of teleost fishes, whose

enamel organs must also be of endodermal origin, as Cook &
Neal have contended.

The method of origin of the taste buds is precisely comparable
to that of the enamel organs. Landacre claimed that in *Ameiurus*
the taste buds are formed from the ectoderm in the epidermis
and from the endoderm in the pharynx. The fact that the maintenance and regeneration of taste buds is dependent on the
presence of the nerve innervating them, as Olmsted showed,
suggests that here also the primary factor in inducing the formation of a taste bud is extraneous to it, viz. the nerve.

Lastly, the thymus presents a case in which a structure can
arise from different germ layers. The thymus of *Salmo* arises
from ectoderm and endoderm as Deanesley has described. In
Trichosurus, Fraser and Hill have shown that the anterior thymus
rudiment is derived from both ectoderm and endoderm, while
the posterior rudiments are solely endodermal in origin. On the
other hand, in *Lepus* and *Homo* the anterior thymus is entirely
endodermal, while in *Sus* and *Talpa* it is entirely ectodermal.
Here again it appears very likely that an organizer is at work,
inducing the differentiation of a thymus out of whatever material
is available at the place in question.

The failure of attempts to apply the principles of homology to
early stages of development, when the only structures present are
germ layers, is a further indication that the germ-layer theory is
of no value to the concept of homology. It is not because the
rudiments arise from the same germ layer (if they do) that organs
are homologous. Rather, as Pasteels (1937) has observed, the
proposition should be reversed. Organs arise from the same germ
layer in an organism when the presumptive rudiments of these
organs occupy adjacent regions in the egg. And if in different
organisms homologous structures have rudiments which occupy
corresponding regions in the egg, they will tend to pass through
the same germ layer, but not always.

The presumptive organ-forming regions and the germ layers

It is now necessary, therefore, to go to earlier stages of ontogeny, and to consider the presumptive regions of origin of homologous structures in the blastula before the formation of the
germ layers. Except for the notochord and segmented mesoderm, these presumptive regions are not determined in the

blastula, and their demarcation represents only a conceptual projection into early stages of the normal fates of any given parts at later stages. But these presumptive regions vary in different forms and it becomes important to see whether such variation is correlated with corresponding variations in the germ layers.

It is of importance to realize that the correspondence between homologous structures cannot always be pressed back to identical similarity of position of the cells in the embryo, or of the regions of the egg out of which the structures are ultimately composed. It is sufficient to compare the maps of presumptive regions in the eggs of different groups of animals to be convinced of this. The presumptive mesoderm lines the ventral lip of the blastopore of tunicates but the sides of the dorsal lip in craniates: the larval mesenchyme is derived from different quadrants of the second quartette of micromeres in Polyclada, Nemertini, and Annelida; the gut may be formed, as Jenkinson (1913) pointed out, from the roof of the archenteron (Selachii, Teleostei), the floor of the archenteron (Cyclostomata, *Ceratodus*, Urodela), roof and floor of the archenteron (*Lepidosiren*, Anura), yolk cells in the floor of the cleavage cavity (Gymnophiona), or from the lower layer of the blastoderm (Amniota).

A difference in position of origin of the material which gives rise to structures undoubtedly homologous can been seen in the development of the mesodermal somites in *Amphioxus* and in the remainder of the vertebrates. In the latter the row of mesodermal somites is formed as a continuous band of cells, quite separate from the endoderm, which becomes invaginated and then undergoes metameric segmentation. In *Amphioxus*, however, the foremost somite, the so-called anterior head cavity, is at first separated from the more posterior mesoderm and lies like an enclave in the territory of the endoderm from which it subsequently becomes separated. That this anterior head cavity is serially homologous with the first somite of other vertebrates has been proved by Goodrich (1917) who showed from its relation to the 'proboscis pore' that it corresponds. It cannot therefore be claimed that the other vertebrates have lost the original foremost somite, and it must be concluded that in *Amphioxus* the rudiment of the mesoderm has undergone fragmentation, and that part of it reaches its definitive position via the endoderm. But nobody would for this reason claim either that the foremost somite of *Amphioxus* was formed 'from the endoderm', or that it was not homologous with the foremost somite of other vertebrates.

Another case of difference in site of formation of a rudiment is provided by the cells which give rise to the neurons forming the general cutaneous component of the trigeminal nerve. The typical method of origin of these cells in vertebrates is from the neural crest. But in the frog, Knouff has shown that they arise from the epidermal placode, and not from the neural crest.

It is true that in this last case the change in site of origin is not very great and does not transcend the germ layer (ectoderm) from which the structure is formed, but it raises the question of principle whether (as in *Amphioxus* as shown above) it may not be possible in some cases that the site of origin may involve a change in the germ layer through which the material passes to reach its destination.

In all these cases, if the sources of origin are plotted back into the egg, it is obvious that they occupy different regions. This is evidence, therefore, that homologous organs can 'arise' from different regions of the egg, and the reason for this must be that in the succession of ontogenies there have been changes in the morphogenetic processes of determination. An interesting example of this is provided by the animal pole of the egg, which in all cases gives rise to the anterior end of the organism. But whereas, as Conklin (1932) emphasized, in invertebrates the animal pole is generally located at the free end of the oocyte as it protrudes into the circumambient water or coelomic fluid, in *Amphioxus* and Tunicata it is located at the attached end of the oocyte. Nobody would dream, for that reason, of denying the general homology of the anterior ends of all these forms, and in this case there are grounds for believing that the location of the animal pole of an egg is determined *de novo* in each generation by the orientation of the oocyte to differential stimulation by the surrounding medium, in accordance with Child's principle of axiation. Since development is known to partake of the nature of epigenesis, there is nothing surprising in that the sites of origin of structures should change.

Further, there is the fact, well demonstrated by E. B. Wilson's (1904) classical investigations on *Dentalium*, that qualitatively determined organ-forming substances can and do undergo marked changes of position in the egg after fertilization.

The significance of all this is that structures which arise from corresponding portions of the egg do not always pass through the same germ layers to reach their final destination. A further example of this fact is provided by the tail muscles in Amphibia. In the urodele blastula the region of the presumptive tail mesoderm is continuous with that of the trunk mesoderm and occupies a region corresponding to that which in Cyclostomata is completely invaginated through the lip of the blastopore. But in Urodela, the tail mesoderm does not become invaginated. It arrives at the lip of the blastopore as the latter closes; it is, as it were, just too late to get in, so it remains on the outer surface of the gastrula and becomes the floor of the hindmost part of the 'neural' plate, as Bijtel first showed. In this position the presumptive tail mesoderm is carried beneath the outer surface of the neurula as the neural folds rise up and fuse above it, and it finds itself in prolongation of the trunk mesoderm which was invaginated in the normal manner for mesoderm. Here then is a case of structures, tail muscles, which are undoubtedly homologous with those of other vertebrates, which originate from corresponding presumptive areas in the blastula, and end up in corresponding positions in the neurula, but which in the gastrula have not been involved in the same layer as in other forms.

Before leaving the question of presumptive organ-forming regions, it should be noted that studies on homology have in the past been confined to the comparison of formed structures with one another. But it has become increasingly clear from researches in embryology that the processes whereby the structures are formed are as important as the structures themselves from the point of view of evolutionary morphology and homology. For instance, as Pasteels (1937) has shown, a comparison between the structures of the gastrula stages of the different types of vertebrates leads to unsatisfactory results. But a comparison between the processes involved in gastrulation and the movements of regions—extension of area of ectoderm, convergence and stretching of notochord and mesoderm, invagination of endoderm—provides a system showing certain fundamental similarities throughout, though differing in extent, intensity, and time relations, and therefore in the structure of the product to which these processes give rise. It is the processes that are homologous, and thanks to the work of Holtfreter (1943, 1944) something is now known of the nature of these 'mass-movements' of regions of the embryo.

That the presumptive regions of the egg or blastula can vary in extent in time and space in different organisms, is, of course, merely a further illustration of the fact that, contrary to the theory of recapitulation, variations of evolutionary significance can and do arise at the earliest stages of development.

Lastly, the extent of presumptive regions can be affected experimentally, as shown by the experiments of Herbst and of Lindahl on 'endodermization' and 'ectodermization' of sea-urchin larvae by exposure of the eggs to lithium salts and to sodium thiocyanide, respectively. These results are a salutary reminder of the fact that development is epigenetic and consists of a series of responses by the organism to its environment.

The conclusion to be drawn from these facts is that, while the germ layers frequently segregate the different presumptive organ-forming regions from one another, they do not invariably do so and therefore do not function as determinants of differentiation in development.

The evolution of the coelenterates

The extent to which the theory of recapitulation has established its hold over the minds of zoologists, even subconsciously, may be gauged from a consideration of the coelenterates. If asked which are the most primitive Metazoa apart from the sponges, most zoologists would reply unquestioningly the coelenterates. Their reasons would be that the coelenterates are simple in structure, consist of only two layers of tissue, and resemble the gastrula stage through which so many of the Metazoa pass. In accepting this view, certain other corollaries are also necessarily accepted, viz. that the two layers of tissue are as old as the Metazoa and that they are in fact two of the definitive germ layers of higher forms, the ectoderm and the endoderm; that the original Metazoa were radially symmetrical, i.e. that bilateral symmetry had not yet been evolved; and that the Metazoa arose from the Protozoa by aggregation of separate cells into a morula which became converted into a gastrula, primitively, by the method of invagination.

All these conclusions might appear to be so firmly established that they were unassailable, and yet Hadži (1944, 1953) has recently challenged every one of them. Starting from the facts that the coelenterates are not strictly bilaminar, for the meso-glaea contains cells and in some forms there is a parenchyma; that 'gastrulation' occurs by the most diverse means in the coelenterates; that bilateral symmetry already exists in the Protozoa; that prototypes of that supposedly characteristic coel-enterate organ the nematocyst are found in the Protozoa and also occur in Turbellaria and Nemertina; that tentacles con-taining an 'endodermal' core are found in the Turbellaria; that the gut of Turbellaria is lobulated by re-entrants of parenchyma; and that the origin of Metazoa from Protozoa is better conceived as an internal cellularization of the protozoan body rather than as an aggregation of separate protozoan individuals, because the maintenance of the all-important integration of the organism is thereby preserved: from all these facts Hadži has been led to formulate the following hypothesis.

By internal cellularization polynuclear Protozoa gave rise to Turbellaria. Then by adoption of a sessile habit, Rhabdocoel Turbellaria gave rise to coelenterates of which the Anthozoa are the most primitive by reason of their bilateral symmetry, possession of a pharynx, hollow 'endoderm-lined' tentacles, lobulated gut restricted by 'mesenteries', and absence of medu-soid stage. The germ layers were not yet definitively established, and the material for the construction of the body got into place either as a direct result of cleavage, delamination, immigration, or invagination. The sessile habit brought about loss of a central nervous system. In the subsequent evolution of the Scyphozoa and Hydrozoa from Anthozoan-like ancestors, radial symmetry was fully established and all traces of bilateral symmetry were lost except in the planula larva; the pharynx and mesenteries were progressively lost; a medusoid stage was introduced as an adaptation to dispersal, and asexual reproduction and colony-formation as an adaptation to sessile life; the germ-cells became incorporated in the outer layer in Hydrozoa and in the inner layer in Scyphozoa as these layers became progressively and independently established; these layers do not correspond exactly to the germ layers of higher forms.

The polyp, Hadži thinks, is more primitive than the medusa,

and therefore the Narcomedusae and Trachomedusae in which the polypoid form is suppressed are neotenous.

The Ctenophora Hadži derives from Polyclad Turbellaria by neoteny: they must, as we have seen (p. 67), have evolved from forms like Müller's larva by retaining many of its features. The Platyctenea and particularly *Coeloplana* may now acquire a new significance. The Cydippid Ctenophora may be neotenous Platyctenea, in which case the sequence made out by Komai would have to be read the other way.

At first sight, such a view may appear revolutionary and extravagant, and yet, the more it is considered, the more does the old-fashioned view appear to be vulnerable. This is hardly the place to make a definitive pronouncement on the results of Hadži's forty years of expert study devoted to these problems, but it is worth noting that by freeing the field of discussion from the recapitulatory incubus of the gastraea theory and Haeckel's views, much that was obscure in Zoology acquires the possibility of formal explanation.

Haeckel's 'blastaea' and 'gastraea' theory

From the fact that during their ontogeny many animals pass through the stage of a single-layered hollow ball, the blastula, which is then converted into a double-layered hollow sac, the gastrula, Haeckel (1874, 1875 A) insisted that the single-layered hollow ball represented the original ancestral adult stage which he called the blastaea. This, he considered, was then succeeded in evolution by the double-layered sac (containing an archenteron opening to the outside by a blastopore) which he called the gastraea. It followed that an animal like *Hydra*, which is something like a persistent gastrula, must be primitive. Reasons have already (p. 165) been given to show why this argument is unsound, and Lankester pointed this out in 1877.

Perhaps unconsciously, zoologists have continued to regard the hollow gastrula as a primitive form, and the germ layers as of equal age as the gastrula. But it is very doubtful if the original Metazoa were hollow at all, and it is much more probable that they resembled organisms like the Turbellaria Acoela, using the phagocytic method of feeding (as in Protozoa) and composed of an outer layer of cells which may be regarded as ectoderm, and an inner mass in which the endoderm cannot be distinguished from the other parenchymatous tissue which has been called the mesohyle. Even in the Protozoa there is a differentiation into outer, inner, and intermediate material, and this was before the subdivision of the body into cells, which process constituted the evolution of Metazoa from Protozoa. This means that the regions of the body represented by the germ layers are phylogenetically older than the Metazoa and much older than the stage of evolution at which the gastrula was first formed.

In Turbellaria Acoela, cleavage of the egg results in the production of ectoderm, endoderm, and mesohyle *in situ*, without the formation of any germ layers at all. The same is true in the Rotifera; and the formation of similar 'solid' gastrulae is common in Coelenterata and Porifera. In the development of Cephalopoda, Sacarrão (1953) has shown that there is no two-layered stage at all. Nor is it possible to speak of a gastrula stage in insects such as *Calandra*, as Tiegs has demonstrated.

It has already been mentioned that in the Coelenterata, gastrulation takes place by one or more of a variety of methods, immigration, delamination, etc., of which invagination is the least frequent. In other words, the commonest method of gastrulation in Coelenterata involves the presence of no blastopore and is therefore the most different from Haeckel's 'gastraea'.

While the *movements* of cells which take place during the gastrulation (spreading of ectoderm, convergence and epiboly of chorda-mesoderm, and ingrowth of endoderm) are fundamentally similar in different groups of animals, as has just been seen, the *structures* to which they give rise are so variable, owing to differences in time-relations, amounts of tissue involved, and extents of movements, that comparisons between them are unprofitable. Pasteels (1940) has been led to conclude that 'if there is one embryonic type of structure that is not repeated, it is the two-layered hollow sac'. The fact is that the gastrula as a morphological concept is a pure abstraction, useless and misleading as a guide to evolutionary history and as a criterion of primitive and secondary conditions.

If the concept of the gastrula does not rest on an objective foundation, there is no reason why the idea of the constancy of the two layers of which the gastrula is supposed to consist should have any firmer basis of fact. From the morphological point of view the position has been admirably summarized by Sacarrão

(1952) as follows: 'In fact the two transitory first "layers" do not have the same value throughout the Vertebrata; they have been described as ectophylle and entophylle, two neutral (and therefore advantageous) terms proposed by Celestino da Costa (1947).' For comparable reasons Hadži (1949) has proposed the term mesohyle for mesoderm.

The theory of recapitulation and the germ-layer theory are each of them fallacious: their combination in the theory of the gastraea is all the more unacceptable.

Conclusions

The position is, therefore, that the germ layers do not equate perfectly either with the presumptive regions of the egg or blastula from which the various adult structures will arise, or with these structures when formed. It may well be asked, therefore, what value remains in the germ-layer theory. Looking at it from the point of view of causal embryology, there can be no doubt that the germ-layer theory was misconceived in its attempt to provide an embryological criterion of homology and in its assumption that the fates of the germ layers were universally equal and limited. 'The facts forbid us to see in these elementary organs of the embryo that definite predetermination for the performance of certain ontogenetic functions', wrote Jenkinson (1906). 'The germinal layers', he continued, 'are not sets of cells of universally identical origin which necessarily and invariably give rise to certain fixed parts of the adult organization.'

What, then, are the germ layers? In Oppenheimer's view they are 'the embryo's method of sorting out its constituent parts', and the problem consists in the elucidation of the limitation of the potencies of the germ layers to their normal accomplishment. Interesting as this problem is, it does not, however, appear to be exclusive to the germ layers. Rather should the germ layers be considered as a problem of the anatomy of embryos, and less as a problem of the production of the anatomy of the adult. Even allowing for the possibility that in the lowest Metazoa (Turbellaria and coelenterates), as mentioned above (p. 165), the germ layers have not become definitively established, in all animals above these, germ layers exist and they correspond in widely different types of organisms, regardless of the exact topographical localizations of the materials of which they are composed and of the ultimate fate of such materials. As Holtfreter (1943) has shown, germ layers owe their origin, segregation, and the maintenance of their distinctness to the distribution in the blastula of the physical and other conditions which produce expansion, convergence, and stretching, invagination, adhesiveness, and non-adhesiveness of the cells.

There is just sufficient constancy in the origins and fates of the materials of which the germ layers are composed to endow the ghost of the germ-layer theory with a provisional, descriptive, and limited didactic value in systematizing the description of the results of the chief course of events in the development of many different kinds of animals; provided that it be remembered that such systematization is without bearing on the question of the causal determination of the origin of the structures of an adult organism.

Lastly, it may be pointed out that the abandonment of the germ-layer theory in embryology is of more than academic interest, for attempts have frequently been made to base classifications of tumours on it. There is every reason to believe that pathology will benefit rather than suffer from a realization of the incompetence of the germ-layer theory to contribute to an understanding of the causes of morphological and histological differentiation in development. The same is doubtless true of the study of developmental genetics. The notion that correlation of developmental effects can be explained by community of origin from the same germ layer of the structures in question has already been severely criticized by Grüneberg; it can now be seen to have no basis.

XIX

CONCLUSIONS

THE line of argument which forms the subject of this book may be summarized as follows:

Ontogeny is the result of the action of external factors in evoking responses from the internal factors of an animal to which the latter were transmitted by inheritance from its parents.

Phylogeny is provisionally to be regarded as a series of adult forms, which are disconnected and causally unrelated to one another, each adult form being the result of an ontogeny which differs from the previous one.

Successive ontogenies are related to one another by the transmission of internal factors from fertilized egg to fertilized egg.

Modifications in ontogeny (in a constant environment) are due to changes in the internal factors.

Phylogeny is therefore due to modified ontogeny.

Phylogeny plays no causal part in determining ontogeny.

The internal factors exert their effects at certain definite rates.

Modification of the rate of action of the internal factors in successive ontogenies may result in heterochrony.

Evolution is brought about by acquisition of qualitative novelties and by the production of novel situations by quantitative alteration of the rate of action of the internal factors.

New characters may appear at all stages of ontogeny, and by heterochrony they may be retarded or accelerated so as to appear later or earlier in subsequent ontogenies.

Characters present in the early stages of ontogeny (provided that they are not too specialized) have played an important part in evolution by paedomorphosis, resulting in large structural changes without loss of plasticity.

Characters present in the late stages of ontogeny have played an important part in evolution by gerontomorphosis, resulting in relatively small structural changes with loss of plasticity.

Paedomorphosis and gerontomorphosis may act alternately in the phylogeny of a race, the former producing racial 're-juvenescence', the latter racial 'senescence'.

Recapitulation, i.e. the pressing back of adult ancestral stages into early stages of development of descendants, does not take place.

Paedomorphosis explains gaps in the fossil record.

It is a confusion of categories to assume that a character which is embryonic in ontogeny must also be primitive in phylogeny, or that a character which develops early in ontogeny must also have evolved early in phylogeny. The possession of an embryonic character may be, and very often is, the result of a secondary retention of prolongation of embryonic features, and a character which appears early in ontogeny may have been evolved recently in phylogeny.

Repetition of ancestral ontogenetic stages in the ontogeny of the descendant, whether retarded or accelerated, is due to the transmission of inherited internal factors from ancestor to descendant.

Similarity in ontogeny between any animals is a proof of their affinity, and no evidence as to the adult structure of the ancestor.

Atavism is due to the re-establishment in the ontogeny of the descendant of a set of circumstances which was present in the ontogeny of the ancestor.

Classification schemes based on the characters of larval and of adult forms may be discrepant, but they coincide best in the case of members of a species.

Embryological and genetic criteria fail to provide a satisfactory basis for the interpretation of homology to which the surest guide is comparative anatomy.

The germ-layer theory is no longer tenable as an absolute guide to the origin of structures.

It goes without saying that even if the views set forth here are correct, they do not provide an 'explanation' of evolution, for there remains the problem of how and why novelties arise, and why they show heterochrony in those cases in which they do. But it is claimed that after dethroning the theory of recapitulation we are able to make a better synthesis of our knowledge of embryology and evolution.

In the first place, we are able to consider possibilities other than the repetition of ancestral adult characters by youthful descendants, and, as we have seen, these possibilities are interesting and important. The relations of evolutionary plasticity to genetic plasticity encourage the hope that progress in knowledge of the latter, which is accessible to experimental investigation, will increase our knowledge of the former. And in both cases the variability which plasticity denotes will have to be studied from the embryological aspect.

In the second place, we are rid of a mental strait-jacket which has had lamentable effects on biological progress. It is no exaggeration to say that although Haeckel's theory of recapitulation may have stimulated research into the development of many animals, yet it has thwarted and delayed the introduction of causal analytic methods into embryology. For instance, when Wilhelm His attempted to analyse ontogenetic processes into simpler components, such as growth, expansion, adhesions, perforation, &c., Haeckel (1875 B: 24) ridiculed them on the grounds that 'each of these simple ontogenetic processes of unfolding is the result of an extremely complicated series of historical events. It is causally determined by the thousands of phylogenetic changes, by the innumerable hereditary and adaptive alterations, which the ancestors of the organism in question have undergone during the course of millions of years.'

As His himself woefully complained, his contemporaries considered that they had 'better things to do in embryology than to discuss tensions of germinal layers and similar questions, since all embryological explanations must of necessity be of a phylogenetic nature'.

Clearly, if phylogeny was the mechanical cause of ontogeny as Haeckel proclaimed, there was little inducement to search for other causes, and until this point of view was swept away, there could be little interest in experimental embryology.

J. S. Huxley has pointed out that it is essential to realize the difference between the descriptive historical and the causal analytic methods of study of living organisms. The analytical and experimental study of embryology is providing an increasing body of information concerning the chains of linked causes the result of which is ontogenetic development. On the other hand, morphological and palaeontological studies are providing an increasingly precise description of the results of phylogenetic evolution. We may now ask ourselves the question, what is the nature of the assistance which each study can bring to the other?

Clearly, phylogeny does not give any causal explanation of

the succession of events in ontogeny at all. Even if we had a *complete* phylogenetic series of adults ancestral to any given descendant, it would not help us to understand the processes of fertilization, cleavage, induction, differentiation, organogeny, &c., which take place in the ontogeny of that descendant. The historical descriptive study of evolution has no bearing on the causal analytic study of embryology. To use an analogy suggested by Woodger, rockets go up on November the 5th (*a*) because of an historical tradition in virtue of which the practice of firing rockets is repeated each year on this day, (*b*) because the rockets contain charges of a substance, gunpowder, whose properties are to undergo rapid combustion and to produce powerful gaseous expansion resulting in the exertion of force on the rockets. The details of the properties of gunpowder are not deducible from a study of the biography of Guido Fawkes; nor are those of a fertilized egg from a study of the phylogenetic series of adults in the evolutionary history of its species.

Evolution therefore does not explain embryology.

On the other hand, if we had preserved for us the stages of ontogeny gone through by a complete phylogenetic series of adults, we should find close similarities between the repeated early stages, and we can be certain that such similarities are due to common inheritance of genetic factors. Therefore, although the past evolution of a race cannot explain why one embryo develops today, it can explain why there are similarities by inheritance between ontogenetic stages of ancestors and descendants.

Conversely, if we knew all the processes involved in the causal chain of events of ontogeny of any given animal, such knowledge would not of itself provide an explanation of the phylogeny of that animal. For past phylogeny no method of study other than the historical descriptive is possible. This is why the concept of homology cannot be based on genetics or embryology, but must rest on comparative anatomy and palaeontology. But since phylogeny is but the result of modified ontogeny, there is the possibility of a causal analytic study of present evolution in an experimental study of the variability and genetics of ontogenetic processes.

The eight possible types of relation between ontogeny and phylogeny enumerated in Chapter V, described in Chapters VI to XIII, and discussed in Chapter XIV, are morphological modes. *They describe the course* which evolutionary change is believed to have taken in various groups of plants and animals, but *they do not explain the mechanism* by which these evolutionary changes took place. It is now recognized that evolution is the result of selection acting on heritable variation in the form of mutation and recombination of Mendelian genes. These processes must have been at work in all the evolutionary changes considered in this book. The morphological modes describe aspects of the course which the changes took, but it was variation and selection which caused them.

The advantages which accrue from a recognition of the morphological modes of relation between ontogeny and phylogeny are twofold. First is the fact that the material on which the factors of evolution work is not restricted to a single type in each species, but consists of all the structures presented at all the stages of the life-history of each species. In other words, an organism shows variation in its own life-history. Second, the effects of heterochrony produce important results even without the introduction of numerous evolutionary novelties in the form of new structures. By ringing the changes along the time-axis of ontogeny, evolutionary changes can take place. And when new structures and functions are added to the effects of heterochrony, especially those described under the name of paedomorphosis, such evolutionary changes may be very important and far-reaching.

Finally, it may even be possible that, freed from the trammels and fetters of the theory of recapitulation which have so long confined thought, the whole of the animal kingdom may appear in a new light, more homogeneous and compact than had been imagined, and with the gaps between its major groups less formidable and perhaps even bridgeable.

BIBLIOGRAPHY

ABERCROMBIE, M. (1951). 'Editor's Notes on Problems of Adaptation', *New Biology*, **11**, 25.

ADAMS, A. E. (1924). 'An Experimental Study of the Development of the Mouth in the Amphibian Embryo', *Journal of Experimental Zoology*, **40**, 311.

AGASSIZ, L. (1850). *Lake Superior*, p. 195. Boston.

ALLIS, E. P. (1936). 'Comparison of the Latero-sensory Lines', *Journal of Anatomy*, **70**, 293.

ANNANDALE, N. (1917). 'Zoological Results of a Tour in the Far East. Batrachia', *Memoirs of the Asiatic Society of Bengal*, **6**, 115.

—— (1918). 'Some Undescribed Tadpoles from the Hills of Southern India', *Records of the Indian Museum*, **15**, 118.

ARISTOTLE, in SINGER, C. (1922). *Greek Biology and Greek Medicine*, p. 45. Oxford.

ASHLEY-MONTAGU, M. F. (1935). 'The Premaxilla in the Primates', *Quarterly Review of Biology*, **10**, 32, 181.

BAER, K. E. VON (1828). 'Über Entwicklungsgeschichte der Thiere', *Beobachtung und Reflexion*. Königsberg.

—— (1866). 'De la découverte de larves qui se propagent', *Bulletin de l'Académie Impériale des Sciences de St. Petersbourg*, **9**, 64.

BALTZER, F. (1950). 'Entwicklungsphysiologische Betrachtungen über Probleme der Homologie und Evolution', *Revue Suisse de Zoologie*, **57**, 451.

BARCROFT, J. (1938). *The Brain and its Environment*. Yale University Press.

BATESON, W. (1913). *Problems of Genetics*, p. 67. Yale.

BAUR, A. (1864). 'Beiträge zur Naturgeschichte von Synapta digitata', *Verhandlungen der Kaiserlichen Leopoldino-Carolinischen Akademie für Naturforscher*, **31**, (3).

BEECHER, C. E. (1893). 'Some Correlations of Phylogeny and Ontogeny in Brachiopoda', *American Naturalist*, **27**, 599.

DE BEER, G. R. (1937). *The Development of the Vertebrate Skull*. Oxford.

—— (1938). 'Embryology and Evolution'. In *Evolution: Essays presented to E. S. Goodrich*. Edited by G. R. de Beer. Oxford.

—— (1947). 'The Differentiation of Neural Crest Cells into Visceral Cartilages and Odontoblasts in Amblystoma, and a Re-examination of the Germ-layer Theory', *Proceedings of the Royal Society*, B, **134**, 377.

—— (1948). 'Embryology and the Evolution of Man', *Robert Broom Commemorative Volume*, p. 181, Cape Town.

—— (1949). 'Caruncles and Egg-teeth', *Proceedings of the Linnean Society of London*, **161**, 218.

—— (1956). 'The Evolution of Ratites', *Bulletin of the British Museum (Natural History): Zoology*, **4**, 57.

—— & GRÜNEBERG, H. (1940). 'A Note on Pituitary Dwarfism in the Mouse', *Journal of Genetics*, **39**, 297.

DE BEER, G., & SWINTON, W. E. (1958). 'Prophetic Fossils', *Studies on Fossil Verbrates*, p. 1. London.

BENGTSSON, S. (1927). 'Die Larven der nordischen Arten von Carabus', *Lunds Universitets Årsskrift*, **24**, 1.

BERG, L. (1926). *Nomogenesis or Evolution determined by Law*. London.

BERRILL, N. J. (1945). 'Size and Organization in the Development of Ascidians', *Essays on Growth and Form presented to D'Arcy Thompson*, edited by W. E. Le Gros Clark and P. B. Medawar, p. 231, Oxford.

—— (1955). *The Origin of Vertebrates*. Oxford.

BEURLEN, K. (1930). 'Vergleichende Stammesgeschichte', *Fortschritte der Geologie und Paläontologie*, **8**, 317.

BIJTEL, J. H. (1931). 'Über die Entwicklung des Schwanzes bei Amphibien', *Archiv für Entwicklungsmechanik*, **125**, 448.

BOAS, J. E. V. (1896). 'Über Neotenie', *Festschrift für C. Gegenbaur*, **2**, 1, Leipzig.

BODENHEIMER, F. S. (1932). 'Ökologische Beobachtungen an Cimbex quadrimaculata in Palästina', *Zeitschrift für Pflanzenkrankheiten*, **42**, 351.

BOLK, L. (1926). *Das Problem der Menschwerdung*. Jena.

BONNET, C. (1764). *Contemplation de la nature*. Amsterdam.

BOTNARIUC, N. (1948). 'Contribution à la connaissance du développement des Phyllopodes Conchostracés', *Bulletin biologique de la France et de la Belgique*, **82**, 31.

BOULENGER, G. A. (1891). 'A Contribution to the Knowledge of the Races of Rana esculenta and their Geographical Distribution', *Proceedings of the Zoological Society of London*, 374, 593.

—— (1893). 'Description of New Reptiles and Batrachians observed in Borneo . . .', *Proceedings of the Zoological Society of London*, 522.

—— (1908). 'A Revision of the Oriental Pelobatid Batrachians . . .', *Proceedings of the Zoological Society of London*, 407.

BRINKMANN, R. (1929). 'Statistisch-biostratigraphische Untersuchungen an Mitteljurassischen Ammoniten über Artbegriff und Stammesentwicklung', *Abhandlungen der Gesellschaft der Wissenschaften zu Göttingen*. Math.-Phys. Kl., N.F. **13**, 1.

BRISCHKE, C. G. A., & ZADDACH, G. (1882). 'Beobachtungen über die Arten der Blatt- und Holzwespen', *Schriften der Physikalisch-Ökonomischen Gesellschaft zu Königsberg*, **23**, 127.

BROMAN, I. (1920). *Das sogenannte biogenetische Grundgesetz*. München und Wiesbaden.

BROOM, R., & SCHEPERS, G. W. H. (1946). *The South African Fossil Ape-men. The Australopithecinae*, Pretoria.

BULMAN, O. M. B. (1933). 'Programme-evolution in the Graptolites', *Biological Reviews*, **8**, 311.

BUTLER, P. M. (1937). 'Studies of the Mammalian Dentition', *Proceedings of the Zoological Society of London*, B, 103.

—— (1951). 'Molarization of the premolars in the Perissodactyla,' *Proceedings of the Zoological Society of London*, **121**, 819.

BUXTON, L. H. D., & DE BEER, G. R. (1932). 'Neanderthal and Modern Man', *Nature*, **129**, 940.

BUXTON, P. A. (1938). 'Anopheles and the Species Problem', *Proceedings of the Zoological Society of London*, C, 57.

CALMAN, W. T. (1909). *A Treatise on Zoology, Crustacea*. London.

CALMAN, W. T., & GORDON, I. (1933). 'A Dodecapodous Pycnogonid', *Proceedings of the Royal Society*, B, **113**, 107.

CANNON, H. G. (1926). 'On the Post-embryonic Development of the Fairy Shrimp (Cheirocephalus)', *Journal of the Linnean Society, Zoology*, **36**, 401.

CARPENTER, G. D. HALE (1912). 'Synaposematic Resemblance between Acraeine Larvae', *Transactions of the Entomological Society*, **45**, 702.

CASTLE, W. E., & GREGORY, P. W. (1931). 'The Embryological Basis of Size Inheritance in the Rabbit', *Journal of Morphology*, **48**, 81.

CHAMPY, C. (1924). *Sexualité et hormones*. Paris.

CHEN, S. H. (1946). 'Evolution of the Insect Larva', *Transactions of the Royal Entomological Society of London*, **97**, 381.

CHILD, C. M. (1915). *Senescence and Rejuvenescence*, p. 464. Chicago.

—— (1924). *Physiological Foundations of Behaviour*. New York.

CLOUD, P. E. (1948). 'Some Problems and Patterns of Evolution exemplified by Fossil Invertebrates', *Evolution*, **2**, 322.

COCKAYNE, E. A. (1928). 'Annual Address: Larval Variations', *Proceedings of the South London Entomological and Natural Society*, 55.

CONKLIN, E. G. (1922). *Heredity and Environment*. Princeton.

—— (1932). 'The Embryology of Amphioxus', *Journal of Morphology*, **54**, 69.

COOK, M. H., & NEAL, H. V. (1921). 'Are the Taste-buds of Elasmobranchs Endodermal in Origin?', *Journal of Comparative Neurology*, **33**, 45.

COPE, E. D. (1868). 'On the Origin of Genera', *Proceedings of the Academy of National Science, Philadelphia*, 242.

COSTA, A. CELESTINO DA (1947). *Éléments d'embryologie*. Paris.

COUPIN, F. (1925). 'Étude du cerveau du chimpanzé nouveau-né', *Bulletin de la Société d'Anthropologie de Paris*, **6**, 20.

COUSIN, G. (1938). 'La Néoténie chez Gryllus campestris', *Bulletin biologique de France et de Belgique*, **72**, 79.

CROFTS, D. R. (1955). 'Muscle morphogenesis in primitive gastropods and its relation to torsion', *Proceedings of the Zoological Society of London*, **125**, 711.

CROW, W. B. (1926). 'Phylogeny and the Natural System', *Journal of Genetics*, **17**, 129.

DARWIN, C. *The Origin of Species* (World's Classics edition).

DEANESLEY, R. (1927). 'The Structure and Development of the Thymus in Fish', *Quarterly Journal of Microscopical Science*, **71**, 113.

DETWILER, S. R. (1926). 'Experimental Studies on Morphogenesis in the Nervous System', *Quarterly Review of Biology*, **1**, 61.

DEVAUX, E. (1933). *Trois problèmes: l'espèce, l'instinct, l'homme*. Paris.

DIVER, C. (1939). 'Aspects of the Study of Variation in Snails', *Journal of Conchology*, **21**, 91.

DOLLO, L. (1922). 'Les Céphalopodes déroulés et l'irréversibilité de l'évolution', *Bijdragen tot de Dierkunde*, **22**, 215.

DRENNAN, N. R. (1931). 'Pedomorphism in the Pre-Bushman Skull', *American Journal of Physical Anthropology*, **1** , 203.

DROOGLEVER FORTUYN, A. B. (1922). 'Verklebung von Leberzellbalken in Säugetieren', *Bijdragen tot de Dierkunde*, **22**, 13.

DUERDEN, J. E. (1924). 'Methods of Evolution', *Science Progress*, **18**, 560.

EALES, N. B. (1931). 'The Development of the Mandible in the Elephant', *Proceedings of the Zoological Society of London*, 115.

EHRENBERG, K. (1932). 'Das biogenetische Grundgesetz in seiner Beziehung zum biologischen Trägheitsgesetz', *Biologia generalis*, **8**, 547.

EIMER, G. H. T. (1890). *Organic Evolution*. (English translation.) London.

EKMAN, G. (1930). 'Über Entwicklung und Vererbung', *Annalia Societatis Zoologicae-botanicae Fennicae*, **10**, (1).

ELLES, G. L. (1924). 'Evolutional Palaeontology', *Report of the British Association for the Advancement of Science for 1923*, p. 83.

ELLIOT SMITH, G. (1927). *Essays on the Evolution of Man*. Oxford.

EMDEN, F. I. VAN (1929). 'Über den Speziesbegriff vom Standpunkt der Larvensystematik aus,' **3**. *Wandersammlung deutscher Entomologen*, 47.

—— (1946). 'Egg-bursters in Some More Families of Polyphagous Beetles, and Some General Remarks on Egg-bursters', *Proceedings of the Royal Entomological Society of London*, **21**, 89.

ENSLIN, E. (1917). 'Die Tenthredinoidea Mitteleuropas', *Deutsche Entomologische Zeitschrift*, 539.

ERIKSSON, S. (1934). 'Studien über die Fangapparate der Branchiopoden nebst einigen phylogenetischen Bemerkungen', *Zoologiska Bidrag från Uppsala*, **15**, 23.

ESSEX, R. (1927). 'Studies in Reptilian Degeneration', *Proceedings of the Zoological Society of London*, 879.

FENTON, C. L. (1931). 'Studies of Evolution in the Genus Spirifer', *Publications of the Wagner Free Institute*, **2**, 8.

DE FERRÉ, Y. (1952). 'Les Formes de Jeunesse des Abiétacées. Ontogenie-Phylogenie'. *Travaux du Laboratoire Forestier de Toulouse*, II, **3**, Toulouse.

FISHER, R. A. (1935). 'Dominance in Poultry', *Philosophical Transactions of the Royal Society*, B, **225**, 195.

FIZE, A. (1956). 'Observations biologiques sur les Hapalocarcinidés', *Annales de la Faculté des Sciences, Université nationale du Viêt-Nam*, Saigon. Contribution 22.

FORD, E. B. (1928). 'The Inheritance of Dwarfing in Gammarus chevreuxi', *Journal of Genetics*, **20**, 93.

—— (1937). 'Problems of Heredity in the Lepidoptera', *Biological Reviews*, **12**, 461.

—— (1954). 'Problems in the Evolution of Geographical Races'. *Evolution as a Process*, p. 99. London.

FORD, E. B., & HUXLEY, J. S. (1927). 'Mendelian Genes and Rates of Development in Gammarus chevreuxi', *British Journal of Experimental Biology*, **5**, 112.

FOXON, G. E. H. (1936). 'Notes on Recapitulation in the Larvae of Decapod Crustacea', *Annals and Magazine of Natural History* (10), **18**, 117.

FRANZ, V. (1927). 'Ontogenie und Phylogenie', *Abhandlungen zur Theorie der organischen Entwicklung*. Berlin.

FRASER, E. A., & HILL, J. P. (1915). 'The Development of the Thymus,

Epithelial Bodies, and Thyroid in the Marsupialia. . .', *Philosophical Transactions of the Royal Society*, B, **207**, 1.

FRIEDMANN, H. (1955). 'The Honey-Guides', *United States National Museum Bulletin*, **208**, Washington.

FUCHS, H. (1930). 'Beiträge zur Entwicklungsgeschichte und vergleichenden Anatomie des Brustschultergürtels', *Morphologisches Jahrbuch*, **64**, 1.

GARSTANG, S. L., & W. (1926). 'On the Development of Botrylloides and the Ancestry of Vertebrates', *Proceedings of the Leeds Philosophical Society*, **1**, 81.

—— (1928). 'On the Development of Botrylloides, and its Bearings on some Morphological Problems', *Quarterly Journal of Microscopical Science*, **72**, 1.

GARSTANG, W. (1894). 'Preliminary Note on a New Theory of the Phylogeny of the Chordata', *Zoologischer Anzeiger*, **17**, 122.

—— (1922). 'The Theory of Recapitulation. A Critical Restatement of the Biogenetic Law', *Journal of the Linnean Society of London, Zoology*, **35**, 81.

—— (1928 A). 'The Origin and Evolution of Larval Forms', *Report of the British Association for the Advancement of Science for 1928*, 77.

—— (1928 B). 'The Morphology of the Tunicata, and its Bearings on the Phylogeny of the Chordata', *Quarterly Journal of Microscopical Science*, **72**, 51.

—— (1946). 'The Morphology and Relations of the Siphonophora', *Quarterly Journal of Microscopical Science*, **87**, 103.

—— (1954). 'Amphioxus, a Cephalaspid Paedomorph', *Evolution as a Process*, London, 140.

GAUSSEN, H. (1937). 'Jeunesse et Evolution', *Revue générale des sciences pures et appliquées*, Paris, **48**, 293.

—— (1942). 'Évolution et retour aux formes ancestrales', *Revue générale des sciences pures et appliquées*, Paris, **52**, 4.

GEGENBAUR, C. (1880). 'Kritische Bemerkungen über Polydactylie als Atavismus', *Morphologisches Jahrbuch*, **6**, 584.

GEORGE, T. N. (1933). 'Palingenesis and Palaeontology', *Biological Reviews*, **8**, 125.

GEROULD, J. H. (1921). 'Blue-green Caterpillars. . .', *Journal of Experimental Zoology*, **34**, 385.

GIARD, A. (1887). 'La Castration parasitaire', *Bulletin scientifique du Département du Nord*, 2e ser., **10**, 23.

—— (1905). 'La Poecilogonie', *Bulletin biologique de la France et de la Belgique*, **39**, 153.

GILFORD, H. (1911). *The Disorders of Postnatal Growth and Development*. London.

GOEBEL, K. (1889). 'Über die Jugendzustände der Pflanzen', *Flora*, **72**, 1.

GOLDSCHMIDT, R. (1923). 'Einige Materialien zur Theorie der abgestimmten Reaktionsgeschwindigkeiten', *Archiv für mikroskopische Anatomie und Entwicklungsmechanik*, **98**, 292.

—— (1924). 'Untersuchungen zur Genetik der geographischen Variation', *Archiv für Entwicklungsmechanik*, **101**, 92.

—— (1927). *Physiologische Theorie der Vererbung*. Berlin.

—— (1933). 'Untersuchungen zur Genetik der geographischen Variation, VII', *Archiv für Entwicklungsmechanik*, **130**, 266.

—— (1934). 'Lymantria', *Bibliographia Genetica*, **11**, 4.

GOODRICH, E. S. (1895). 'On the Coelom, Genital Ducts, and Nephridia', *Quarterly Journal of Microscopical Science*, **37**, 447.

—— (1913). 'Metameric Segmentation and Homology', *Quarterly Journal of Microscopical Science*, **59**, 227.

—— (1917). 'Proboscis-pores in Craniate Vertebrates', *Quarterly Journal of Microscopical Science*, **62**, 539.

—— (1924). *Living Organisms*, p. 61. Oxford.

—— (1930). *Studies on the Structure and Development of Vertebrates*. London.

GOODRICH, H. B., & HANSEN, I. B. (1931). 'The Postembryonic Development of Mendelian Characters in the Goldfish', *Journal of Experimental Zoology*, **59**, 337.

GRAVE, C. (1944). 'The Larva of *Styela* (*Cynthia*) *partita*: Structure, Activities and Duration of Life', *Journal of Morphology*, **75**, 173.

GREGORY, W. K. (1925). 'The Biogenetic Law and the Skull Form of Primitive Man', *American Journal of Physical Anthropology*, **8**, 373.

—— (1946). 'The Role of Motile Larvae and Fixed Adults in the Origin of Vertebrates', *Quarterly Review of Biology*, **21**, 348.

GROBBEN, K. (1892). 'Zur Kenntnis des Stammbaumes und des Systems der Crustaceen', *Sitzungsberichte der Mathematisch-naturwissenschaftlichen Klasse der Kaiserlichen Akademie der Wissenschaften in Wien*, **101**, 1.

GRÜNEBERG, H. (1947). *Animal Genetics and Medicine*. London.

GUILLAUMIN, A. (1910). 'L'Étude des germinations appliquée à la classification des genres et à la phylogénie des groupes', *Revue générale de botanique*, **22**, 449.

—— (1912). 'L'Étude des germinations et la loi de Fritz Müller', *Comptes rendu du Congrès des Sociétés Savantes de Paris et des Départements*, 186.

GURNEY, R. (1933). *British Fresh-Water Copepoda, III*. London.

—— (1942). *Larvae of Decapod Crustacea*. London.

HADŽI, J. (1944). 'Turbelarijska Teorija Knidarijev', *Slovenska Akademija Znanosti in Umetnosti v Ljubljani*, **3**, 1.

—— (1949). 'Problem mezoderma in celoma v luči turbelarijske teorije knidarijev', *Razprave Slovenske Akademije Znanosti in Umetnosti v Ljubljani*, **4**, 5.

—— (1953). 'An Attempt to Reconstruct the System of Animal Classification', *Systematic Zoology*, **2**, 145.

HAECKEL, E. (1866). *Generelle Morphologie der Organismen*. Berlin.

—— (1874). 'Die Gastraea-Theorie, die phylogenetische Classification des Thierreichs und die Homologie der Keimblätter', *Jenaische Zeitschrift für Naturwissenschaft*, **8**, 1.

—— (1875 A). 'Die Gastrula und die Eifurchung der Thiere', *Jenaische Zeitschrift für Naturwissenschaft*, **9**, 402.

—— (1875 B). *Ziele und Wege der heutigen Entwicklungsgeschichte*, Jena, 1875.

HAECKER, V. (1925). 'Aufgaben und Ergebnisse der Phänogenetik', *Bibliographia Genetica*, **1**, 95.

HALDANE, J. B. S. (1932 A). 'The Time of Action of Genes and its Bearing on some Evolutionary Problems', *American Naturalist*, **66**, 5.

—— (1932 B). *The Causes of Evolution*, p. 150. London.

HALL, F. G. (1934). 'Haemoglobin Function in the Developing Chick', *Journal of Physiology*, **83**, 222.

HANDLIRSCH, A. (1908). *Die fossilen Insekten.* Leipzig.

HARDY, A. C. (1954). 'Escape from Specialization', *Evolution as a Process,* p. 122. London.

HARLAND, S. C. (1936). 'The Genetical Conception of the Species', *Biological Reviews, Cambridge,* 11, 83.

HARVEY, W. (1645). 'Exercitatio anatomica de motu cordis et sanguinis in animalibus' in *Adriani Spigelii Anatomica,* p. lxiii. Amsterdam.

HATT, P. (1932). 'Essais expérimentaux sur les localisations germinales dans l'œuf d'un Annelide (Sabellaria alveolata)', *Archives d'Anatomie Microscopique,* 18, 81.

HEDGPETH, J. W. (1947). 'On the evolutionary significance of the Pycnogonida', *Smithsonian Miscellaneous Collections,* 106, (18).

HERBST, (1895). 'Experimentelle Untersuchungen über den Einfluß der veränderten chemischen Zusammensetzung des umgebenden Mediums auf die Entwicklung der Thiere, 2-er Theil', *Mitteilungen der Zoologischen Station, Neapel,* 11, 136.

HERTWIG, O. (1906). 'Über die Stellung der vergleichenden Entwicklungslehre zur vergleichenden Anatomie, zur Systematik und Deszendenztheorie', *Handbuch der vergleichenden und experimentellen Entwicklungslehre der Wirbeltiere,* III. 3, 149. Jena.

—— (1916). *Das Werden der Organismen,* p. 216. Jena.

HERTWIG, O., & HERTWIG, R. (1880). 'Die Coelomtheorie', *Jenaische Zeitschrift für Naturwissenschaften,* 15, 1.

HILL, J. P. (1932). 'The Developmental History of the Primates', *Philosophical Transactions of the Royal Society,* B, 221, 45.

HILL, J. P., & DE BEER, G. R. (1950). 'Development of the Monotremata. VII. The Development and Structure of the Egg-tooth and the Caruncle in the Monotremes and on the Occurrence of Vestiges of the Egg-tooth and Caruncle in Marsupials', *Transactions of the Zoological Society of London,* 26, 503.

HIS, W. (1874). *Unsere Körperform und das physiologische Problem ihrer Entstehung.* Leipzig.

HOLMES, S. J. (1944). 'Recapitulation and its Supposed Causes', *Quarterly Review of Biology,* 19, 319.

HOLMGREN, N., & STENSIÖ, E. A. (1936). 'Kranium und Visceralskelett der Akranier, Cyclostomen und Fische', *Handbuch der vergleichenden Anatomie,* 4, 233.

HOLTFRETER, J. (1936). 'Regionale Induktionen in xenoplastisch zusammengesetzten Explantaten', *Archiv für Entwicklungsmechanik,* 134, 466.

—— (1943, 1944). 'A Study of the Mechanics of Gastrulation', *Journal of Experimental Zoology,* 94, 261; 95, 171.

HOPKINS, G. H. E. (1936). *Mosquitoes of the Ethiopean Region.* London, 1936.

HOSKER, A. (1936). 'Studies on the Epidermal Structures of Birds', *Philosophical Transactions of the Royal Society,* B, 226, 143.

HUNTER, J. (1861). *Essays and Observations,* 1, 203. London.

HUPÉ, P. (1953). 'Quelques remarques sur la croissance et la segmentation des trilobites', *Bulletin de la Société Géologique de France,* 6ᵉ sér., 3, 3.

HURST, C. H. (1893). 'The Recapitulation Theory', *Natural Science,* 2, 195.

HUXLEY, J. S. (1923). 'Time Relations in Amphibian Metamorphosis', *Science Progress*, **17**, 606.

―― (1924). 'Constant Differential Growth-Rates and their Significance', *Nature*, **114**, 895.

―― (1926). 'The Study of Growth and its Bearings upon Morphology and Evolution', *British Association for the Advancement of Science, Sectional Transactions*, 35.

―― (1932). *Problems of Relative Growth*. London.

HUXLEY, T. H. (1855). 'On Certain Zoological Arguments commonly adduced in favour of the Hypothesis of the Progressive Development of Animal Life in Time', *Proceedings of the Royal Institution*, **2**, 82; reprinted in *The Scientific Memoirs of Thomas Henry Huxley*, London, 1898, **1**, 300.

HYATT, A. (1872). 'Fossil Cephalopods', *Bulletin of the Museum of Comparative Zoology, Harvard*, **3**, 59.

―― (1894). 'The Phylogeny of an Acquired Characteristic', *Proceedings of the American Philosophical Society*, **32**, 349.

IMMS, A. D. (1936). 'The ancestry of insects,' *Transactions of the Society for British Entomology*, **3**, 1.

JAEKEL, O. (1901). 'Über verschiedene Wege phylogenetischer Entwickelung', *Verhandlungen des V. internationalen Zoologen-Congresses*, Berlin, 1058.

JENKINSON, J. W. (1906). 'Remarks on the Germinal Layers of Vertebrates and on the Significance of Germinal Layers in General', *Memoirs of the Manchester Literary and Philosophical Society*, **50**, (3).

―― (1913). *Vertebrate Embryology*. Oxford.

JEZHIKOV, J. J. (1937). 'Zur Rekapitulationslehre', *Biologia generalis*, **13**, 67.

KAPPERS, C. U. A. (1928). *Three Lectures on Neurobiotaxis and Other Subjects*. Copenhagen.

KEIBEL, F. (1897). 'Das biogenetische Grundgesetz und die Cenogenese,' *Ergebnisse der Anatomie und Entwicklungsgeschichte*, **7**, 722.

KEITH, SIR A. (1939). 'A Resurvey of the Anatomical Features of the Piltdown Skull with Some Observations on the Recently Discovered Swanscombe Skull', *Journal of Anatomy*, **73**, 155 and 234.

KIESLINGER, A. (1924). 'Neotenie, Persistenz, Degeneration', *Proceedings of the Academy of Sciences of Amsterdam*, **27**, 761.

KLEINENBERG, N. (1886). 'Die Entstehung des Annelids aus der Larve von Lopadorhynchus', *Zeitschrift für wissenschaftliche Zoologie*, **44**, 212.

KNIGHT, J. BROOKES (1952). 'Primitive Fossil Gastropods and their Bearing on Gastropod Classification', *Smithsonian Miscellaneous Collections*, **17**, (13).

KNIGHT-JONES, E. W. (1952). 'On the Nervous System of *Saccoglossus cambrensis* (Enteropneusta)', *Philosophical Transactions of the Royal Society*, B, **236**, 315.

KNOUFF, R. A. (1927). 'The Origin of the Cranial Ganglia of Rana', *Journal of Comparative Neurology*, **44**, 259.

KÖLLIKER, A. (1864). 'Über die Darwin'sche Schöpfungstheorie', *Zeitschrift für wissenschaftliche Zoologie*, **14**, 174.

―― (1884). 'Die embryonalen Keimblätter und die Gewebe', *Zeitschrift für wissenschaftliche Zoologie*, **40**, 179.

KOLLMANN, J. (1882). 'Das Überwintern von Frosch- und Tritonlarven und die Umwandlung des mexikanischen Axolotl', *Verhandlungen der naturforschenden Gesellschaft, Basel,* **7,** 387.

KOMAI, T. (1922). *Studies on Two Aberrant Ctenophores, Coeloplana and Gastrodes.* Kyoto.

KRYŽANOWSKY, S. G. (1939). 'Das Rekapitulationsprinzip', *Acta Zoologica,* **20,** 1.

KÜKENTHAL, W. (1897). 'Vergleichend-anatomische und entwicklungs-geschichtliche Untersuchungen an Sirenen', *Semons Forschungsreisen* **4,** *Jenaische Denkschriften,* **7,** 74.

KUMMER, B. (1952). 'Untersuchungen über die ontogenetische Entwicklung der menschlichen Schädelbasiswinkel', *Zeitschrift für Morphologie und Anthropologie,* **43,** 331.

LAMARCK, J. B. P. A. DE M. DE (1809). *Philosophie zoologique.* (Édition C. Martins, **1,** 223. Paris, 1873.)

LANDACRE, F. L. (1907). 'On the Place of Origin and Method of Distribution of Taste-buds in Ameiurus melas', *Journal of Comparative Neurology,* **17,** 1.

LANG, W. D. (1919). 'The Evolution of Ammonites', *Proceedings of the Geological Association,* **30,** 50.

LANKESTER, E. R. (1877). 'Notes on the embryology and classification of the animal Kingdom', *Quarterly Journal of Microscopical Science,* **17,** 399.

—— (1894). 'Acquired Characters', *Nature,* **51,** 102.

LATREILLE, P. A. (1825). *Familles naturelles du règne animal.* Paris.

LEACH, W. E. (1817). *The Zoological Miscellany,* **3,** 57, London.

LEBEDKIN, S. (1937). 'The Recapitulation Problem', *Biologia generalis,* **13,** 391, 561.

LEHMANN, F. E. (1938). 'Die morphologische Rekapitulation des Grund-plans bei Wirbeltierembryonen', *Vierteljahrsschrift der naturforschenden Gesellschaft in Zürich. Beiblatt* **30,** 187. *(Festschrift Karl Hescheler.)*

LELOUP, E. (1929). 'Recherches sur l'anatomie et le développement de *Vellella spirans* Forsk', *Archives de biologie,* Paris, **39,** 397.

—— (1939). 'A propos de l'hydraire *Margellopsis haeckeli* Hartlaub', *Annales de la Société royale Zoologique de Belgique,* **60,** 97.

LEMCHE, H. (1948). 'Northern and Arctic Tectibranch Gastropods', *Konge-lige Danske Videnskabernes Selskab,* **5,** (3), 24.

LENZ, F. (1926). 'Die Chironomiden-Metamorphose in ihrer Bedeutung für die Systematik', *Entomologische Mitteilungen,* **15,** 440.

LEWIS, W. H. (1920). 'The Cartilaginous Skull of a Human Embryo Twenty-one mm. in Length', *Contributions to Embryology of the Carnegie Institution of Washington,* **9,** 299.

LILLIE, F. R. (1908). *The Development of the Chick.* New York.

LINDAHL, P. E. (1933). 'Über animalisierte und vegetativisierte Seeigel-larven', *Archiv für Entwicklungsmechanik,* **128,** 661.

LOWE, P. R. (1928). 'Studies and Observations bearing on the Phylogeny of the Ostrich and its Allies', *Proceedings of the Zoological Society of London,* 185.

—— (1933). 'On the Primitive Characters of the Penguins', *Proceedings of the Zoological Society of London,* 483.

Lunz, A. (1935). *Das sogenannte biogenetische Grundgesetz und seine Bedeutung in der modernen Biologie*. Moskau-Leningrad.

MacBride, E. W. (1914). *Text-book of Embryology*. I. *Invertebrata*, p. 650. London.

—— (1918). 'The Artificial Production of Echinoderm Larvae with Two Water-vascular Systems', *Proceedings of the Royal Society*, B, **90**, 323.

Mackebras, I. M., & Mackebras, M. J. (1948). 'Revisional Notes on Australasian Simuliidae (Deptera)', *Proceedings of the Linnean Society of New South Wales*, **73**, 372.

Mangold, O. (1923). 'Transplantationsversuche zur Frage der Spezifität und der Bildung der Keimblätter', *Archiv für mikroskopische Anatomie und Entwicklungsmechanik*, **100**, 198.

Mansour, K. (1927). 'The Development of the Larval and Adult Mid-gut of *Calandra oryzae*', *Quarterly Journal of Microscopical Science*, **71**, 313.

Manton, S. M. (1928). 'On the Embryology of a Mysid Crustacean', *Philosophical Transactions of the Royal Society*, B, **216**, 363.

—— (1934). 'On the Embryology of the Crustacean Nebalia bipes', *Philosophical Transactions of the Royal Society*, B, **223**, 163.

—— (1953). 'Locomotory Habits and the Evolution of the Larger Arthropodan Groups', *Symposia of the Society for Experimental Biology*, Cambridge, 339.

Margalef, R. (1949). 'Importancia de la neotenia en la evolución de los crustaceos de agua dulce', *Publicaciones del Instituto de Biología Aplicada*, (Barcelona), **6**, 41.

Matthew, W. D. (1926). 'The Evolution of the Horse', *Quarterly Review of Biology*, **1**, 139.

Mazenot, G. (1940). 'La "loi" de l'accélération phylogénique ou de la précession des caractères', *Bulletin Mensuel de la Société Linnéenne de Lyon*, **9**, 74.

Meckel, J. F. (1811). *Beyträge zur vergleichenden Anatomie*. **2**. *Entwurf einer Darstellung der zwischen dem Embryozustande der höheren Thiere und dem niederen Statt findenden Parallele*. Leipzig.

Medawar, P. B. (1951). 'Problems of Adaptation', *New Biology*, **11**, 10.

Mehnert, E. (1898). *Biomechanik*. Jena.

Metschnikoff, E. (1874). 'Embryologie der doppeltfüßigen Myriapoden', *Zeitschrift für wissenschaftliche Zoologie*, **24**, 253.

Morant, G. M. (1938). 'The Form of the Swanscombe Skull', in 'Report on the Swanscombe Skull', *Journal of the Royal Anthropological Institute*, **68**, 67.

Morgan, T. H. (1916). *A Critique of the Theory of Evolution*. Princeton, 1916.

—— (1924). 'Heredity of Embryonic Characters', *Scientific Monthly*, **18**, 5.

—— (1926). *The Theory of the Gene*. Yale.

Morgan, T. H., Bridges, C., & Sturtevant, A. H. (1925). 'The Genetics of Drosophila', *Bibliotheca Genetica*, **2**, 1.

Mortensen, T. (1921). *Studies of the Development and Larval Forms of Echinoderms*. Copenhagen·

Mossman, H. W. (1939). 'The Epithelio-chorial Placenta of an American Mole, *Scalopus aquaticus*', *Proceedings of the Zoological Society of London*, B, **109**, 373.

MÜLLER, FRITZ (1864). *Für Darwin.* Leipzig.

MÜLLER, H. J. (1927). 'Artificial Transmutation of the Gene', *Science,* **66,** 84.

MÜLLER, L. (1933). 'Pieris bryoniae O. und napi L.', *Internationale entomologische Zeitschrift,* **27,** 93.

MÜLLER, W. (1873). 'Über die Hypobranchialrinne der Tunikaten und deren Vorhandensein bei Amphioxus und den Cyklostomen', *Jenaische Zeitschrift für Naturwissenschaften,* **7,** 327.

NAEF, A. (1917). *Die individuelle Entwicklung organischer Formen als Urkunde ihrer Stammesgeschichte.* Jena.

—— (1919). *Idealistische Morphologie und Phylogenetik.* Jena.

NAME, W. G. VAN (1921). 'Budding in Compound Ascidians and Other Invertebrates, and its bearing on the Question of the Early Ancestry of the Vertebrates', *Bulletin of the American Museum of Natural History,* **44,** 275.

NAUCK, E. T. (1931). 'Über umwegige Entwicklung', *Morphologisches Jahrbuch,* **66,** 65.

NEEDHAM, J. (1930). 'The Biochemical Aspect of the Recapitulation Theory', *Biological Reviews,* **5,** 142.

NICHOLS, J. T., & BRADER, C. M. (1928). 'An Annotated List of the Synentognathi', *Zoologica,* New York, **8,** 423.

NICOLOFF, T. (1910). 'Sur les feuilles juvéniles des jeunes plantules et des rameaux adventifs', *Revue générale de botanique,* Paris, **22,** 113.

NOBLE, G. K. (1925). 'An Outline of the Relation of Ontogeny to Phylogeny within the Amphibia', *American Museum Novitates,* No. 165.

—— (1926). 'The Importance of Larval Characters in Classification of the South African Salientia', *American Museum Novitates,* No. 237.

OLMSTED, J. D. (1920). 'The Results of Cutting the Seventh Cranial Nerve in Amiurus', *Journal of Experimental Zoology,* **31,** 369.

OPPENHEIMER, J. M. (1940). 'The Non-specificity of the Germ-layers', *Quarterly Review of Biology,* **15,** 1.

OSBORN, H. F. (1902). 'The Law of Adaptive Radiation', *American Naturalist,* **34,** 353.

—— (1915). 'Origin of Single Character Differences', *American Naturalist,* **49,** 193.

PANDER, C. (1817). *Beiträge zur Entwickelungsgeschichte des Hühnchens im Eye.* Würzburg.

PASTEELS, J. (1937). 'Études sur la gastrulation des vertébrés méroblastiques', *Archives de biologie,* **48,** 381.

—— (1940). 'Un aperçu comparatif de la gastrulation chez les chordés', *Biological Reviews,* **15,** 59.

PAVLOV, A. P. (1901). 'Le Crétacé inférieur de la Russie et sa faune', *Nouveaux Mémoires de la Société impériale des Naturalistes de Moscou,* N.S., **16,** 87.

PAVLOV, M. (1888). 'Études sur l'histoire paléontologique des Ongulés. II. Le développement des Equidae', *Bulletin de la Société Impériale des Naturalistes de Moscou,* **2,** 135.

—— (1892). 'Études sur l'histoire paléontologique des Ongulés. VI. Les Rhinoceridae de la Russie et le développement des Rhinoceridae en général. *Bulletin de la Société Impériale des Naturalistes de Moscou,* **6,** 137.

PYCRAFT, W. P. (1900–1903). 'Some Points on the Morphology of the Palate of the Neognathea.' *Journal of the Linnean Society of London, Zoology,* **28,** 343.

—— (1907). 'III. On Some Points in the Anatomy of the Emperor and Adélie Penguins', *National Antarctic Expedition 1901–1904,* London, 1907, **II,** Zoology, 1.

RAW, F. (1927). 'Ontogenies of Trilobites and their Significance', *American Journal of Science,* **14,** 7, 131.

RAY, J. (1710). *Historia Insectorum.* Londini.

REES, W. J. (1939). 'The Hydroid of the Medusa Dipurena halterata (Forbes)', *Journal of the Marine Biological Association,* **23,** 343.

—— (1941). 'Notes on British and Norwegian Hydroids and Medusae', *Journal of the Marine Biological Association,* **25,** 129.

—— (1956). 'A Revision of the Hydroid Genus *Perigonimus*', *Bulletin of the British Museum (Natural History), Zoology,* **3,** 335.

—— (1957). 'Evolutionary Trends in the Classification of Capitate Hydroids and Medusae', *Bulletin of the British Museum (Natural History), Zoology,* **4,** 453.

REES, W. J., & RUSSELL, F. S. (1937). 'On Rearing the Hydroids of Certain Medusae, with an Account of the Methods Used', *Journal of the Marine Biological Association of the United Kingdom,* **22,** 61.

REEVE, E. C. R., & MURRAY, P. D. F. (1942). 'Evolution in the Horse's Skull', *Nature,* **150,** 402.

REGAN, C. T. (1911). 'A Classification of the Teleostean Fishes of the Order Synentognathi', *Annals & Magazine of Natural History,* Ser. 8, **7,** 639.

REICHERT, C. B. (1838). *Vergleichende Entwickelungsgeschichte des Kopfes der nackten Amphibien.* Königsberg.

REMAK, R. (1855). *Untersuchungen über die Entwickelung der Wirbelthiere.* Berlin.

RIDDLE, O. (1928). 'Internal Secretions in Evolution and Reproduction', *Scientific Monthly,* **26,** 216.

ROBB, R. C. (1935–7). 'A Study of Mutations in Evolution', *Journal of Genetics,* **31,** 39, 47; **33,** 267; **34,** 477.

ROMER, A. S. (1942). 'Cartilage an Embryonic Adaptation', *American Naturalist,* **76,** 394.

—— (1949). *The Vertebrate Body.* Philadelphia & London.

RUBNER, M. (1908). *Das Problem der Lebensdauer und seine Beziehungen zu Wachstum und Ernährung.* München und Berlin.

RUNNSTRÖM, J. (1925). 'Zur experimentellen Analyse der Entwicklung von Antedon', *Archiv für Entwicklungsmechanik,* **105,** 63.

—— and S. (1918–19). 'Über die Entwicklung von Cucumaria frondosa Gunnerus und Psolus phantapus Strussenfelt', *Bergens Museums Aarbok, Naturvidenskabelig række,* **5,** 1.

RUSSELL, E. S. (1916). *Form and Function.* London.

RUSSELL, F. S. (1953). *The Medusae of the British Isles.* Cambridge.

RUTIMEYER, L. (1863). 'Über die historische Methode in der Paläontologie. Beiträge zur Kenntnis der fossilen Pferde und zur vergleichenden Odontographie der Hufthiere überhaupt', *Verhandlungen der naturforschenden Gesellschaft in Basel,* **3,** 558.

SACARRÃO, G. DA FONSECA (1952). 'The Meaning of Gastrulation', *Aquivos do Museu Bocage*, Lisbon, **23,** 47.

—— (1953). 'Sur la formation des feuillets germinatifs des Céphalopodes et les incertitudes de leur interprétation', *Revista da Faculdade de Ciências*, Lisbon, Ser. 2, C, **3,** 311.

SARRA, R. (1918). 'Intorno ad un Imenothero Tentredinide (Cimbex quadrimaculata Müll.) dannoso al mandorlo', *Bollettino del Laboratorio di Zoologia Generale e Agraria*, Portici, **12,** 275.

SCHINDEWOLF, O. H. (1936). *Paläontologie, Entwicklungslehre und Genetik.* Berlin.

—— (1937). 'Beobachtungen und Gedanken zur Deszendenzlehre', *Acta Biotheoretica*, **3,** 195.

SCHLESINGER, G. (1909). 'Zur Phylogenie und Ethologie der Scombresociden', *Verhandlungen der kaiserlich-königlichen zoologisch-botanischen Gesellschaft in Wien*, **59,** 302.

SCHMIDT, G. A. (1934). 'Ein zweiter Entwicklungstypus von Lineus gesserensis-ruber', *Zoologische Jahrbücher, Abteilung für Anatomie und Ontogenie*, **58,** 607.

SCHULTZ, A. H. (1926). 'Fetal Growth of Man and other Primates', *Quarterly Review of Biology*, **1,** 465.

—— (1949). 'Ontogenetic Specialisations in Man', *Archiv der Julius Klaus-Stiftung für Vererbungsforschung, Sozialanthropologie und Rassenhygiene*, **24,** 197.

—— (1950). 'The Physical Distinctions of Man', *Proceedings of the American Philosophical Society*, **94,** 428.

SCHULZE, P. (1922). 'Über nachlaufende Entwicklung (Hysterotelie) einzelner Organe bei Schmetterlingen', *Archiv für Naturgeschichte*, **88,** A. (7), 109.

—— (1937). 'Trilobita, Xiphosura, Acarina', *Zeitschrift für Morphologie und Ökologie der Tiere*, **32,** 181.

SEDGWICK, A. (1894). 'On the Law of Development commonly known as von Baer's Law, and on the Significance of Ancestral Rudiments in Embryonic Development', *Quarterly Journal of Microscopical Science*, **36,** 35.

—— (1909). 'The Influence of Darwin on the Study of Animal Embryology', *Darwin and Modern Sciences*, ed. A. C. Seward. Cambridge.

SELENKA, E. (1899). *Studien über Entwicklungsgeschichte der Tiere. II. Menschenaffen.* Wiesbaden, 143.

SERRES, M. (1824). 'Recherches sur l'anatomie comparée des animaux invertébrés. **1.** Que sont par rapport aux vertébrés et à l'homme les animaux invertébrés?' *Annales des Sciences Naturelles*, II. **2,** 248.

SEWERTZOW, A. N. (1927). 'Über die Beziehungen zwischen der Ontogenese und der Phylogenese der Tiere', *Jenaische Zeitschrift für Naturwissenschaft*, **63,** 51.

—— (1931). *Morphologische Gesetzmäßigkeiten der Evolution.* Jena.

SHUMWAY, W. (1932). 'The Recapitulation Theory', *Quarterly Review of Biology*, **7,** 93.

SIMPSON, G. G. (1953). *The Major Features of Evolution.* New York.

SINNOTT, E. W., & DUNN, L. C. (1935). 'The Effect of Genes on the Development of Size and Form', *Biological Reviews*, **10**, 123.

SLIJPER, E. J. (1936). 'Die Cetaceen vergleichend-anatomisch und systematisch', *Cupita Zoologia*, **7**, 1.

SMITH, J. P. (1914). 'Acceleration of Development in Fossil Cephalopoda', *Leland Stanford Junior University Publications*.

SMITH, P. E., and MACDOWELL, E. C. (1930). 'An Hereditary Anterior Pituitary Deficiency in the Mouse', *Anatomical Record*, **46**, 249.

SMITH WOODWARD, A. (1923). *Presidential Address, Proceedings of the Linnean Society of London*, 135th Session, 1923, 30.

SOUTH, R. (1908). *Moths of the British Isles*. London.

SPATH, L. F. (1923). 'The Ammonoidea of the Gault', *Memoirs of the Palaeontographical Society*, **75**, 65.

—— (1924). 'The Ammonites of the Blue Lias', *Proceedings of the Geological Association*, **35**, 186.

—— (1925–6). 'Notes on Yorkshire Ammonites', *The Naturalist*, Sept. 1925, 268, and May 1926, 137, 139.

—— (1933). 'The Evolution of the Cephalopoda', *Biological Reviews*, **8**, 418.

—— (1936). 'The Phylogeny of the Cephalopoda', *Palaeontologische Zeitschrift*, **18**, 156.

—— (1938). *A Catalogue of the Ammonites of the Liassic Family Liparoceratidae*. British Museum, London.

SPEMANN, H. (1938). *Embryonic Development and Induction*. New Haven.

SPUHLER, N. J. (1954). 'Ape-men more like men as babes than as adults,' *Science News Letter*, **65**, 233.

ST. HILAIRE, E. G. (1818). *Philosophie Anatomique*. Paris.

STAFF, F. (1910). 'Organogenetische Untersuchungen über Criodrilus', *Arbeiten aus dem Zoologischen Institut in Wien*, **18**, 227.

STEINER, H. (1918). 'Das Problem der Diastataxie des Vogelflügels', *Jenaische Zeitschrift für Naturwissenschaften*, **55**, 221.

—— (1938). 'Der "Archaeopteryx"-Schwanz der Vogelembryonen', *Vierteljahrsschrift der Naturforschenden Gesellschaft in Zürich*, **83**, 279 (*Beiblatt*).

STEINER, H., & ANDERS, G. (1946). 'Zur Frage der Entstehung von Rudimenten. . .', *Revue Suisse de Zoologie*, **53**, 537.

STOCKARD, C. R. (1910). 'The Influence of Alcohol and other Anaesthetics on Embryonic Development', *American Journal of Anatomy*, **10**, 369.

—— (1930). 'The Presence of a Factorial Basis for Characters lost in Evolution', *American Journal of Anatomy*, **45**, 345.

STØRMER, L. (1941). 'Studies on Trilobite Morphology, II', *Norsk Geologisk Tidsskrift*, **41**, 49.

STRASBURGER, E. (1872). *Die Coniferen und die Gnetaceen. Eine morphologische Studie*, 1. Jena, 1872.

STUBBLEFIELD, C. J. (1936). 'Cephalic Sutures and their Bearing on Current Classification of Trilobites', *Biological Reviews*, **11**, 407.

SWAMMERDAM, J. (1669). *Algemeene Verhandeling van bloedeloosen diertjes*. Utrecht.

SWINNERTON, H. H. (1938). 'Development and Evolution', *Report of the British Association for the Advancement of Science for 1938*, p. 57.

TAKHTAJAN, A. L. (1945). 'An Essay of Application of the Theory of

Phyllembryogenesis to the Interpretation of Monocotyledonous Embryo', *Proceedings of the Academy of Sciences of the Armenian S.S.R.*, **3**, 53.

TAN SIN HOK (1932). 'On the Genus Cycloclypeus', *Wetenschapliche Mededeelingen*, **19**, 3.

THOMPSON, D'A. W. (1917). *On Growth and Form*, pp. 54, 549. Cambridge.

THOMPSON, J. V. (1830). 'On the Cirripedes or Barnacles', *Zoological Researches*, **1**, 69, Cork.

—— (1836). 'Natural History and Metamorphosis of Sacculina carcini', *Entomologist's Magazine*, **3**, 452.

THOMSON, A. (1924). 'Facial Development', *The Dental Record*, **44**, 119.

TIEGS, O. W. (1938). 'The Embryonic Development of *Calandra oryzae*', *Quarterly Journal of Microscopical Science*, **80**, 159.

—— (1947). 'The development and affinities of the Pauropoda', *Quarterly Journal of Microscopical Science*, **88**, 165 & 269.

TOPSENT, E. (1910). 'Sur les affinités des Halichondria et la classification des Halichondrines d'après leurs formes larvaires', *Archives de Zoologie expérimentale et générale (Notes et revues)*, **7**.

TOTTON, A. K. (1954). 'Siphonophora of the Indian Ocean together with Systematic and Biological Notes on Related Specimens from other Oceans', *Discovery Reports*, **27**, 1.

TRUEMAN, A. E. (1922). 'The Use of Gryphaea in the Correlation of the Lower Lias', *Geological Magazine*, **59**, 256.

TUNG, T. C. (1934). 'L'Organisation de l'œuf fécondé d'Ascidiella', *Comptes rendus de la Société de Biologie*, Paris, **115**, 1375.

UBISCH, L. VON (1928). 'Über Lage, Entwicklung, Induktionswirkung und Funktion·von Chorda und Hydrocöl, *Verhandlungen der deutschen zoologischen Gesellschaft*, **33**, 83.

—— (1933). 'Untersuchungen über Formbildung, III', *Archiv für Entwicklungsmechanik*, **127**, 216.

VERSLUYS, J. (1922). 'Über die Rückbildung der Kiemenbogen bei den Selachii', *Bijdragen tot de Dierkunde*, **22**, 95.

WADDINGTON, C. H. (1957). *Strategy of Genes*. London.

WAGNER, G. (1949). 'Die Bedeutung der Neuralleiste für die Kopfgestaltung der Amphibien', *Revue Suisse de Zoologie*, **56**, 519.

WARDLAW, C. W. (1955). *Embryogenesis in Plants*. London.

WEDEKIND, R. (1920). 'Über Virenzperioden', *Sitzungsberichte der Gesellschaft für Beförderung der gesammten Naturwissenschaften zu Marburg*, 18.

WEIDENREICH, F. (1904). 'Zur Kinnbildung beim Menschen', *Anatomischer Anzeiger*, **25**, 314.

WEISMANN, A. (1876). *Studien zur Descendenz-Theorie*, **2**. Leipzig.

—— (1904). *The Evolution Theory*, pp. 177, 186. (English translation.) London.

WELLER, G. L. (1933). 'Development of the Thyroid, Parathyroid, and Thymus Glands in Man', *Contributions to Embryology of the Carnegie Institution*, **24**, 93.

WHITE, E. I. (1957). 'The original environment of the Craniates', In *Studies on fossil vertebrates*, edited by T. S. Westoll, London.

WILSON, C. B. (1911). 'North American Parasitic Copepods', *Proceedings of the United States National Museum*, **39**, 189.

WILSON, E. B. (1894). 'The Embryological Criteria of Homology', *Biological Lectures*, Woods Hole, 101.

—— (1904). 'Experimental Studies on Germinal Localisation, I. The Germ Regions in the Egg of Dentalium', *Journal of Experimental Zoology*, **1**, 1.

WOLTERECK, R. (1904). 'Beiträge zur praktischen Analyse der Polygordius-Entwicklung nach dem "Nordsee-" und dem "Mittelmeer-typus" ', *Archiv für Entwicklungsmechanik*, **18**, 377.

—— (1905). 'Wurmkopf, Wurmrumpf und Trochophora', *Zoologischer Anzeiger*, **28**, 273.

WOOD, A., and BARNARD, T. (1946). 'Ophthalmidium: A Study of Nomenclature, Variation, and Evolution in the Foraminifera', *Quarterly Journal of the Geological Society of London*, **102**, 77.

WOOD JONES, F. (1916). *Arboreal Man.* London.

—— (1947). 'The Premaxilla and the Ancestry of Man', *Nature*, London, **159**, 439.

WÜRTENBERGER, L. (1880). *Studien über die Stammesgeschichte der Ammoniten.* Leipzig.

YOUNG, J. Z. (1938). 'The Evolution of the Nervous System and of the Relationship of Organism and Environment', *Evolution: Essays on Aspects of Evolutionary Biology presented to E. S. Goodrich.* Oxford, 179.

ADDENDA TO BIBLIOGRAPHY

DE BEER, G. R. (1958). 'Darwin's Views on the Relations between Embryology and Evolution', *Journal of the Linnean Society of London, Zoology*, **44**, 15.

—— (1959). 'Paedomorphosis', *Proceedings of the XVth International Congress of Zoology*, 927.

DALCQ, A. (1949). 'L'Apport de l'embryologie causale au problème de l'évolution', *Portugalliae Acta Biologica*, p. 367.

LOVEJOY, A. O. (1959). 'Recent Criticism of the Darwinian Theory of Recapitulation', in *Forerunners of Darwin*, Baltimore, 438.

OPPENHEIMER, J. M. (1959). 'An Embryological Enigma in the *Origin of Species*', in *Forerunners of Darwin*, Baltimore, 292.

TOTTON, A. K, (1960). 'Studies on *Physalia physalis*', *Discovery Reports*, **30**, 301.

VANDEL, A. (1954). 'L'Évolution considérée comme phénomène de développement', *Bulletin de la société zoologique de France*, **79**, 341.

INDEX

PRINTED IN GREAT BRITAIN
AT THE UNIVERSITY PRESS, OXFORD
BY VIVIAN RIDLER
PRINTER TO THE UNIVERSITY